Avatar Bodies

Electronic Mediations

Katherine Hayles, Mark Poster, and Samuel Weber, series editors

Avatar Bodies

A Tantra for Posthumanism

Ann Weinstone

Electronic Mediations, Volume 10

University of Minnesota Press
Minneapolis • *London*

Poetry from *Songs of Ecstasy* by Hugh B. Urban copyright 2001 by Hugh B. Urban. Reprinted by permission of Oxford University Press, Inc.

Excerpts from letters and teachings of Dharmanidhi Sarasvati, spiritual director of Tantric College of America, reprinted with permission.

Correspondence from Chris Kraus reprinted with permission.

Published by the University of Minnesota Press
111 Third Avenue South, Suite 290
Minneapolis, MN 55401-2520
http://www.upress.umn.edu

Library of Congress Cataloging-in-Publication Data

Weinstone, Ann (Lalita Sarasvati).
    Avatar bodies : a tantra for posthumanism / Ann Weinstone.
        p.   cm. — (Electronic mediations ; v. 10)
    Includes bibliographical references.
    ISBN 0-8166-4146-3 (hc : alk. paper) — ISBN 0-8166-4147-1 (pbk. : alk. paper)
        1. Philosophical anthropology.   2. Body, Human (Philosophy).
    3. Humanism.   I. Title.   II. Series.
    BD450.W445   2003
    128—dc22   2003021040

Printed in the United States of America on acid-free paper

The University of Minnesota is an equal-opportunity educator and employer.

12 11 10 09 08 07 06 05 04   10 9 8 7 6 5 4 3 2 1

For Elaine and Nicola

Contents

Acknowledgments

Many people have contributed to this book and to the person I have become through writing it.

Thanks to Jeffrey T. Schnapp for superb intellectual guidance and generous, unflagging support of all varieties.

Thanks to Marjorie Perloff, N. Katherine Hayles, and Michael Wood for their years of expert mentoring and unstinting support.

Thanks to Chris Kraus for her letters, her friendship, her courage, and her deep kindness.

Thanks to Niklas Damiris, Helga Wild, and Sha Xin Wei for years of friendship and for inspiring me and challenging me through the course of many productive conversations.

Thanks to Vicki Kirby and Richard Doyle for going first.

Thanks to Arlene Stein, Judith Jackson Fossett, Meg Worley, Monica Moore, Lesley Ruda, Jennifer Gonzalez, and Daniel Peltz for their friendship and sage advice.

Thanks to Eduardo Cadava, Stefanie Harris, Helen Tartar, and Haun Saussy for additional assistance and comments during the writing process.

Thanks to the anonymous readers for the University of Minnesota Press who helped to reshape this project and make it better.

Thanks to Timothy Lenoir and Diane Middlebrook for their enthusiasm and support.

For financial support, thanks to the Alice B. Kaplan Center for the Humanities at Northwestern University, the Northwestern University

Faculty Development Grant, the Program in Modern Thought and Literature at Stanford University, the Stanford Humanities Center, the Whiting Foundation, the Stanford Postdoctoral Fellowship Program, Chris Kraus, Nicola McIntyre, Rowan and George Rowntree, David Weinstone, Mella Mincberg, and Scott Johnson.

For assistance in preparing this manuscript, thanks to Abigail Derecho.

Thanks to the *Jñānagni Kula* worldwide, and especially to my Bay Area brothers and sisters. You have blessed my life.

Thanks to Anodea Judith, without whose example I would not have had the courage to attempt this project.

Thanks to my guru, Dharmanidhi Sarasvati, for his teachings, his grace, and his love.

Finally, thanks to my mother, Elaine Weinstone, for bequeathing me her optimism and intellectual passion, and to Nicola McIntyre for her friendship, her insight, and her unparalleled kindness during the past fifteen years.

▼ Pleasure Ψ

I can scarcely tolerate the word *pleasure*.
—Gilles Deleuze, "Desire and Pleasure"

Pleasure is, perhaps, a love child of the 1960s. Wafting lavenderesque from cracks in the cosmic egg, pleasure recalls indulgence, mild intoxication, a polymorphous romp well shy of the imperatives of desire. Pleasure comes and goes; it manifests in the grain, the bubbling up, the tingle, the fractional slip. Compared to desire, pleasure is hedonistic, rambling, familiar, and, according to some, subject to manipulation by various economic and political regimes. Freud tells us that pleasure must be overridden in the name of a survivalism that always asks us to delay, delay, delay. Desire, on the other hand, must be crushed and cannot be delayed as its very structure is delay, and delay only intensifies desire. Desire drags and feeds on its own deferrals. It is a condition of excitation that seeks more excitation. Desire insists, and the one who contains the insistence of desire commands. Desire initiates power struggles. Mostly, desire wins.

This victory constitutes desire's purchase in contemporary critical and literary theory. Desire is what cannot be calculated, attained, fixed, or stabilized. Whether it is calibrated to a constitutive lack, as in the writings of Jacques Lacan, or promoted as a salutary, autonomous movement anterior to arrangements of power, as for Gilles Deleuze, desire is called upon to do the antihumanist, anticolonialist, anti-Enlightenment work of disrupting the sovereign self and oppressive organizations such as the normative body and the state. Desire promulgates a necessary and ongoing failure of the agency of the Western privileged subject. It functions as a line of movement that disrupts and redirects. While less imperious than desire, pleasure, as satisfaction, as resolution, as a lowering of thermodynamic tension, is nevertheless dangerous. It connotes the cessation of anxiety, a cessation of the vigilance deemed necessary to ward off a future of genocide, murder, assimilation, colonialism, projection, and introjection. We are lulled by pleasure into literal self-satisfaction; we are driven by desire into recognitions of that which we cannot maintain or definitively obtain. Pleasure gratifies; desire becomes.

In March of this year, my Guru, Dharmanidhi Sarasvati, wrote to me: *Be with yourself like the sweet anticipation of peeling the pomegranate on a hot summer day in the desert, almost tasting the sweet, juicy fulfillment and **rasa** pouring down your fingers ... soon to be taken in and become a part of you.*

Within the Tantric tradition of which I am an initiate, both desire and pleasure are the engines of creation. Nothing is rejected. Nothing is renounced. A self-aware energy, pulsing with spontaneous desire, emanates the manifest universe and then experiences pleasure upon encountering itself in all its multiplicity. *I desire. I anticipate. The other appears. We recognize each other. I taste her sweetness. We are distinct; we are one body. An identity inside a difference; a difference inside an identity. An expression, an emanation. Beyond resolution. Paradoxical. Trembling.* The Tantras or written scriptures most often describe this trembling, this creation inside the edge of the multiplicity and oneness, as *delight*.

Delight taken in the act of assimilation, in the act of eating, may be the paradigmatic transgression for post–World War II ethical theory and its heir, posthumanism. In an interview with Jean Luc Nancy that will figure heavily here, Derrida writes that we will eat, we cannot help but eat. The ethical question is: *How may we eat well?* (1991, 114). Certainly the colonialisms, genocides, and violent appropriations associated with Western humanism are cases of *eating badly*. For Derrida, eating well consists of respect, caution, a feeling for or of justice, and a hospitality that welcomes unconditionally while preserving the strangeness of the meal, the otherness of the other. Resonating with much postwar Continental philosophy, and particularly in his later work, there is little room for gustatory pleasure.

Ψ Every Relation but One: Part I

Humanist discourses of epistemological and ontological transcendence and their brutal real-life effects have deeply marked, and I would even say scarred, postwar ethical thinking with the imperative to avoid at all costs the breaching of human-human boundaries. Not only are human relations viewed primarily as scenes of wounding and violence, but as Peter Hallward has noted, many contemporary philosophers and cultural theorists share *a profound distrust of the very concept of a community. For these thinkers, "community" often connotes a notion of* ***fascism*** (89). Those writing under the sign of posthumanism have perhaps exercised the greatest restraint, the most consistent asceticism. Theorists of the posthuman generally avoid scenes of human-human relations altogether in favor of exploring questions of relationality and ethics at the edges where humans and nonhumans or technologies join. Posthumanism sutures people together out of variegated components. It links people to technologies, to nonhumans, to forces, to animals, and even, as we shall see, to insects. Rarely, however, does posthumanism explicitly or primarily connect people to each other, regardless of how "person" is conceived and even when such connections are an urgent concern.

Humanism, in by now well-rehearsed arguments, produces oppressive institutions and discourses because it presumes that one sort of person (usually male, white, educated, and wealthy) is exemplary, and/or that there exists a "human nature" that is "the same" for all. Simultaneously, it excludes certain people and all nonhumans from that elite class or common inheritance and fails to recognize and value cultures that do not comport with itself. As such, humanism is the eager inheritor and vehicle of Western metaphysics, of *the Greek domination of the Same and the One. . . . an oppression certainly comparable to none other in the world, an ontological or transcendental oppression, but also the origin or alibi of all oppression in the world* (Derrida 1978, 83). During World War II, terrifying imputations of "sameness" and "difference" were concomitant with mystic fascist statecraft and acts of genocide. To avoid the worst in the postwar period, human-human relations have been insistently figured as the locus of an unbridgeable ontological and epistemological gap, a juncture marked with prophylactic concepts of "absolute otherness" and "radical alterity" deployed rather like moats to deter violence. At the same time, *affectively*, in their potential for the blurring of self-other boundaries, human relations remain the site of a potential eruption of a dangerous, and perhaps dangerously seductive sameness. This leads to a situation within posthumanist discourses in which human relations mark *both unbridgeable difference and dangerous similarity*. We may freely engage with nonhuman others as these others cause difference to appear and be legible in a way that human-human relations may scarily fail to do. At the same time, we must be radically other to each other. This paradox makes it difficult, or better, prohibitively uncomfortable, to locate questions of ethics directly at the scene of human relations, at the scene of two.

Posthumanism, sometimes called "transhumanism," is a field of inquiry and a set of practices that, in light of the political critique of humanism and Western metaphysics of the past fifty years, asks not "Who or what is a person?" but "How is a person?" In many versions of posthumanism, the distinctions (of species, genre, gender, class, race, and so on) that lent substance and value to the question "Who?" have given way to a view of a person as a set of processes, performances, or decentralized agents coupled with or distributed across an environment. In keeping with much postwar thinking about ethics, posthumanism wants to prevent violence by undermining notions of a superior, self-willing, self-possessed person and its march toward ontological and epistemological transcendence. Posthumanism's specific style of rethinking concepts of the person and the human proceeds by considering how subjectivity, bodies, agency, and cognition are altered by engagements with communications technologies and networks; by the changing technological conditions for the production of language; by new media generally; by the artificial life sciences and computer science; and by related concepts extant in science studies and philosophy such as sociotechnical systems, rhizome, and machinic assemblage. Each of these domains provides opportunities for decentering, destabilizing, and complicating categories of the human and the person.

N. Katherine Hayles: *The posthuman subject is an amalgam, a collection of heterogeneous components, a material-informational entity whose boundaries undergo continuous construction and reconstruction* (1999, 3).

Chris Hables Gray and Steven Mentor: *The cyborg body politic is at times a web, a shifting chain of inter-related bodies, some human-machine some machine* (230).

Rosi Braidotti: *The feminist subject of knowledge . . . is rhizomatic, embodied, and, therefore, perfectly artificial; as an artifact it is machinic, complex, endowed with multiple capacities for interconnectedness in the impersonal mode* (1994, 162).

Cary Wolfe: *The moment is irredeemably post-humanist because of the boundary breakdowns between animal and human, organism and machine, and the physical and the non-physical* (1995, 36).

Bruno Latour: *I simply try to present, in the space left empty by the dichotomy between subject and object, a conceptual scenography for the pair human and nonhuman* (viii).

Brian Rotman: *Circa 2000 technology ushers out the human race to produce a divergent plurality of "species." The result? A parallel co-evolution and deferred coalescence of machines and humans* (1997, 3).

Despite their sometimes significantly different sources, the authors cited above exemplify posthumanism's near-exclusive focus on the human-nonhuman touch and its preference for routing questions of ethics through relationships between people and technologies or other non-human entities, including animals. Most of the authors invoked in this text, including myself, would agree with Cary Wolfe when he writes that the politics of posthumanism are *of a piece with larger liberationist political projects that have historically had to battle against the strategic deployment of humanist discourse against other human beings for the purposes of oppression* (1995, 36). Human/nonhuman "cuts" produce most of the desired political gains for posthumanism by laminating technologized, heterogeneous, networked versions of the person with a politics of difference. The cyborg is perhaps the exemplary figure of posthumanism. According to Donna Haraway's now classic definition, the cyborg is *a cybernetic organism, a hybrid of machine and organism, a creature of social reality as well as a creature of fiction* (1985, 65). By disrupting notions of a stable, autonomous, uniquely human self, posthumanist theorists hope to create the conditions for the emergence of less hierarchical and less violent social and political relationships. However, for those specifically working under the banner of posthumanism, hopes for mitigating human violence have expressed themselves, not only as productive engagements with difference and its vector, the nonhuman, but also as an aversion to speaking of human-to-human relationships at all. The cyborg is never a hybrid of two or more *people.*

When theorists of the posthuman do approach human-to-human relationships, they tend to do so indirectly, exercising a great deal of caution. This tendency is evident, for example, when Donna Haraway suggests that *hypertext is an instrument for reconstructing common sense about relatedness* (1997, 125). Or when Alexandra Chasin proposes that *the progressive emergence of machines that work electronically has coincided with the progressive theoretical displacement of hierarchical humanisms, and with the proliferation of theories about identity* (94). Or when M.I.T. roboticist Rodney Brooks told me during the 1997 Society for Literature Conference that he is building humanoid robots because he believes they will teach us to get along with those who are "different." Or when N. Katherine Hayles writes that the *cyborg puppet* or avatar in cyberspace *has the potential to become more than a puppet, representing instead a zone of interaction that opens the subject to the exhilarating realization of Otherness* (1993, 188). In these examples, human relationships with nonhumans serve as salutary pedagogical models or moments in ways that more direct (and dangerous) relationships between humans no longer may.

If humanism asks "Who is?" for the purposes of generating both the exemplary human individual and the species-entity "Man," posthumanism asks "How is a person?" with the intention of cutting into the intoxicant "Man" with a destabilizing "difference": the nonhuman. However, if the posthuman solution is to produce difference only at the site of the human-nonhuman touch, and concurrently there is not a vocabulary for relationships between people, then the person-person touch is left to stand as the unreconstructed site from which might erupt all the violent effects attributed to humanism. Of course, it is precisely anxiety about provoking such eruptions that underpins posthumanist circumspection with regard to speaking of relations between people.

For those of us engaged in thinking and experimenting with a possible posthuman ethics, it would seem crucial to attempt to move beyond this impasse and to begin to develop vocabularies and strategies for engaging in human relations in ways that do not demand such austerities of contact. I take it as axiomatic that the effects of *exemption* are at the heart of posthumanism's complaint against humanism. Here I want to begin to develop a vocabulary of concepts and a set of practices that will be hospitable to a posthumanism, and to a postdeconstruction as Derrida hints at it, that will not be required to obey the injunction that ethics arise only from the respectful maintenance of an irremediable gap between self and others, or, in the case of posthumanism, to situate itself everywhere but at the scene of human relationships. I want to create the conditions that will make it possible to think and practice an ethics that does not rely on what I believe are *untenable* concepts of the radically unassimilable and absolute or even legible differences and identities. What I want to arrive at is an altered syntax of self-other relations that is *more faithful* to the critiques of elitism and exemption that both posthumanism and deconstruction enact.

Ψ (Post)Humanism Ψ

In 1976, the same year that *Of Grammatology* appeared in English for the first time, critic and cultural theorist Ihab Hassan delivered the keynote address at the International Symposium on Postmodern Performance organized by the Center for Twentieth-Century Studies at the University of Wisconsin in Milwaukee. Hassan opened by announcing the eclipse of the postmodern by the posthuman. Despite the greater intellectual reach and impact of Donna Haraway's "A Manifesto for Cyborgs," it is likely Hassan who first explicitly identified the cyborg with the posthuman (848). He described the posthuman as a creative, Promethean trickster split by language, in intimate, shaping contact with technology, obeying only the law of change, and charged with the Nietzschean task of evolving humankind beyond humanism's dangerously oppressive "Man." *We need first to understand that the human form—including human desire and all its external representations—may be changing radically, and thus must be re-visioned. We need to understand that five hundred years of humanism may be coming to an end, as humanism transforms itself into something that we must helplessly call posthumanism* (843).

In *The End of Education: Toward Posthumanism*, William Spanos positions posthumanism as an outflux of the social protest movements that led up to and shaped the Vietnam War era: the Black Power movement, feminism, and movements of other *ethnic minorities* (xiii). He employs posthumanism as an umbrella term that subsumes both Continental philosophy and postmodernism (xiv). His purpose is to draw from these domains related projects that he supports even as he argues that they have been incompletely realized by posthumanist thinkers and activists thus far. These projects are the decentering of the human or the *anthropologos*, the articulation of difference and otherness, and the project of rendering porous disciplines of knowledge and therefore, academic disciplines (187–90). While Spanos places posthumanism exclusively within the purview of U.S. social movements and the Continental European philosophical response to liberal humanism and Western metaphysics, N. Katherine Hayles has focused her extensive writings on the reconfiguration and decentering of concepts of the human and the person emerging from post–World War II sciences and social sciences such as cybernetics, systems theory, and artificial intelligence. In *How We Became Posthuman,* Hayles argues that *the posthuman appears when computation rather than possessive individualism is taken as the ground of being* (34). Hayles aptly coins *the computational subject* to denote a view of the person that *privileges informational pattern over material instantiation . . . considers consciousness . . . as an epiphenomenon . . . thinks of the body as the original prosthesis . . . and configures human being so that it can be seamlessly articulated with intelligent machines* (1997, 242). The inaugural moment of *this* posthuman might be 1948 when cyberneticist Norbert Wiener opined that he saw no reason why a human being might not be sent through a telegraph wire (1948, 144–54).

Both Spanos and Hayles use the term "posthumanism" to denote critical orientations toward Western humanisms as advanced by philosophers, scientists, critics, and activists whether or not the term "posthumanism" is explicitly employed. I take a somewhat different approach. I use "posthumanism" to denote those who specifically invoke the term in their work. The addition of "progressive" distinguishes the commitments of my interlocutors from those of technophiles who long for digital, disembodied immortality: a variety of posthuman that is not at issue here. I also include those who engage with the figure of the cyborg, as this figure has been central to posthumanist thinking generally. By doing so, I hope to give you a sense of the range of concerns of those working under the rubric of posthumanism. I also hope to avoid pinning the term on those I believe would actively reject it, those Spanos groups, somewhat injudiciously I think, under the banner of "poststructuralism." Here I am thinking most vigorously of Derrida, who has generally declined to endorse the ruptures and surpassings indicated by the prefix "post." Distinguished from those who explicitly use the term posthumanism are the major philosophical and technoscientific sources for progressive posthumanism. These include Michel Foucault, Deleuze and Guattari, cognitive scientist Francisco Varela, and social systems theorist Niklas Luhmann.

While posthumanism responds to the legacies of humanism by breaking up, fracturing, distributing, and decentralizing the self-willing person, questioning its subjectival unity and epistemological conceits, like its humanist, Enlightenment, and Romantic progenitors, posthumanism is passionately concerned with creativity and freedom. Posthumanist figurations of freedom range from the beatitude of autonomous self-creation found in the writings of Deleuze and Guattari to states of libertarian noninterference inspired by the systems theory of sociologist Niklas Luhmann. Despite posthumanism's interest in undermining the humanist subject, Hassan's invocation of a singular, salvific, and renegade figure, that of Prometheus, still serves as an index of contemporary posthumanism's reliance on solo figures of creative and often heroic autonomy. These figures—a poet, a trickster, a cyborg, a scientist, an engineer of self—are triply charged with maintaining an ethical stance with respect to others, with preserving a zone of human freedom without which respect for difference would not matter, and with carrying forward what is explicitly, or simply by virtue of a kind of posthumanist rhetorical zeal, the project of posthuman creative differentiation. Keith Ansell Pearson makes this point with respect to the machinic assemblages of Deleuze and Guattari, and I think it applies to much of posthumanist theorizing. *In many of the examples given of ethological assemblages that involve supposedly nonhuman becomings of the human the crucial component in the assemblage is more often than not the human one. It is, in fact, the technicized human that provides the unifying and privileged point of consistency in such an assemblage* (185–86). The focus on the human individual "part" derives, I believe, from posthumanism's concern with freedom—freedom *from* oppression, freedom *for* self-creation. Posthumanist iterations of the person often assume that control of creative transformative capacity is the engine of freedom. Despite other dislocations and attenuations, the human part effects this control, and this control is, as we shall see, guaranteed by the closure of the individual, by maintaining a legible gap, a legible difference between one and another. Posthumanism emerges, then, from a tension between the urge to disperse the subject into decentralized agents or more autonomous, anonymous forces and the urge to find a locus for the pursuit of freedom founded on practices of creative self-constitution.

In light of the above, posthumanism retains the logic of humanism in several ways. First, posthumanist inquiries are still addressed to closed entities or individuals, even when closure is narrowly delimited. Posthuman theorists write about the posthuman as an entity in contact with many other entities and substances, yet *the difference must be told*. In the final analysis, each "part" must do its work of maintaining clearly legible instances of difference, the sine qua non of postwar ethics. While Cary Wolfe writes of "boundary breakdowns" between the human and the animal or the technological, the boundaries may never be truly violated or difference would be put at an untenable risk. Second, while the individual is often simply *a* posthuman, he or she is just as often a heroic, special individual, such as a poet or an "engineer of self," charged with carrying out the creative self-constituting work on which freedom is predicated. Posthumanism remains firmly within the purview of humanism insofar as it tends to retain at the center of its narratives the *one* who becomes and the one who owns those becomings. Third, posthumanism asks a great many questions in which the Other or alter or alien or animal or nonhuman or technological feature as active terms. Relationships between these entities and a "human" individual are the relationships that appear most frequently in posthumanist texts. Yet in general, the urge of these questions is to formulate something about a "human" individual, however human is figured. Finally, posthumanism places great faith in the idea that a reformulation of the concept of *an* individual will produce better politics or ethics: the courtier and *l'uomo universale* of humanism are supplanted by the exemplary, differentiating posthuman.

▼ Suspension

I cannot bear the word *desire.*
—Michel Foucault as remembered by Gilles Deleuze,
"Desire and Pleasure"

This project, while it invokes pleasure only sporadically, is nonetheless written under pleasure's auspices. *Pleasure's force of suspension,* Roland Barthes insists, *can never be overstated* (1975, 65). Barthes illustrates the suspensive effects of pleasure with scenes of reading. *For example, in reading Zola's Fécondité, the ideology is flagrant, especially sticky: naturism, family-ism, colonialism; nonetheless I continue reading the book* (32). Here, pleasure suspends or defers the distinction between work and luxury, between useful time and wasted time, between my sensations and my opinions, and, importantly, between the time of enjoyment and the time of politics. Such *narrative luxuries that take time and waste time,* writes Kathryn Bond Stockton, constitute a *sign of a fascinating sacrifice* (n.p.). Many of us have branded pleasure's sacrifices as apolitical or anti-intellectual. The main complaint against pleasure is that it does not adequately respect difference. Pleasure has been associated with the worst aristocratic propensities of high modernism, with fascist aestheticizations and mystifications of nation and state, and with approaches to literature that depoliticize and dehistoricize. Within posthumanist theory, the expectation and seeking of pleasure within human relationships, relationships which include reading, writing, being read, and being written, have gone largely untheorized, unacknowledged, rejected, and even feared. Yet pleasure persists. As the persistent supplement, even at the scene of violence, pleasure points me toward what I hope to convince you is the paradigmatic posthuman ethical gesture: a paradoxical sacrifice of renunciation, the renunciation of exemption.

Inaugurating procedures of nonexemption, pleasure opens me, you, and this text, to forms of relationality that sometimes suspend the imperatives of trauma and the prohibitions that would protect from the assimilative touch. These momentary pleasures hint at a *capacity* for ontological confusion that ultimately undermines an ethics based on concepts such as "radical" difference or "absolute" otherness. I call these moments of "weak" transcendence. Roland Barthes's friend, the French-Cuban Buddhist Tantric Severo Sarduy, calls the state of weak transcendence *beeromania*, a mild intoxication, *that aspires only to the state of "happiness," to momentary irresponsibility, to a letting go, around the brief noon hour, of the weight of one's self, of the punctual watchfulness of the Other in the omnipresent shape of the Law* (1995, 12). Putting it one way out of many yet to come, the question for me is, in attending to pleasure and its weak transcendence of self-other boundaries, can I further a posthumanist and, following Derrida, postdeconstructive ethics? As I elaborate it here, such an ethics would waive the demand that others and "the Other" do the work of ethics as such and would invite the consideration of forms and moments of relationality that proceed from the subjection of categories of both self and other to suspension.

This shift in emphasis and attention prepares the way for a meeting of the two conceptions of ethics that have been most important to contemporary progressive thought. Posthumanist concepts of ethics center on the multiplication of individual capacities via technologies of self. These have been most clearly articulated by Gilles Deleuze in his engagements with Spinoza and Foucault. Brian Massumi describes Deleuzian self-capacitation *as ethical experimentation and as an invitation to recapitulate, to repeat and complexify... the real conditions of emergence, not of the categorical, but of the unclassifiable, the unassimilable, the never yet felt.... The implied ethics of the project is the value attached—without foundation, with desire only—to the multiplication of powers of existence, to ever-divergent regimes of action and expression* (1995, 94–95). I intend to examine instances in which an ethics of self-capacitation tries, and in my opinion fails, to become an ethics of responsibility, skirting dangerously close to narcissism and simple insufficiency with respect to the task of imagining a posthumanist ethics that would not repeat the humanist logic of elitism and exemption. I will then focus on that thread of ethical thinking running from Emmanuel Levinas to Derrida. This thread winds itself around the problem of responsibility and indebtedness and generally takes human relationality as its primal scene. I believe that deconstruction also relies on a kind of prophylaxis, on a restraining or yoking of categories of self and other for the purpose of grounding a discourse on responsibility. This yoking presents us with an untenable end of deconstruction, an end of *différance*. Routing my argument through Derrida's anomalous invocation of *a new (postdeconstructive) determination of the responsibility of the "subject"* (Derrida and Nancy, 105), I suggest that we might find our way out of these conundrums by suspending the closure of the human individual deployed to maintain a legible and founding difference between self and other. In order to create the conditions for the emergence of a nonexemptive, nonelitist ethics of both capacitation and responsibility, we will have to give up our reliance on concepts of the radically other, or the other as such, and also on a *zero-point* of calculation of the responsibility of the self. My method, with respect to both Deleuze and Derrida, is to show that figures of closure, of the inviolable zone that guarantees ethics, do not hold up even, or especially, on their own terms. I hope to clear a space in which an *otherwise* might appear as livable.

Ψ Deconstruction and Posthumanism? Ψ

Despite the fact that the (mostly) North American theorists who write under the banner of posthumanism rarely engage with Derrida or his interlocutors, posthumanism and deconstruction are inseparable in profound ways. Posthumanists and deconstructionists position colonialism, racism, and genocide as the logical outcome of the broad sweep of Western logocentrism. Along with many of their interlocutors, they view fascism, with its dangerous concatenation of techno-spirituous merges and violent ejections, as humanism's limit case. In the most fundamental and pervasive sense, their shared urge is to contravene Western humanisms comprehended as elitist and exemptive valuations of the human and propagated via a series of related iterations of empire—political, social, cultural, economic, spiritual, and epistemological. Throughout this text, I will view both posthumanism and deconstruction as critiques of a double logic of elitism and exemption.

In a more specific sense, both posthumanism and deconstruction respond to the precepts and effects of largely nineteenth-century elaborations of humanism. Since the time of what has been deemed the origin of Western thought—that is, the time of ancient Greek philosophy—the destiny of the human has been conceived within the domain of metaphysics. This entrainment of an exclusively human destiny to the possibility of attaining comprehensive, transcendent knowledge also entrains all other species, and the planet itself, to the human and has propagated itself through the valorization of the powers of mind at the expense of respecting the powers of bodies and the material world.

Nineteenth-century critics and theorists such as Matthew Arnold, Jacob Burckhardt, and Arthur de Gobineau extended the privilege and range of the Enlightenment's "Man" by constructing a multilayered typology of Greek, Roman, Renaissance, and contemporary European cultures for the purpose of justifying empire, elitism, racialism, essentialism, and a cult of *l'oumo universale* (Burckhardt 152). Nineteenth-century "anthropological" typologies of human beings and the racist mappings of human bodies, existing as they did alongside a discourse of human virtue, freedom, and power, are, of course, the co-constructors of colonialism, and further on, of fascist-sponsored genocide.

Posthumanism's links to American cultural studies, queer theory, and U.S. sociopolitical movements tend to focus it more on problems of colonization and representation, broadly conceived, and less on the legacy of World War II and fascism in general. Its responses to the problems of colonization and representation most often rely upon conceptions of human-technology relations that work to "unseat" the colonizer at the same time that they preserve altered notions of self-capacitation, autonomy, and creativity. Despite the fact that human relationships are posthumanism's urgent concern, and, as I propose here, because of a pressing anxiety about human relationships and their inevitable violence, posthumanism has failed to develop a vocabulary with which it might speak of care, of responsibility. Instead, it tends to celebrate figures of Deleuzian creativity, *human* figures directing or participating in processes of self-creation. Deconstruction, on the other hand, finds its ethical horizon in responsibility for what Derrida repeatedly terms "the worst," that is, with the genocides of World War II. Can we now weave these two modes of thinking ethics together: both self-capacitation *and* responsibility? One of the meanings of *Tantra* is a weaving.

▼ Nonphilosophy Ψ

> When it seems in his texts that Deleuze is making a claim about the
> way things are, most often he is not—and he does not take himself
> to be—telling us about the way things are. Instead, he is offering
> us a way of looking at things.
> —Todd May, "Difference and Unity in Gilles Deleuze"

In the beginning is a performance, a staging: a dialogue. Two people or
more head toward realization, a series of realizations led by an auteur,
an author, an actor. And there is always an audience, an assembly. I see,
by now, a rather epicized image of the bearded old man. The city serves
as proscenium for the conversation underway. *Socrates seemed to spend
all his time in the streets, the marketplace, and more particularly, the gym-
nasia. He cared little for the country* (*Encyclopaedia Britannica* n.p.). The
philosopher-character is ironic, knowing, deliberate, wry, never vulnerable or immersed. Or I see the author, Plato, nearly synonymous with
the book, its tissue-thin pages, their vanilla church scent. The ritual of
past readings renders my own readings in the epic mold. I set out on
the adventure once again with the odd mingling of security and thrill.
Treading the ancient stones, through the inexorable alleys, toward the
inevitable clearing bathed in an outlandish light.

The conjunction of argument, knowledge, and virtue constitutes
Socrates' conceit: the assumption that the virtuous voice and knowledge stick, cohere in a way that empowers both. But I really want to ask
about the performance. Is Socrates' "conceit" the occasion for the necessity of Plato's performance? *Plato's irony, I believe, is more disturbing*

than Socrates': it is deep, dark, and disdainful (Nehamas 72). But disdainful
of whom? Of Socrates or his interlocutors? Nietzsche accuses Plato of
being a corrupt artist, of placing art at the service of an ascetic, life-
slandering philosophy, of corrupting art in the service of truth (Nietzsche
1994, 121). And I do first think of the stifling inevitability of the written
dialogues. How much time, how many fits and starts, misunderstandings,
inchoate tailings are finished off, smoothed, condensed? This smooth-
ness, this knowingness, is the performance of philosophy as such. But it
is performed by Socrates alone, his acerbic, urban certainty pitted against
the uncertainty or inarticulateness of his auditors.

Socrates' logic presumes to surpass art, to surpass performance. The
beyond is silence. In the Western philosophical tradition, silence marks
the edge of logic, where it takes you and where it drops you off: the
Real. Silence = *logos* = the end of performance = transparency = transcendence. Silence = revelation. Inarticulateness is quite another thing.
Socrates' auditors, those comely young men, are often inarticulate. I am
inarticulate when I don't know or can't say. But I am also inarticulate in
the face, not of lack, but of *too much.* Sometimes, such as in the neo-
baroque fiction of Sarduy, the too much is precisely the sensual, inarticulate pleasure of reading: washed over by words. In the dialogues, inarticulateness becomes commentary otherwise; it works through blanks
and interspacings, through delinquencies, through the setting into motion of flows and tensions between volumes of too much positive speech.

Socrates appears to orchestrate the silence of his pupils in order to
mark a lack, in order to open a space for instruction, a space for truth to
enter. The dramatic art of Plato uses inarticulateness to limn and comment on Socrates' brand of truth, his too much that is, nevertheless, not
enough. Here I think of any number of scenes in which the monosyllabic
answers of Socrates' interlocutors interleaf his speeches with shifting
and shifty affects, sarcastic commentary, deflections from the "point."
Those metronomic answers, "I do," "Yes," "Obviously," "That is so," are
the punctum, what punctures the arguments, opening them to else-
wheres and otherwises. The cheerful, nearly seductive, nearly burlesque
servility of these performances draws attention to Socrates' egotism, his
need for subservience, and the terms under which his method may succeed. *Philosophy has a horror of discussions. . . . Socrates constantly made
all discussion impossible. . . . He turned the friend into the friend of the*

single concept, and the concept into the pitiless monologue that eliminates the rivals one by one (Deleuze and Guattari 1994, 29).

Socrates is Plato's concept of certainty dramatized. Foolishness, the inchoate, the lapse, and the fall are on the side of philosophy's interlocutors. Plato, as I wish to read him, knows that these are also philosophy's friends. He wreaks a certain vengeance on Socrates by placing him (philosophy) in a relationship not of his own choosing, a relationship to fiction, the fiction of the sufficiency of argument, its autonomy. *The dramatic setting engages forms of life, not just arguments, and because philosophy must be practical, not dependent solely on foundational claims, Socrates elaborates a relation to contradiction more powerful than that usually available to philosophers* (Altieri 255). Many interpreters of Plato have faulted Socrates' frigid intellectualism. What if the conjunctions philosophy/nonphilosophy and philosopher/nonphilosopher friends were meant to raise just this critique, a critique of philosophy's sufficiency played out on the stage of a city among a society of friends in the genre of dramatic art?

Under the auspices of a series of related humanistic discourses and practices concerned with the question of mastery, the common elements of successive waves of humanism derive from these dramatized scenes of Socratic pedagogy. Marked at one end by the Roman reinvention and glorification of Greek epigraphy, humanism proceeds through a series of appropriations and reimaginings of a heroic Greco-Roman past. These center on the city as the objective correlative of an elite vantage point; on the society of elite friends and the raising up of a virtuous androcentric friendship above all other relations; on the commonwealth of propertied men as the origin of empire; on the association of the learning of arts and letters with a homoerotic relationship between an older man and a younger one; on the valuation of the autonomy and power of the individual condensed in the figure of the philosopher-king; and on the presumptive relations that obtain between orality, logical and formal coherence, and transparency to truth.

While it might seem as if I am offering you an argument, a proposal, a demonstration that wants to rout out the last vestiges of the humanist subject and its political problems, I am not. Instead, my aim is to make it possible for posthumanism to claim what I will call, following both Tantra and Spinoza-Deleuze, the *capacities* of humanism by detaching them from a logic of exemption and elitism and putting them into play within a milieu that recognizes the ethicopolitical necessity of differentiation, of incoherency, of incompletion, of play, and of modes expressivity based, not on capitulation or accommodation, but on delight. My method throughout will be to extend existing ideas and tendencies within posthumanism and deconstruction beyond their currently acceptable, currently *thinkable* terrain and thus invigorate what I see as their liberatory, ethicopolitical potentials. This method must derive from procedures of nonexemption that recirculate the central tropes and values of humanism: the city, the friend, the pedagogical relation, and, as much of progressive posthumanism has rejected or critiqued narratives of personality in favor of an emphasis on the impersonal or antipsychological, the capacity to create subjects, the capacity to tell and enact baroque personality stories. One additional "capacity" of humanism that I wish to relocate within posthumanism is the ability to speak of the One, here recalculated as the nonlocal or *oceanic.*

▼Ψ Tidal Kneeplay Ψ▼

The theology of [Tantric] **prakasa** [consciousness] *speaks not only the language of scientific prose, but also in what one might call a language of spiritual and emotional liquidity. It hints at the dissolution of ordinary ego consciousness, at immersion in the cave, the bottomless center of all phenomena; it seems to speak of overflowing, being brimful, of being afloat in the depths of the sea.* **Prakasa** *as liquidity has, however, as its counterpoint* **prakasa** *as solidification. Dissolution is balanced by the emitting of the material world. . . . This counterpoint is reflected in practice: . . . the dissolution of ordinary consciousness, is never sought for its own sake; it is sought for the sake of the return. The "deep," and the solid world of multiplicity are to be seen as both the same and different . . .*

I am tempted to call the theology of **prakasa** *. . . a "tidal" theology, for it is a theology which seems to serve as a sustained meditation upon the inexorable, unfathomable rhythms of in and out, open and shut, filling and emptying, some of the subliminal regularities, ambivalences, and antinomies underlying human life* (Alper 385).

Letter to Chris Kraus

undated

Dear Chris,

Don't you think that too often, we read philosophers programmatically for the purpose and pleasure of extracting a coherent system of ideas or series of usable concepts? We are asked to do this, of course. Not asked:

ordered. Even those, such as Deleuze and Derrida, who explicitly engage in experiments of writing, must be taken seriously. (Read as Men and not Girls?) But perhaps Derrida, who I love, and Deleuze, who fascinates, perhaps they would want me to notice how desire conflicts with concept, how anger, bitterness, compassion, fear of death, and the yearning for transcendence crack and flow through. Perhaps they would take pleasure in finding themselves engaged along the grain of the skin, in the lungs, the fluids: the inexorable, unfathomable rhythms of in and out, open and shut, filling and emptying, some of the subliminal regularities, ambivalences, and antinomies . . .

Love, Ann

▼ Deleuze and Derrida: *You Are Other* Ψ

Postwar ethics emerges from an intensified sensibility to wounding and human violence. For both Deleuze and Derrida, the violent "subject" of any relation must be protectively closed off from its fellows in limited, but critical ways. In the case of Deleuze, a concept of positive, absolute, and ontologically-generated difference is what creates individuals, and also what individuals create. Deleuze insists we may take on the capacities of other individuals, or participate in zones of involvement, but we may not actually *be the other*. Deleuze's concept of difference also enables and undergirds his *affective* investment in heroic human figures who have ownership of insistently active capacities for proliferating and controlling self-expressions. These expressions include capacities drawn from other people, animals, and things. Derrida's ethical thinking also relies on concepts of the singular and the unalterably other, where the other is, in Levinasian fashion, constitutive of the self, of experience itself: an always unassimilable exterior-interior. And as does Deleuze, Derrida also maintains that the other may not be myself. Only via this closure is the subject able to congeal at a "zero point" on which responsibility, at least in theory, may be calculated.

Posthumanism inherits this protective gesture. Despite the involvement of "alien," "other," and "nonhuman" in processes of self-creation, a legible difference, a gap, between individual entities is preserved, even if that gap has been relocated to an altered, composite, and in some cases, alien-ized interior. As Vicki Kirby has written about the cyborg, the *recipe for cyborg graftings is utterly dependent upon the calculus of one* *plus one, the logic wherein pre-existent identities are **then** conjoined and melded* (147). Demonstrating Kirby's point, Camilla Griggers argues in exemplary posthumanist mode that *if we accept that the body exists in an assemblage with technology, the "human" body itself may well appear subordinate to the cyborg body of which it is a part* (55). In the interest of preserving legible difference, the identities of parts are often quite strenuously marked by a highly cathected insistence that the alien remain alien and the other remain tantalizingly other. If true confusion were allowed, difference would tremble too violently. This marking constitutes the individual, reinstating the logic of humanism and the necessity to pose questions of ethics, when they are posed, in the usual form: How might we induce caretaking, or more commonly, guarantee responsibility for others when we are fatally separate, self-interested individuals? The unstable, tidal vocabulary I have offered thus far, "weak transcendence" and "suspension," emphasizes what happens in more unbounded relations of contact, of touch. It points us toward the task of imagining a more rigorously nonexemptive posthumanist ethics, one that *includes* our capacities for uncertain mergers. Baudrillard, in his ironic, curmudgeonly way, writes: *Otherness has become sociodramatic, semiodramatic, melodramatic* (125). In some quarters, yes. But even the most devoted philosophers, the most devoted and loving theorists and activists, have sensitized themselves and us to otherness at the expense of its suspension, to wounding at the expense of pleasure, at the expense of an incoherence that risks events of contact. Is there a way to teach us that our bodies are not dumb woundings or, on the other hand, furnaces?

Ψ To Have

Thus far, the logic of the humanist subject and humanist political life has been a logic of elite ownership: ownership of knowledge, land, material and psychic resources, and sociopolitical entitlements. Even concepts such as consensus and intersubjectivity are based on ownership, either ownership of singularities that might be communicated, or an essentialized, self-present ownership of a common psychic, cognitive, or spiritual inheritance. Writing of Leibniz and citing Gabriel Tarde's recapture of Leibnizian monadology for a democratic sociology, Deleuze notes favorably Tarde's *substitution of having for being, as a true inversion of metaphysics that issues directly from the monad* (1993, 158n20). "To have," as opposed to "to be," Deleuze argues, is a formulation of "to fold." Writing with and across Spinoza, Leibniz, Foucault, and, as we shall see, Indian Tantra, Deleuze develops the concept of folding or involution (involvement) that underwrites processes of self-capacitation and self-expansion. Elizabeth Grosz calls this a *postmodern ethics* based not on a Levinasian (and Derridian) *subject-to-subject, self-to-other, relation, the relation of a being respected in its autonomy from the other, but on the ability to increase or decrease one's capacities and strengths and abilities* (1994, 196–97). These processes consist of entering into blocks of becoming with others, of adding their capacities or forces to one's own, and of differentiating in ways that resist regimes of oversignification or overcoding.

Deleuze explicitly wants to distinguish *having* from the closure associated with private property. *This new domain of having does not put us into an element of calm, which would be a relation of the proprietor and property that could be easily established once and for all. What rules in the domain of having are moving and perpetually reshuffled relations among monads.* However, Deleuze notes the casuistry of Leibniz's claim that monads may be considered *each and every one for each other:* for to have must always also be a domination and an appropriation. To have, at a certain point, puts an end to the reshuffling, there is *a strange linkage, a bracket, a yoke, a knot, a complex relation that comprises variable terms and one constant term . . . Because every relation has a subject* (1993, 109–11). Despite disclaimers with respect to proprietorship, this *yoke,* a word whose root is shared with *yoga,* this *constant term,* this *human* subject, controls matters of its own becomings through yogas of self-mastery and philosophical practices that hold individuals prophylactically apart, disallowing the mistaking of one individual for another. This self mastery is the condition for a Deleuzian ethics based on expanding one's capacities for expression. *The expressive is primary in relation to the possessive; expressive qualities, or matters of expression, are necessarily appropriative and constitute a having more profound than being* (Deleuze and Guattari 1987, 316). And, *one becomes a master of one's speed and, relatively speaking, a master of one's molecules and particular features* (1988a, 123). The question remains: Can practices of self-mastery and self-capacitation, especially those that are founded on a philosophy of difference, *also* answer to or reach toward responsibility for others?

In keeping with procedures of nonexemption, I want to question this logic of possession, not by eschewing the "to have," or the subject, but by pushing them to extremes and asking about the necessity of "to have" with respect to creativity, to expression, to responsibility, to the "I am," and the relationship of two. Spinoza has famously said that *we have only a completely confused knowledge of our body* (124). Much of posthumanism concerns bodies and their powers or limits. However, we have even less of an idea of what two bodies are capable, or of what language and bodies are capable. This indicates that there may be problems with assigning loci of possession in any relationship, particularly at such undecodable membrane/edges as word and flesh. Kirby makes this point in *Telling Flesh: The Substance of the Corporeal.* Arguing for a *corporeography,* or general bio-graphics, she disrupts the presumption that writing is *an essentially human technology* and argues for the literacy of *flesh, blood, and bone—literate matter—[that] never ceases to reread and rewrite itself through endless incarnations* (148). Kirby suggests that corporeography constitutes *a constitutive breaching, a recalling and differentiating within the subject, that hails it into presence. As impossible as it may seem, the ethical relation to radical alterity is to an other that is, also, me, and in which alterity is not radically outside knowledge and understanding* (95; 99).

While I am uncomfortable with the assimilation of the world's differentiating activities to the notion of a global writing, my motivations are very much in keeping with Kirby's. I, too, am concerned with the *impossible* situation of an "other" who is a "me" to the extent that the whole notion of *radical alterity* would be compromised. In other words, I am concerned with events that suspend the terms self and other and with the ethical consequences that flow from these events-in-common. Such events, which to my mind signal a general capacity for and condition of suspension, are trauma, pleasure, love, devotion, illness, inebriation, and multiple forms of incorporation and transmission that constitute a kind of ongoing, ontogenic pedagogy punctuating our days.

To Belong ▼

In my posthuman experiment, I consider the posthuman (entity, person, system) not as a singular "to have," but as an undecidably multiple, undecidably possessed "to belong." To belong subsumes to have, opening it up. Under the rubric of "to belong," "to have" is always deferred, always differing, always trembling, always subject to *différance*. To belong refers, simultaneously, to belonging, belongings, and belonging to. This move breaks the frame "individual," a frame that remains axiomatic for both deconstruction and posthumanism, even when "individual" connotes a system or heterogeneous assemblage. To belong detaches from "having" or "belonging" accomplished in the present. To belong neither rejects nor settles into present belonging; it introduces an uncertainty coupled to a movement in time, a movement of deferral, a movement that opens to an uncertain abundance. The general operational mode of to belonging is *suspension,* a holding things together in such a way that they may move in and out of states of more or less difference, more or less disjunction depending on conditions.

To belong does not operate at a deficit of possession, but at a surfeit. Its "contents"—a gesture, a skill, a memory, a topology, a sensation, a belief, an affect, a longing, a rhythm of speech, an illness—travel around, gathering signatures and never settling down even when they are "stuck" in a traumatized pattern. In light of the above, to belong is suspended with respect to its possessions: what I yoke is what passes through me is what I shelter. These modes of to belonging are never impersonal, prepersonal, presubjective, or asubjective because they never depend on any one origin or destination or component that could be named as such. Instead, they might be deemed *nonlocal,* a designation indicating modes of being in the world, of *worlding,* that circulate among the living, the nonliving, the human, the nonhuman and that serve as multiply-signed capacities for some or all of these. The nonlocal includes the impersonal, the asubjective, the prepersonal, and the presubjective as potential modes or styles.

Provoking the undecidability of the question "to whom?" the quality of deferral of to belonging renders me always uncertain about what belongs to myself or to another. Crucially, to belonging reanimates the question of our belonging to each other, of our nonseparation in specific ways that neither deconstruction nor posthumanism nor recent identity-based sociopolitical movements have been willing to risk. Rather than the poles "self" and "alterity" or "other," to belonging moves from the familiar to the strange, from an affective register of familiarity to estrangement. These are not states of ownership, but mark self-strangeness and the uncanny or canny familiarity of others. Rather than interruption or spacing, the syntax of to belonging is vibration, stretching, porosity, oscillation, stickiness.

The question of to belonging is always a question of two to an unpredictable abundance. As such, it provokes, within posthumanism and deconstruction, the question of love. Philosopher Alain Badiou makes this point when, in a very different kind of an argument, he writes: *We can thus say that love is precisely this: the ad-vent [l'avènement] of the Two as such, the stage of the Two.... This stage of the Two is a work, a process. It only exists as a track through the situation, under the supposition that there are Two. The Two is the hypothetical operator, the operator of an aleatory enquiry, of such a work or such a track.... There is here a numerical schema proper to the amorous procedure. This schema states that the Two fractures the One and tests the infinity of the situation. One, Two, infinity: such is the numericity of the amorous procedure* (2000, 272). Amorous procedures of love, illness, and inebriation induce porosity, induce uncertain abundances which must not (normally) flow through. This illicit flow, occasioned by lapses in the ability to make distinctions between self and other, between objects, between objects and thoughts or flesh and words, has been linked, in the writings of artists, scientists and philosophers to periods of intense creativity and raises the question of whether distinguishing one's possessions, even the possession of "making distinctions," is necessary for an ethics based, in part, on expressivity. Most importantly, the to belonging of expressivities, capacities, creations, bodies, gestures, and so on, raises, from the outset, the possibility of an ethics that does not start from irremediable separation or social antagonism and then move, in some miraculating fashion, toward love, but that includes love in its concept: a t(w)o belonging.

Cyberneticist Norbert Wiener wrote of a bout of pneumonia: *It was impossible for me to distinguish among my pain and difficulty of breathing, the flapping of the window curtain, and certain as yet unresolved parts of the potential [mathematical] problem on which I was working.* After his recovery, Wiener explained the efficacy of this loss of distinction between a pain, an object, and an abstraction as arising from its value as a *temporary symbol for a mathematical situation which has not yet been organized and cleared up* (1956, 85–86). Deleuze and Guattari also speak of invention occasioned by category breakdowns: *Thinking... implies a sort of groping experimentation and its layout resorts to measures that are not very respectable, rational, or reasonable. These measures belong to the order of dreams, of pathological processes, esoteric experiences, drunkenness, and excess. We head for the horizon, ... and we return with bloodshot eyes* (1994, 41). But what if we don't return? What if we don't organize, don't clear things up? What if I fall devotedly in love, here, with you, inside the undecodable, inarticulable edge?

▼▼ Fiora Raggi Kneeplay

I attended what used to be called an "experimental" high school, part hippie, part Marxist. We took small seminar classes on topics such as the Victorian Novel and the French Revolution. Mike, my biology teacher, became interested in the work of Wilhelm Reich. In the mid-seventies, lots of people were interested in Reich's ideas about interlacings of sexuality, biophysical energy, and fascism. Reich viewed the body as an energetic/muscular/socio-political system that stored experiences and that could be transformed on an energetic level. He called this bioenergy "orgone," but it has also been called other names such as *kundalini* and *qi*. Mike offered a seminar in Reich's major works, and I took it. This, believe it or not, set me on a spiritual path, only I didn't know it yet.

At the time, I had a job waiting tables at a local diner. I used the money to begin Reichian therapy. Philadelphia boasted the highest concentration of classically trained Reichian therapists in the world. Fiora Raggi, my therapist, had been a student of Reich's, but she left the official Reichian organization because she found their approaches to be too rigid. Fiora had earned a degree in veterinary science before she became a doctor. She invented a bovine flu shot. She was also a resistance fighter in Italy during World War II. After therapy, we would sit in her kitchen and drink coffee made with instant Nescafé and hot tap water. She would tell me stories of the resistance movement and of her fear as she crouched in roadside trenches, bombs exploding around her. As I did, Fiora wrote science fiction.

I decided I wanted to be a Reichian. Fiora offered to train me. I read everything I could find and attended a laboratory seminar offered by the College of Orgonomy, the official Reichian association. I went off to college and began preparations to go to medical school.

In 1985, when I had long since abandoned the idea of medical school because writing was more important to me, when Fiora had died of cancer, when I was living in New York City and working in the tenant's rights movement, I stumbled into a workshop called something like "Develop Your Intuition." My immersion, since high school, in thinking psychology, politics, and body together, and my acceptance, via Reich, of the idea of the body as an energetic system, prepared me for everything that was to follow from this workshop.

The teacher never described the tradition that informed her work. Now, looking back, I understand that the exercises she taught us were derived directly from classical Indian Tantra. In the early 1990s, I was living in California and working with another teacher, Anodea Judith. She finally told me that the meditation, psychotherapy, and energy exercises I'd been practicing for so many years were Tantric in origin. I woke up one day and discovered I had a spiritual life.

▼ Tantra for Posthumanism Ψ

Indian Tantra was an amalgam of orally transmitted Indian village practices and traditional Vedic beliefs that began to emerge as a written tradition around 500 C.E. (Gupta 5; Feuerstein ix–x). Most contemporary scholars agree that due to its complex history and baroquely variegated forms of expression, any definition of Tantra must be one that generalizes as to a shared set of characteristics, tendencies, or more or less identifiable resemblances. A short list of these resemblances or, better yet, values would include an acceptance of the material, phenomenal world as a real, and not illusory, manifestation of consciousness *(Śiva)* and power *(Śakti)*; a commitment to nonexclusivity of caste, class, and gender; the belief that the human body is a valuable tool in seeking liberation; and the insistence that enjoyment *(bhukti)* and liberation *(mukti)* are not mutually exclusive.

The scholarly literature on Tantra is often structured, explicitly or implicitly, as an argument about to what extent and in which historical time periods Indian Tantra can be viewed as an oppositional response to Brahmin-dominated socio-religious hierarchies or should be understood as a means through which Brahminical power and privilege were reinforced and defended (see Padoux 32–35; Urban 1997). It is certainly true that from about the eighth century onward, upper-class Hindu Brahmins vigorously absorbed and altered Tantra, synthesizing it, but not obliterating it, with more conservative, post-Vedic Hinduism. However, this does not invalidate the ways in which Tantric values and philosophy have already, may in the future, or do simultaneously support more egalitarian, liberatory social and spiritual practices. For instance, Hugh B. Urban, writing across a pair of essays, argues that the centrality of *secrecy* to Tantric practice and culture *offered a new source of status, prestige, and identity for a large number of poor, lower-class, and marginalized individuals at the same time that it opened up a secret realm in which Brahmins could retain their traditional power and privilege, yet without losing their orthodox authority in the exoteric social sphere* (1988, 212; 1997, 5).

My use of Indian Tantra closely resembles Foucault's invocation of Greco-Roman technologies of self. These include letter writing and comprise a set of attitudes and techniques for *performing a certain number of operations on . . . bodies and souls, thoughts, conduct, and way of being* (1988, 18). Tantra, too, comprises a set of techniques or technologies of self. Most Tantras consist of instructions for meditation and bodily practices aimed at sensitizing the practitioner to ontogenic relationships between self and others, self and world. Tantra is a practice of relationality par excellence. Nothing happens outside of relationship; all practices are practices within and of intensified relationality. No relationship is exempt. This is the reason why the Guru-disciple relationship is so central to Tantric practice. The Guru provides the disciple with an experience of and a model for unconditional relationality with everything. As I will discuss later, within Tantric philosophy, a dynamic, processual understanding of relationship is tantamount to both cosmology and ontology. Tantric *sādhāna* (practice) demands what my teacher calls *effortful surrender:* the surrender of static, limiting self concepts, of the limited self, *into* the world, a world whose intrinsic character is that of continually becoming. The goal of *sādhāna* is total participation in the world process.

Alexis Sanderson has begun to illuminate the complex social, political, and religious nexus that gave rise to the systemization and synthesis of many streams of Tantric thought and practice by the early eleventh-century Kashmiri philosopher, yogi, and householder Brahmin Abhinavagupta and his followers. This synthesis, called since the nineteenth century Kashmiri Śaivite Tantra or Kashmir Śaivism, *excluded both the illusionism of the Vedantins and the atheistic autonomism of the [Tantric] ritualists* (197). At the same time, Kashmir Śaivism drew together four extant schools of Tantra and Śaivism. According to Sanderson, Abhinavagupta sought to create a system of metaphysics and practice that would, simply put, outbid all other systems by encompassing them. In the process, he, and even more so his followers, inaugurated what Sanderson terms a *deodorizing* of Tantra, or what another scholar, Andre Padoux, has called the *brahminization* of Tantra (Sanderson 203; Padoux 35). On the one hand, this consisted, according to Sanderson and Padoux, of introducing more purist, abstract notions into Tantric metaphysics and of reinterpreting texts and practices so that unsavory aspects of Tantra were reread as symbolic or deleted altogether. On the other hand, the task of synthesizing several distinct schools and of attempting, as Abhinavagupta does most profoundly, to create a language and a system of thought that might somehow do justice to the *experience* of Tantric practice, resulted in a stunningly fluid, relational, and nondoctrinaire view of the person and the cosmos. As Harvey P. Alper writes: *Does Abhinava have a system in the strict sense? I think so, though I am not certain. He does seem to have a coherent but unstated goal: to encompass— without reconciling—contradictions, that is, to attempt to be faithful to the confusion of experience, to be consistent to inconsistency* (383).

Those complexities and possibilities being noted, across its many permutations, Tantra *has* retained its core values. It consistently counters the body negativism of post-Vedic Hinduisms, viewing the body as a literal, and generally not a symbolic, modality of the cosmos. As such, the body is the best vehicle for achieving both success and enjoyment in this life and spiritual liberation. Describing the ideal female practitioner, an eleventh-century Tantra states: *She is beautiful, cheerful, fair of face, pleasant of brow, devoted to Kulāgama, free from fear, very calm, with a lovely nature, speaking the truth and free from doubts . . . a Devi with a lovely body, grounded in her own body (lit. "having faith in her own body"). Such is a heroine who is Rudra Sakti, the root devata* [both the cosmogonic Sʹakti and the internal goddess] (Bagchi n.p.). Tantra, perhaps infamously, takes antinomian positions with respect to the Vedantic emphasis on renunciation, purity, and with respect to bars on certain forms of relationship within Indian society. Tantric rituals prescribe indulgence in forbidden foods, such as meat and alcohol, and sexual contacts between those married to other people, between strangers, and especially between people of different castes or classes. Central texts and teaching stories emphasize that self-realization, and thus divine realization, is available to anyone, in any walk of life, without renunciation. Tantric lore is replete with stories of washerwomen and other servants who experience liberation while performing their everyday tasks. *The Tantric movement embraced people not ordinarily credited with spiritual knowledge or refinement, namely, outcasts and social rejects like rag-pickers, street-sweepers, thieves, gamblers, bartenders, entertainers, and menial laborers of all types* (Shaw 22). *What all Tantras have in common is that they are scriptures for common folk, unanimous in rejecting the elitism of caste Hinduism. This is in part a reflection of the fact that the great Mother Goddess and her consort Śiva have dark aboriginal origins, and were for a long time not admitted to the Vedic Religion* (Sinha 17). In more recent times, the Bengali Tantric sect, the Kartābhajās, responded directly to both the caste system and to colonialist hegemony: *All members stand on the same footing and distinctions based on caste, wealth, etc. are not recognized. . . . Degraded humanity finds a cordial welcome and ready recognition* (1910; a Kartābhajā spokesperson, quoted in Urban 2001, 20). Today, Tantra is a pan-Asian, indeed a global phenomenon that survives through various teacher lineages and schools, including Tantric Buddhisms, and through disseminated practices such as mantra repetition, visualization, and yogas that have become central to other traditions generally.

Ψ Speaking of Assimilation Ψ

Each of these traditions, Tantra and posthumanism, is primally concerned with the ethics and ontology of relationship, and, despite posthumanism's near-monomaniacal focus on human-technology relations, ultimately with the ethics of human relationships. Each tradition views itself as not just a set of concepts or theories, but as an elaborator and teacher of technologies of self and world transformation. Both Tantra and posthumanism emerged in response to experiences of violence: the violence of exclusion, of representation, of oppressive social hierarchy, of colonialism, and, in the case of posthumanism, of genocide. Both Tantra and posthumanism confront and seek to alter a political-social orthodoxy definitive of their respective culture's spontaneous, normative consciousness. Crucially for this project, in each of these traditions, questions of ethics are tantamount to the problems and paradoxes of difference and sameness, oneness and multiplicity, transcendence and immanence. Tantra, under the influence of Abhinavagupta, is the great thinker of difference, oneness, transcendence, and immanence in Indian culture; posthumanism and its interlocutors are the great thinkers of these in contemporary Western culture. In each tradition, ethics emerges from ontology; ontology replaces or supersedes epistemology.

Of course, you may deem me irresponsible for bringing these traditions together simply because they share some important concerns and several generally similar socio-political contexts. However, it is also true that Tantra, Hinduism, Taoism, and Buddhism have already made significant appearances in the work of the Western philosophers and scientists whose thinking has most shaped posthumanism. For instance, as I will discuss at length, some of Gilles Deleuze's most influential concepts and figures are explicitly Tantric, a situation that has not, as far as I know, been commented upon until now. So, one of the ways that this book works is to make visible and thus more usable the Tantra that is already present within posthumanism.

At the same time, I have noticed that the appearances within posthumanism of Tantra and other Eastern philosophical and spiritual traditions are of a *certain kind*. They generally draw from versions or inflections of these traditions that support what I have already described as the ascetic bent of current posthumanisms, an asceticism that continues a general asceticism about human relationships that has structured Continental philosophy in the post–World War II period. To put again briefly what I will elaborate on at length elsewhere: Experiences of genocide and understandings of violence in the postcolonial period, especially the violence of representation, created the conditions for a view of human relationality and ethics whose prime imperative is the preservation of zones of radical difference, of absolute otherness. This insistence on some zone of inviolability—ontological and epistemological—between one person and another, a demilitarized zone perhaps, is meant as a preventative, guarding against the complete assimilation (murder) of the other. The Tantra that we find imbedded in the eleventh-century synthesis preserves no gap between one person and another: there is no untouchable zone; everything, everyone touches all the way down. At the same time, touch does not dissolve into a static or final transcendental oneness. Tantra holds difference and multiplicity, and oneness or nonduality in the same thought, in the same body. It rejects nothing, exempts nothing, and ultimately resolves nothing in favor of a general cosmology and ontology of pervasive and undecidable relation, one that delights in its own paradoxes. Thus, liberation, or *mokṣa,* can only be realized via an intensification of our sensitivity to the relationality we always already are. Importantly for any service that Tantra could provide to posthumanism, Tantric practices always begin with human relationships. For these, Tantra has a highly developed vocabulary. Yet human relations are viewed as a microcosmic gateway to experiencing the fundamental and pervasive ontological undecidability that *is* our cosmos, one that cuts through the human and the nonhuman world alike.

My project here is to introduce you to the possibility that less ascetic Tantric conceptions of difference and Tantric nonexemptive technologies of relationality have vocabularies and practices of great value to offer posthumanism. Tantra is intimately engaged, both as a philosophy and a practice of freedom, with the terms most productive of posthumanist and deconstructionist ethics. Yet Tantra moves us through and past the exclusions wrought by current formulations of difference and otherness, by the general rejection of pleasure at the scene of human-human relations. Tantric philosophy and practice encourages us to think of and experience ourselves as composed of circulating and partial personalities, feelings, gestures, skills, memories, topologies, sensations, beliefs, affects, and longings which we do not own, but with whose care and development we are charged. This formulation breaks the frame "individual," and demands an enlarged, albeit altered, concept of responsibility that comprises both self-care and the care of others. From a Tantric viewpoint, these are, in fact, the same.

▼ Avatar Bodies Ψ

Over thousands of years, Tantra has demonstrated an extraordinary flexibility, adaptability, and mutability. At the same, its most "Tantric" features have survived relatively unscathed. It has managed to evade the grasp of both historians and those who seek to statically interpret its metaphysics and practices, continually breaking out of the confines of coherent definition and, in keeping with the eleventh-century synthesis, expanding into and absorbing aspects of other traditions. In a hopeful sense, this history gives a degree of license to practitioners and scholars who come to the tradition at this late date and from far-flung locations: the capaciousness and catholicism of Tantra is inherent in its most deeply held beliefs and its metaphysics. My focus here will be on generalizable features of Tantric concepts and practices of relationality, difference, and differentiation, that is, on the aspects of Tantra that have the most direct bearing on the central ethical "pressure points" of contemporary thinking, and which, as we shall see, have already found their way into posthumanist discourse. The history of Tantra further, and I think usefully, complicates the whole question of authenticity and assimilation. Given Tantra's mutability and its durability, and without abandoning my responsibility to attempt to represent the tradition with integrity and due effort, I find it humorous to contemplate how the tradition might assimilate *us,* the producers and readers of this book.

Indian Tantra points both deconstruction and posthumanism toward a thinking of the self as a zone of relationality, a zone of expressions or immanent emanations. These are not self-possessed expressions; they come and go, expand and contract, mutate, modulate, *travel*. Within this zone of relationality, the categories of self and other are rendered undecidable, are suspended but not dismissed, and the ontogenic touch of other people is proffered under the sign of pleasure. This "subject," this undecidable zone of relationality, is what I call the *avatar body*, and my formulation has specific consequences for the question of *conduct*. While what counts as ethical conduct in the West is largely conveyed, at least in theory, via gestures of restraining, negotiating, and offering, Tantric ethics are practiced through gestures of opening and holding. Here, "holding" signifies both waiting and literally touching. The disposition *(bhāva)* of opening and holding acknowledges, expresses, and makes use of the porous, shared, modulated beings we already are. Dharmanidhi Sarasvati: *Tantrics don't believe in reincarnation. You are an infinite event. You think you end here, at your skin? You think this is* **you**? *[pinches his arm] You think* **you** *will be reincarnated? No. You are an event stretching out, out, out. You are an event without end. Isn't that beautiful?*

Avatar Bodies works not against but in the interstices of the vigilance and the anxieties of contact that characterize recent critical and cultural theory. Such vigilance has been described by Eve Kosofsky Sedgwick as one whose affective message is *there must be no bad surprises* (9). Sedgwick suggests a *reparative turn*, one that *skill[s] readers at attending to, rather than having to disavow, the workings of positive affect* (24). She goes on to say that *the vocabulary for articulating any reader's reparative motive toward a text or a culture has long been so sappy, aestheticizing, defensive, anti-intellectual, or reactionary that it's no wonder few critics are willing to describe their acquaintance with such motives* (35). My motives are, perhaps sappily, both reparative and science fictional. I want to attend, in the present, to both mourning and the hope embodied in pleasure that in future times, pleasure will assist, and not arrest, the ethical touch.

But this text is not only an argument: it is also a performance, a provocation, a conversation, and an indulgence that hopes to enact its most urgent assertions and provide, through taking pleasurable risks, a set of strategies for allowing pleasure to more explicitly enter into one of the scenes of relation that is most dear to it: the scene of academic writing. This text is also an avatar body, a thoroughfare of relationality, one that makes explicit the ways in which, even in academia, no text is possessed by its putative author. It takes pleasure in the company of others, creating a space of reception, a space of in-fluences, a space of hospitality. It capacitates itself, stretching the boundaries of what may permissibly take place in a piece of academic writing in ways that also signify the creation of a zone of enlarged, albeit altered, responsibility. As such, it hopes to convince you that when we speak of ethics, we should turn first, or turn with equal enthusiasm, to the forms of life that we inhabit most immediately.

Ψ First City Kneeplay ▼

Foreplay: In the West, the city has most often signified the autonomy of self, the detached vantage point, and a condition of "higher" civic unity. Kant's originary "Idea of a Universal History from Cosmopolitan Point of View" made use of all of these tropic regimes: the macrocosm-microcosm relation of the warring nation and the autonomous, self-interested individual, the "higher" *cosmopolitan condition* represented by the civilizing concept of a league of nations, and the anticipation of future enlightenment as a *moral whole* (*On History* 20, 15). Bruce Robbins writes that *understood as a fundamental devotion to the interests of humanity as a whole, cosmopolitanism has often seemed to claim universality by virtue of its independence, its detachment from the bonds, commitments, and afflictions that constrain ordinary nation-bound lives* (Cheah and Robbins 1). The condensed image of this latter-day Kantian cosmopolitanism is not simply the flaneur—a solo figure, gliding through a crowded urban landscape—but his cool and comprehensive *gaze*. Living within, yet rising above, enfolded yet untouchable, neither foreign nor at home, the flaneur is an impersonal, anonymous arbiter, a commentator who looks always to the future, to the new.

In "Traveling Cultures," James Clifford argues for a different kind of cosmopolitanism or a *dwelling-in-travel* that is not elite, impersonal, untouchable, anonymous, or comprehensive. The organizing figures or *chronotopes* of this refigured cosmopolitanism are entry points, *ways in* to hybrid, diasporic, intra-contaminating *fields* of contact. Clifford suggests, for instance, *the hotel* (96–105). The cosmopolis becomes a

transversal zone, a dense region of shifting intensities and vexed, heterogeneous connections that no one can rise above or glide through. One
may travel *to* the cosmopolis, but cosmopolies may also be *carried*. Travelers are cosmopolitan fields within fields, leaky, multiply attached. The
sticky, heterogeneous point opens to a baroquely differentiated ocean.

For the purposes of this experiment in nonexemptive relations, then,
from the beginning and without building up to anything from smaller,
simpler components, I propose a city. A city is, of course, one kind of
avatar body. In 1902, Georg Simmel imagined a *technique of metropoli-
tan life*, a forced adjustment to intense sensory stimulation. Not only
individuals, but diffuse geographies are affected. *A city consists of its
total effects which extend beyond its immediate confines.* Simmel attributes intellectual hardness and rigid gridifications, especially of time, to
city persons and cities themselves, but *porousness* constitutes the basic
relation between people and a city, a city and not-city. Indeed, it is unclear where these distinctions actually reside or how they might be expressed. In a city, nothing can remain entirely foreign, unalterably alien.
*The qualitative aspect of life is transformed directly into qualitative traits
of character* (419).

A similar dispossession and intensification of categories emerges in
Victor Burgin's writing about Benjamin: *An ambivalence inhabits this
textual fragment: as if two different spaces—one sealed, the other perme-
able—compete to occupy the same moment in time. . . . The metaphor of
porosity competes with a dialectic of interior and exterior that belongs to a
different register* (9). A city is always a membrane/edge, a "place" where
the porous and constrained, the unbounded and contained flicker, where
everything and everyone lives inside the edge, where anxieties about
belonging attest to the ways in which belonging is always deferred,
touched by uneasy possessions. Here, I am inhabited by avatars beyond
human and nonhuman, sameness and difference, incorporated and cor-
poreated in an ambient body, exchanging capacities for wholeness, multiplicity, and distinction. I want to ask you: Will we ever become posthuman if we insist on humanism's meanings and divisions? If we insist
that sameness is sameness? That difference is difference? That alterity is
alterity? *Racism does not exist so long as the other remains Other, so long
as the Stranger remains foreign. It comes into existence when the other becomes merely different—that is to say, dangerously similar* (Baudrillard
129). (Dear JB: I do not believe we can succeed at this end run around

humanism. We cannot "cut" humanism with alterity or technologism; we must stage encounters with the dangerously similar; we must stage encounters with each other. Love, Ann)

Date: Sat, 30 Oct 1999
From: Ann Weinstone
To: Chris Kraus
Subject: invitation

Dear Chris:

Many thanks for sending me the proofs of your wonderful new book, *Aliens and Anorexia*. The sentences do provoke "rapture," but also other disturbances. Your *Aliens* and my *Avatar Bodies* turn out to be such strange, estranged familiars of each other. What an uncanny circulation of the same terms in each: porosity, absorption, decreation, the impersonal, the alien, asceticism, beatitude, attention. I say "estranged" because my text presents an otherwise to an ethicopolitics of asceticism and the impersonal, urging, instead, overpopulation and baroque disciplines of devotion as opposed to your strict, pared-down, "anorexic" rituals. I'm longing for abundance that does not nullify. An Apollonysus surfeit of words and flesh. A city and an ocean, a point and a wave. Together. Suspended. Yet, we both write about love, about care, about outrage at failures of care. So you force me to consider the possibility of an otherwise to my otherwise, which is already responding to asceticism, even asceticism disguised as Dionysianism, in the writings of some contemporary theorists who are sources for whatever may be called progressive posthumanism.

Chris, for some time now I've been pondering certain new writings that I'm tempted to call "extreme realism." Your first book, *I Love Dick*, would be among these. These texts don't worry at the edges of fiction and history, fiction and self, fiction and public life as did their metafictional forebears. They don't pounce on the process of fictionalizing, wielding it, striking out in celebratory, bitter, or wistful modes that always, no matter how activist, end up marking the boundary between the activity of Art and Everything Else. The texts I'm thinking of work through a plainer, quieter address. They assume writings are actors in the world, no less so than bodies, consciousnesses, oil refineries, herds of cattle, boards of directors, chemical reactions, and telephone lines. They seem to *place* themselves in the world in special ways, as forms of experimental ethics, forms of what Geoff Ryman, author of the "extreme" novel *253*, calls "reality editing" (337). But don't think of William Burroughs and his cut ups or scrambled tape experiments. Instead of viral disruption at the limit of sense, these newer experiments make the otherwises, the alternate reals appear so that they can be *lived*. They arrive via modes and capacities we have consigned to the irreal, what brush us, sometimes bruising, as we pass.

In *I Love Dick*, you and Sylvere create love letters born largely of fantasy and then launch them toward their largely unaware object of fantasy. This is the experiment: What will happen if I refuse to distinguish between the genres actual and virtual? What if I proceed from the axiom that the movements and effects of everything on everything else are extremely real, operating along vectors of uncontainable porosity? What can I make from this expanded palette? What will be made of me? What event will overtake my performances as I send letters that might, more normally, be categorized as gross projections, pathological excesses? And what if we stopped categorizing in ways that reduce our capacities for opening ourselves to others and creating a world?

I understood when I read *I Love Dick* that it had something profound to say about letter writing, about e-mail, and about the "virtual" relationships in which so many people engage every day. Considering the centrality of letter writing to the performance of this text, I wonder if you would consider joining me here for another experiment, another event.

Love, Ann

Date: Sun, 12 Dec 1999
From: Chris Kraus
To: Ann Weinstone
Subject: the one I meant to send

Dear Ann,

Thanks for your letter. At first it freaked me out a bit, reading what was actually an amazing essay, addressed, or should I say projected, onto "me." When I fell in love with Dick, I was able to really write for the first time—all I'd ever needed was some "one" to talk to. The fact he didn't answer didn't matter, because then I could invent him as the perfect listener. So when I got your letter, my first reaction was Ahhh, it's Dick's revenge: now it's *my* turn to be the blank screen, the silent partner, the omniscient enabling addressee.

But later on the phone you said you hoped that I'd write back, and that changed everything. Because I love CORRESPONDENCES, I love the way they use the word on the Metro in Paris—a map of corresponding lines drawn through a grid that nostalgically stirs up the panorama of the city.

The first thing I ever wrote was something about cities. It was a poem that went something like: "A man named John Dos Passos bought a bus map to the city. Hurricane fog rolled down the narrow streets . . ." I was living on the Lower East Side of New York City. Now I'm in LA. There is a great romance of cities in your writing that from here seems like an ancient world to me: a midcentury world of sensation and pulse: fleshy bodies pass each other in the street, sexual in their soft decay before the triumph of health clubs and personal trainers, the smell of sweat and wool and gabardine.

Deleuze said something very human once to Sylvere: *We are the last generation to whom things really matter.* This sentiment, to me, has much greater value than all of Deleuze and Guattari's Artaudian recycling of "bodies without organs" because it gives you a glimmer of *who's* really speaking: two old white men sitting around the Café Flores admitting that they're dinosaurs: that they've outlived their time, an era of great cities. Don't you think that correspondences, unlike the programmatic language of philosophy, are always grounded in that "who"?

The romance of cities is the romance of lines and grids moving toward a center. The city is synonymous with centrality: of a certain discourse, class, a rhetoric that has a certain meaning. A rhetoric that is so strong and central, it can live unreferenced to a speaker. And that is what's so weird about Deleuze and Guattari: their exposition of the nomad-state in *Milles Plateaux* is presented in a manner that's so programmatic. As you comment, it is writing that's intended to be "Read as Men and Not Girls." The girl-state—which they so programmatically define as "becoming-woman"—is when I'm letting you watch me find it, rather than showing you what I've found. The girl-state's something close to chaos. And while the followers of Deleuze and Guattari believe this kind of transcendental programmatic rhetoric is capable of describing everything, it misses chaos. Because chaos is what happens in the space between you and me.

Will you write back?

Love, Chris

Date: Tue, 14 Dec 1999
From: Ann Weinstone
To: Chris Kraus
Subject: centrality//chaos

Dear Chris,

Yes.

And thank you for entering into this little experiment with me. Reading your letter, and in keeping with my commitment to nonexemption, I'm wondering what to do with my persistent love for and pleasure in cities. And my love for this city I'm writing in now, the *university.* My city has always been a place of encounter, of touch, of the event, and of chance. The touch of an ocean experienced otherwise. So I offer you this sense memory from my adolescence which, in my typical fashion, I've turned into something like a science fiction.

love,

Ann

. . . On a late afternoon at the end of summer, we leave the island, a pale shimmering strip surrounded by volumes of waves. The ocean is metallic slate, salt green, the beachfront big with mute colors, deferred silences, and swaths of sounds gliding over flat sand. We leave that brushed and trembling space by way of a thin causeway spanning a bay, a sudden, airy tapering that sets us down in a privacy of green New Jersey dwarf pines. A two-lane highway. Seventy miles to home.

Sitting in the back seat of my parents' car, I am already anticipating the city. How old am I? Eight? Nine? I am in love with the city. At some point, the August air loses its infusion of pine, and a different smell seeps in. Dirt. Smoke. Sweat. And gasoline. I roll the window further down. Another bridge, the last one. We sail over a river whose black banks bear the weight of container ship cranes, rotting warehouses, bleak geometries unrecognizable in the fading light of summer's dinnertime. The bridge empties into a swirl of ramps, and then we are here. Our car folds deep into the narrow seventeenth-

century streets. Tourist carriage wheels bounce on tarmac cracked by cobblestones. Horn blasts warp around edges of brickface. The city's music plays in car-windowed measures of murmurs or shouts. Radios at stoplights, fights, horns, and ... and the air touches me with its sticky fingers, currents alive on the hot tan surface of my skin, a grain, intimate, familiar, and strangely ironic, strangely attentive. I lean further out. The city's wind, the wind from its restless body, rifles my hair. I lean my ear closer and listen for its circulatory sounds, its beloved hummmm.

Much later, on another early evening—I don't know the season—I decide to return to the city. I've read that the planners are rebuilding the center, emptying it of its exclusive concentrations in favor of a more dispersed, neighborhood organization. All over, crews have reworked the crumbling faces of the Enlightenment buildings, the ones that used to be so carefully preserved with their proud little brass plaques reading Historical Monument. Engineers are identifying systems and retrofitting them for the new codes. City planners have renamed the river a waterfront zone. This rebuilt city has the advantage of being more resistant to disaster, or so they say. The human population is regularly exhorted to trade with the environment, that is, with everything "else," in the hope that more flexible and expansive collectivities will emerge. But despite the emphasis on collections, living in the city involves various acts of solo heroism. Most important of these is the signal act of recreating oneself as something else. This effect is achieved through the exercise of a singular competence. But who accomplishes this? The question makes "my" head hurt. In any case, I learned that each individual only includes one human part, a strange object like a prayer or an egg. And the collective person ritually observes respect for other collective persons by foregoing touch. A doomsday lump swells in my throat. I think of those August evenings, leaning too far out of the car window, infused with the intimacy of the city, with its undecodable hum.

I prepare to cross the membrane. I walk to the edge where the streets trail off and the junk people don't have room for at home pokes through the rough grass. I feel comforted at the edge. Things rest quietly. I have to listen for movement, for the minute shifts when wind touches, brushing us things with dust. The edge demands a certain hyperattention. My eyes tear up. The membrane emerges from the horizon. It doesn't look like much. Kind of gray, kind of pink. Perhaps. But I feel its force. Like a dangerously reckless lover I've never given up. The pores of my skin begin to radiate. Something pulls a thread through my ...

▼ Insect Threads Ψ

[Tantra:] Its root, tan, means to "stretch," as one would a thread on a loom.

—David Gordon White, *The Alchemical Body*

I'm thinking of Gregor Samsa's story, which Kafka termed *an indiscretion.* Here, a man incarnated as an insect perpetrates a singular offense against the family and the capitalist work ethic. More generally, the unseemly vermin-son undermines the conceit that the human is an unalloyed, irreproachable entity. In their final cleaning frenzy following his death, Gregor's family dismisses the *widow* housekeeper, the only one who had not been repelled by Gregor's transmutation. Her own insect affiliation manifests bodily in a *strong bony frame,* an interior exoskeleton threatening eruption (32–33). It is her removal that will finally restabilize the family and sanctify the impending marriage of the daughter, a union delayed by multiple infestations. *"We'll fire her tonight," said Mr. Samsa, but did not get an answer from either his wife or his daughter, for the cleaning woman seemed to have ruined their barely regained peace of mind* (42). In the *Metamorphosis,* the insect is a singular, a lone "No!" thrown bodily against forces of class, conformity, order, and obedience. Kafka in a letter to Elli Hermann: *In a family in the clutches of the parents, only quite particular kinds of individuals have a place. . . . If they don't conform they are not, say, cast out—that would be very fine, but it is impossible, for after all we are dealing with an organism—but are instead cursed or devoured or both* (*Metamorphosis* 72).

G., my childhood friend, was a refugee from Indonesia. She told me that before her family moved into a new house, they would leave the doors and windows open for several days in order to let insects, and especially spiders, enter. Spiders are good luck in her culture. The family followed after. Western cultures work hard at keeping insects out. They trope aliens and anxieties about contamination from the inside as insects. Arachne occupies a point in a multimillennium negative association of spiders and "difficult" women: the spinsters and the widows. In recent science fictions of evil empires, the hive continues its cold war duty as the locus classicus of the enforced loss of agency and selfhood. Yet insects, with their capacity to incarnate both monstrous singularities and self-less swarms, have spun threads through nearly every major contemporary source for posthumanist theorizing. They dramatize the tensions between the singular, creative individual who guarantees a measure of freedom and the processual, impersonal hordes charged with undermining dangerous humanistic sovereignties.

Case Ψ

Although this particular jumping off point has achieved the status of cliché in narratives of techno-human touches, I want to begin with William Gibson and his 1984 novel *Neuromancer*. Case, *Neuromancer's* overtheorized protagonist, segues between the Sprawl, a gritty, flesh-bound megalopolis, and the abstracted, addicting realms of cyberspace. Despite his dependency on cybersimulations, a nightmare of doing battle with a wasp's nest manifests Case's anxiety about the unnatural clones and artificial intelligences that comprise the reproductive life of the offworld corporation, Tessier-Ashpool.

Case's dream: He's got a fire-spewing **gun** in his hand. After one shot, the papery gray nest falls to the asphalt, breaking open. *Horror. The* **spiral** **birth** *factory, stepped terraces of hatching cells,* **blind** *jaws of the unborn moving ceaselessly, the staged progress from egg to larva, near-wasp, wasp... the biological equivalent of a machine* **gun,** *hideous in its perfection. Alien.... In the dream, just before he'd drenched the nest with fuel, he'd seen the T-A* **logo** *of Tessier-Ashpool neatly* **embossed** *into its side, as though the wasps themselves had worked it there* (126–27; emphasis mine). In a later scene, Case makes love to Linda Lee, Gibson's proper name for romantic (heterosexual) love, human memory, and emotion. Instead of the alien spiral factory, the blind jaws, the machine gun reproduction, here there is sublime immersion in **spiral** *and pheromone, infinite intricacy that only the body, in its strong* **blind** *way, could ever* **read** *... then he was in her, effecting the* **transmission** *of the old* **message** (239–40; emphasis mine). Gibson uses the wasp hive to link a relentless technology of alien reproduction and the "bad" corporate Tessier-Ashpool family with its techno-fascist, incestuous, cloning ways. But these exist in terrible rhetorical proximity to the "good" scene of romantic, proper, and historically sanctioned reproduction. Spiral, blind, gun, transmission. To whom do these signifiers belong? And who embosses the logo? Who sends the transmission? The message? The code? Who dreams? A machine? A corporation? An insect? Case?

Insects manifest Gibson's anxiety about losing his humanity and his human body, made tenuously visible through a display of the "natural" urges and intuitions of heterosexual reproduction. As evidenced by the rhetorical infestation between the two scenes, the threat of loss is a critical, if not a permanent condition. Later, it turns out that the wasp dream is a memory extracted from Case and visited upon him by a computer construct. Can't get closer to the horror than that. But if you feel more like Kafka, or like Clarice Lispector who, in her 1964 "cover" of Kafka's tale, *The Passion According to G.H.,* brings her protagonist to confront the alien by ingesting cockroach protoplasm, the "horror" of the association insect/alien/human/technology works otherwise.

Posthumanism's insects displace rational, transparent communication and a centralized human agency—centerpieces of humanist political theory—with a "hive" of cognitive and other processes that subvert the subject and the subject's bad effects. This displacement of a bounded, self-willing agent with dispersed, autonomous processes operating without central control points toward the urge of the posthumanist invocation of insects, which is to associate the person with what is either explicitly or tonally a technology. Rosi Braidotti: *I . . . take the insect as a figuration of the abject, a borderline figure, capable of having different meanings and associations. It is a generalized figure of liminality and in-betweenness . . . [situated] on the horizon of the "post-human,"* **in closer connection to the technological** *than to the actual animal "kingdom"* (1997, 73; emphasis mine). Steven Shaviro admonishes: *cultivate your inner housefly or cockroach, instead of your inner child. Let selectional processes do their work of hatching alien eggs within your body. And don't imagine for a second that these remarks are merely anthropomorphizing metaphors. We can kill individual insects, as spiders do; but we can't for all that extricate ourselves from the* **insect continuum** *that marks life on this planet* (53). Gibson pairs an alien reproductive technology with ancient, naturalized heterosexual love in a libidinally-charged fight to the death.

Within posthumanist discourses, technology, the self-less, and the non-human dislocate pretensions to cognitive domination and both the rational and mystic transcendence from which some humans and all nonhumans have been violently excluded.

The posthumanist identification of technology, the machinic, the nonhuman or the alien with the asubjective and nonmetaphysical works through a series of replacements and displacements. Consciousness is sidelined as an epiphenomenon of cognitive processes that are generalized, distributed, and attributable to organic, inorganic, technological, social, and human systems alike. Human volition or will is replaced by a concept of agency that emphasizes emergent directional processes distributed across parts and populations. Absolute knowledge is replaced by perspectivalism and a plethora of observer points of view. The attribute "organism" is refashioned or discarded in favor of self-sustaining, generative autopoietic systems or more shifty entities: partial objects composed of the inorganic, the virtual, the conceptual, the technological, and the nonhuman or alien. The conceptual and rhetorical engine of posthumanism is the adequation of the person to the technological, the machinic, the impersonal, and the nonhuman or alien with insects playing all of these roles.

Ψ Insects and Buddhists Ψ

The influential view that the appearance of a unified, centrally controlled (human) individual emerges from a hive of distinct, self-maintaining component systems lies at the heart of the autopoietic systems theory of cognitive scientist, philosopher, and Buddhist Francisco Varela. Varela's earlier work with his mentor Humberto Maturana, and his later work, which focuses more exclusively on human cognition and human-centered ethics, exemplifies many of the ethical and affective investments of posthumanism. As a description of the self-distinction, self-production, and self-maintenance of living systems, Varela's work will help me tell you about the paradoxes and ethical impasses generated by views of the person founded on the imperative to maintain legible distinction.

The history and tenets of autopoietic theory have been aptly described by numerous other writers (see Maturana and Varela, 1980; Luhmann, 1995; Hayles 1999; and Rasch and Wolfe). I will only allude to that history here. Generally, autopoietic theory states that autopoietic systems produce their own identity or organization only with reference to themselves and not with reference to an outside world, and that they come into existence via a distinction between self and non-self or environment that is the result of *self separation* from their environments or a "cut" made by an observer. Maturana and Varela's initial version of autopoiesis was based on color perception research conducted by Maturana and his colleagues. They argued that perception is not representational: the environment acts as a trigger that sets into motion internal processes of an entirely different order, related only to the chemical and neuroelectric organization of visual and cognitive systems. Thus, in autopoietic parlance, the world is not something that an entity discovers "out there" and reconstructs as a model or picture, but it is "enacted" through a process of embodied perception or worlding that has everything to do with the autonomous point of view of the system.

In traditional autopoietic theory, a system is organizationally closed and structurally coupled to the environment. Organizational closure pertains to the internal, self-referential maintenance of the organization that makes something what it presumably *is*. Structural coupling pertains to necessary inputs from an environment figured as *perturbations* or *triggerings*. In his more recent writings, Varela has departed in complicated ways from his earlier positions worked out with Maturana, particularly with respect to the notion of closure. Maturana equates closure with autonomy. Varela, while still depending on a limited notion of closure, speaks of *enaction*, the processes of environmentally engaged systems bringing forth a world. Within the context of progressive posthumanism, N. Katherine Hayles has undertaken the most sustained examination of autopoietic systems theory in its various iterations. As she puts it: *Autopoietic theory sees perception as the system's response to a triggering event in the surrounding medium. Enaction, by contrast, emphasizes that perception is constituted through perceptually guided actions so that movement within an environment is crucial to an organism's development. . . . Whereas autopoietic theory emphasizes the closure of circular processes, however, enaction sees the organism's active engagement with its surroundings as more open-ended and transformative* (1999, 156). Varela's post-Maturana work increasingly focuses on human "systems" and the relationships among cognition, sensation, embodied emotions, and the emergence of a sense of self or "I." In order to accommodate these interrelations, however, closure is still the concept that guarantees the coherence and continuity of an autopoietic system's identity (see 1991, 99).

Varela ostensibly wants to retain a concept of the self as *emergent* from the totality of autopoietic systems that make up the person, but in his later work, this concept of self becomes attenuated in interesting ways. A truly emergent self would be *nothing but a coming from elsewhere:* an emanation or expression, to use terms I will elaborate on somewhat later. Instead, Varela slides into a concept of self based on an unworkable binary: a closed "I" and an empty, selfless self. This tension, generated by an ethical imperative that demands both closure and the undermining of concepts of self-willingness or self-possession, exemplifies the central dilemma of posthumanism.

As Geof Bowker has pointed out, systems theory, from which autopoietic systems theory derives, wants to be a *universal discipline:* it wants to provide *a new set of universal tools* applicable across multiple disciplines from the sciences, the social sciences, to the humanities (107–9). Evidence of the success of systems theory in this regard is its history of application to genetic sciences, military sciences, artificial life sciences, psychology, historiography, and literary theory. Autopoietic systems theory partakes of this urge to become universal; this is its spontaneous consciousness. However, I prefer to say that its urge is to constitute itself as a "smooth theory." As does a "universal discipline," smooth theory wants to account, not just for one class of things or phenomena, but for heterogeneous, seemingly disparate domains with a coherent set of terms or concepts. However, "smooth theory" contrasts with a term such as "universal discipline" in that it points toward the action of such theory in the world, the smoothing over of the lumps, the discontinuities, or toward the procrustean work that goes into assimilating or exiling knotty exceptions. In the case of Varela, the emergent "self" is often spoken of as if it were also a closed, autopoietic system at the same time that autopoietic systems are regularly spoken of as "selves." The sense of self as something autopoietic and closed then *slides* into an understanding of the practical preconditions for ethical behavior as consisting of a kind of internalization and separation akin in its feeling-tone to the autopoietic process itself. The distinction between "self" and "system" is lost. This move reinstates a self-willing (autopoietic) self and entrains the origin of ethical action to the actions of *an* individual operating in important respects *alone.* As in traditional humanist discourses, the figure of *an individual* bears the burden of exemplifying both ethical action and ethical pedagogy.

Varelian autopoiesis is close kin, although by no means identical or non-antagonistic in some of its expressions, to concurrently elaborated theories of difference and technologies of self or self-capacitation associated with Continental philosophers such as Deleuze. The most significant point of contact between autopoietic theory and Deleuzian ontology in particular is that both strive to be rigorous theories of the genesis of individuals and both comprise a set of questions about how individual systems emerge from a "background" or an "environment." They both locate with the individual system creative, neg-entropic processes guaranteed by some form of closure. Here it is important to note that, in the final analysis, both Varela and, as we shall see, Deleuze, rely on a strong, and even a heroic human self with respect to the task of enacting anything that looks like ethics: an ethics of compassion in the case of Varela and of expression in the case of Deleuze. In the writings of both Varela and Deleuze, this individual practices asceticisms of relationality in the form of Buddhist or Tantric yogas.

Ψ The Insect Self

Resonating with a Deleuzian ethic of proliferation, of differentiation, Varela propagates selves or identities, giving these designations to every manifestation of organismic life. Varela: *I guess I've had only one question all my life. Why do emergent selves, virtual identities, pop up all over the place creating worlds, whether at the mind/body level, the cellular level, or the transorganism level? This phenomenon is something so productive that it doesn't cease creating entirely new realms: life, mind, and societies* (Brockman 210). Varela's key metaphor for the emergence of self is the insect colony. *What is particularly striking about the insect colony is that we readily admit that its separate components are individuals and that it has no center or localized "self." Yet the whole does behave as a unit and as if there were a coordinating agent present at its center. This corresponds exactly to what I mean by a **selfless** (or virtual) self: a coherent global pattern that emerges from the activity of simple local components, which seems to be centrally located, but is nowhere to be found, and yet is essential as a level of interaction for the behavior of the whole* (1999, 53). In other words, the autopoietic systems that comprise the *simple local components,* components not necessarily gifted with the "higher" values of subjectivity, reason, and agency, give rise to the appearance of a centralized self that is, as Varela terms it, *selfless.*

Varela's *selfless self,* here compared to a holistic behavioral pattern emerging from an insect colony, carries a completely different set of valuations and valences than does Gibson-Case's wasp nest. The "individuality," "agency," and "autonomy" so threatened by the hive in Gibson's text now are granted to the hive, thus reducing the effects and dangers associated with a centralized subjectivity. The virtual pattern or "whole" emerges from subunits, from the activities of parallel, local agents. Rather than granting the self a positive (pernicious) will or centralized agental force, for Varela, the purposeful behavior of the emergent self comes about through a constitutive lack of signification that is continually challenged from the outside by a series of perturbations or confrontations with the "uncut" world (1991, 99). Each identity creates a world by responding to perturbations, a process of making distinctions and thereby accumulating significations. *Whatever is encountered in the environment must be valued or not and interacted with or not. . . . [Environments] provide a mode of coupling, a perturbation that triggers, that provides an occasion for, the enormous informative capacity of neural networks to constitute sensorimotor correlations and hence put into action their capacity for imagining and presenting* (1999, 56–57).

Varela's person is comprised of a series of *regional selves:* the cellular, the immunological, the cognitive, the socio-linguistic "I", and the collective social multi-individual totality (1991, 80). Like the cyborg, the autopoietic person is conceptualized as an aggregate of persistently self-present "parts." *Organisms have to be understood as a mesh of virtual selves. I don't have one identity, I have a bricolage of various identities. I have a cellular identity, I have an immune identity, I have a cognitive identity, I have various identities that manifest in different modes of interaction. These are my various selves* (Brockman 211). Despite the status of these selves as emergent, their identities are maintained *as if* these were self-referential autopoietic systems. Varela claims that *what we call "I" can be analyzed as arising out of our recursive linguistic abilities and their unique capacity for self-description and narration* (1999, 61). He describes the sense of "me" as being constituted by *linguistic closure and emergent distributed properties* (1991, 101). Here the organization/structure dichotomy of autopoiesis is applied to an emergent "I," repeating the formula of an invariant property X coupled with a zone of openness. This formula also informs Deleuze's and Derrida's view of the person. The emergent property (sense of self) appears to become yet another autopoietic entity dependent on closure for its identity. Varela seems to be reaching for what he cites as Merleau-Ponty's "double perspective": a view of self (or in this case selflessness) that is both a result of "bodily processes" and given as something **already** *there, a* **Dasein,** *constituted* *as an identity* (101). But if this is so, then what can "selflessness" really mean?

The problem comes into sharper focus when considering that, for Varela, ethical behavior—our *natural impulse* for compassion—comes to fruition through a canonical process of self-realization (1999, 68). *Something* must be realized by "me," and this "I," while emergent, is positioned as axiomatically single even while the person can be composed of regional selves. Even for the selfless self, a singular, uninterrupted "I" is the *basic component* of ethical theory and practice. *In purely functionalist logic, "I" can be said to be **for** the interactions with others, **for** creating social life. Out of these articulations come the emergent properties of social life for which the selfless "I" is the basic component* (62).

The Insect Yogi Ψ

This strain between selflessness and I-centeredness intensifies when considering the practical methods by which selflessness is realized. In addition to his commitment to bringing the body back, in this case, back into cognitive science, Varela shares with theorists of the posthuman, and particularly with Deleuze, an intense focus on personal transformation as an individual, creative activity, one that requires great self-possession and self-command. *Praxis is what ethical learning is all about. In other words, if we do not practice transformation, we will never attain the highest degree of ethical expertise. Learning to embody the empty self is certainly difficult, . . . but centrally important* (1999, 63). While Hayles is right to point out the significance for posthumanism of Varela's concept of enaction, particularly as it provides a way to think through and beyond disembodied notions of information as the substrate of all there is, the world, and the other people in it, never actually appear in Varela's work: "praxis" is primarily a solo, introspective affair. The only point at which Varela's selfless self reaches out is in the interest of a compassionate ethical action. Here, the selfless self of autopoiesis somewhat miraculously flips into the selflessness of the enlightened Buddhist, a process which Cary Wolfe calls ethics by *fiat* (1998, 80). A rather technical concept of aggregate selflessness transmogrifies, through the solitary, reflective, ascetic work of an "I," into a subjective stance of selfless compassion. Varela: *As the student practitioner continues [meditating], however, and as his mind relaxes further into awareness, a sense of warmth and inclusiveness begins to appear quite naturally. The street-fighter men-*

tality of watchful self-interest slips away gradually to be replaced by inter-est in others (1999, 66). What Varela does, then, is unseat the possessive self and then reseat "it" in the interest of an individualist ethics. His system is one requiring two revelations: "You" have to realize that "you" don't have a self, "you" have to realize the truth of the not-self to indi-vidually enact a compassionate ethics with respect to others. You have to "own" selflessness. Despite the valuation of emergence and selfless-ness, Varela grants the "I" originary, controlling powers.

Ψ Knowing, Caring ▼

Varela's work illustrates the difficulty of moving from ontological distinction and the helpful recognition that we cannot know to the imperative that we must *care*. Autopoietic systems theory and the posthumanists who employ it thematize the recognition of the failure to *know* as the salutary outcome of constitutive difference. Ultimately, the failure to know emerges from ontology and the presumed inability *to be* other than oneself, even when otherness plays an integral role in the constitution of the self. In *The Tree of Knowledge*, Maturana and Varela write that: *The **knowledge of knowledge compels.** It compels us to adopt an attitude of permanent vigilance against the temptation of certainty* (245). This knowledge of how knowledge is created contingently as the result of the embodied process of bringing forth a shared world prevents us from being seduced by the absolute. Such knowledge of knowledge *lets us **see** the other person and open up for him room for existence beside us. This act is called **love,** or if we prefer a milder expression, the acceptance of the other person beside us in our daily living* (246). Here we have the hope of much postwar ethical thinking: that the understanding that no truth is absolute, that constitutive differences created through distinct but *coupled* processes of worlding must *compel* us to ethics, to what Varela calls love or acceptance. *We affirm that at the core of all the troubles we face today is our very ignorance of knowing* (248).

Cary Wolfe, in his apt critique, terms the sense of this passage *unreconstructed humanism* in that Maturana and Varela obtain the desired result of selflessness by assuming that, underneath our differences, human beings all want the same thing: to get along with each other. As Wolfe points out, the assumption that we all want what appears to some people to be the good evacuates Maturana and Varela's argument for an ethics founded on constitutive difference (Wolfe 1998, 80–81). However, the project of locating the source of a possible posthumanist ethics at a failure to know, even as proximity to others is constitutive, leads us directly to a central ethical conundrum of posthumanism: How do processes such as autopoiesis and creative differentiation equal ethics? How might they have something to say about the modes in which we are all uncertainly each other, about trauma, memory, and our inhabitation by personalities that can never be figured as alien? How do we leap across the gap from understanding problems of knowledge to caring about ourselves and our world? Is this even the right question?

As I have argued, posthumanist theorists, in an unbroken lineage with their humanist forebears, reach for the exemplary figure, one who might, through special efforts, imbue concepts such as emergence and differentiation with the power to reach across a gap that nonetheless must be preserved. This trajectory is evident in Cary Wolfe's response to another systems theorist, the sociologist Niklas Luhmann. Luhmann extends the concept of autopoiesis to social systems. Writing of Luhmann, Wolfe notes that *it is only in the mutual observations of different observers that a critical view of any observed system can be formulated. . . . Although this reformulation is neither, strictly speaking, a compelling politics nor an ethics, it does provide a rigorous and persuasive theorization of the compelling necessity of sociality as such. It offers an epistemologically coherent and compelling model of necessary reciprocal and yet asymmetrical relations between self and other, observer and observed, relations that can no longer be characterized in terms of an identity principle* (1998, 70–71). However, Wolfe rightly critiques *Luhmann's failure to account for the inequities of power that complicate and compromise the formal equivalence of different observers in the social field* (141). At this crucial point, Wolfe cites Kenneth Burke's formulation of a comic perspective and his figure of the poet who *considers human life as a project in "composition," where the poet works with the materials of social relationships. Composition, translation, also "revision," hence offering maximum opportunity for the resources of **criticism*** (quoted in 1998, 142–43). It is unclear to me how this evocation of a special observer, presumably a "poet within" who practices critical self-irony, solves the problem, particularly since at other points,

Wolfe argues quite movingly for the need to account for nonhumans, and especially animals, in the social system. Furthermore, elevating the figure of the poet to the position of ethical exemplar seems to move us further away from addressing *inequities of power that complicate and compromise the formal equivalence of different observers in the social field* precisely because such a move reinforces a notion of ethics as something one does in a solo, detached, humanistic mode, with the benefit of extraordinary training, as a writer working diligently *with the materials of social relationships* rather than more simply, dare I say, with other people.

Returning to Varela's taxonomy of the self, it suggests, rather than the isolated "I," the possibility of a "full" self who is multiply *possessed*. It suggests to me that my *capacity* is to experience, realize, absorb, and create many selves, to experience multiple senses of selves, multiple "I's" or partial "I's" that are not wholly "mine" and whose complex personalities, histories, and uncontainable origins render them undecidable in terms of ownership. A variety of posthumanist theorists and researchers in philosophy of mind have proposed the multiple as the appropriate posthuman model for the self, yet these models of the multiple are still cast in the possessive mold. The multiple selves are "mine" (see Stone; Halberstam and Livingston; Strawson; Rotman, 1999; Braude). In "The Uncut Self," Dorion Sagan and Lynn Margulis move away from possessiveness and suggest that *with the vagaries of memory and experience, it is essentially arbitrary to believe that the zygote and the eighty-year old are the same person, whereas the father and the son have different selves* (374). While posthuman theorists are happy to mingle the human and the nonhuman or alien, it is near apostasy within progressive political theory and philosophy to consider that my father and I do not have different selves.

Varela's linkage of the nomenclature of "self" to a meshwork of systems he oftentimes characterizes as "autonomic," and the idea that we might exchange one sense of self for another, suggests inhabitation by "I's" or senses of self that we did not create and do not own. This "not owning" becomes possible only when untenable assumptions of zones of closure and inordinate powers of distinction or choice give way to the possibility that "personal" selves might emerge from anywhere and leak into anywhere else, gathering styles and inflections along the way. If we have no single, central *or invariant* self, and we *do* have the capacity to work with multiple senses of self, then there is no basis on which to claim ownership of the "materials" over which we nevertheless have some influence. What Varela suggests to me, then, is a capacity for selving that inhabits the membrane/edge between possession and ownership, between *being inhabited* and *having*, that is not closed in any meaningful sense. "I" is always an affair of two to abundance, a porous belonging, belonging, belonging to that cannot "radically" distinguish itself from a constitutive other. The opening of the "I" to undecidably other others significantly, and perhaps frighteningly, alters the entire landscape with respect to questions of conduct and responsibility.

▼ Second City Kneeplay ▼

. . . Call this warble alive in my throat longing. Call this brush the tiniest hairs on my arms flaring. Call this, this myself, the extent, the extension, caught in the cup, flooding and filling. Where are you? If not here, then nowhere? My most urgent question.

If you had not moved first, I would have remained inside the edge. Is our present distance from each other my punishment for that satisfaction? Still, your smile comes to my lips. I admit: I am casting about, for you, for a seepage. But even at this low level of intensity, this faltering start, I wonder how I will finish a proper letter when your smiles won't let me get a word in?

I say "membrane." Perhaps you would say "edge." I could almost get stuck here, wondering what you meant. This is the old question. Have we separated? I mean, have we only literalized our condition of something-to-do-with-separation, something-to-do-with-nonseparation, or have we changed it? This intensity of longing when you are so close.

At the edge of the city, I mistook the guard for a drunken appliance, or a junkie, the way its knees bent too low to the ground when it moved. Barely moving lips. "puh . . . puh . . . ch-ch-ch." That's all I heard before the goo, before the goo changed shape, pulling me "in." The goo had a bluish tinge, a cold stickiness. I felt aroused and ill at the same time. Hot from cold, cold from hot. Right before making love, the moment of having to cross over. The same thing as I am falling ill, right at the edge, having to give into it. The membrane was thickening (itself, me). I felt a (yours?) hand enlarge, engorge in mine. Everything became erectile and also feverish, flying apart, bursting, or melting together. I couldn't tell the difference, except for the fear, that oddly static precipitation. At a certain point, I did give in. Not just a matter of failing resistance, but an assent. Agreeing to cross over. Immediately, the edge pulled me inside. A capture. Captivating. My body vibrated on the brink, then the waves changed. The city's edge "contained" a great body of water, pulsing inside its cup, filling the foreground to the horizon. I looked up at a high, thin bridge stretching over the whitecaps. There didn't seem to be anything supporting the span from above or below. It had a bluish, pearlescent glow.

In contrast, the drab uniforms of the people around me. The workers formed a regular line, moving single file over the bridge. A tired young woman pulled me aside. I hadn't noticed the closet. She opened the door to reveal a rack of identical dull, brown uniforms. Mine didn't fit properly, and it was well worn, the sleeves thready and rimmed with grease.

"We're going to wait tables at the hotel on the other side," she informed me.

(I sense your amusement at the appearance of the table. That philosopher's saw. Yes, kneeplay, please!)

I got into line behind her. We walked slowly along the narrow footpath, step by step, one by one: no touching. The height of the bridge scared me. My guide kept her head down against the wind. The bridge swayed over the water. At the top of the span, I looked down. Ah darling! The surface of the water! Those glistening, shifting colors, those pools of gasoline sun. The shapes swimming sturdily in the depths, under the surface, its heavy weight swelling flirtatiously! I thought of your eyes. I thought of Solaris. These resemblances are not . . . any thing . . . just the things I find there, falling into each other.

Even though the leap terrified me, I didn't belong in the line. And waiting tables was just a past I had forgotten to forget. I stood at the edge, spread my arms, and jumped. The spread arms, I admit, were a bit of unnecessary drama. And the fall itself, I honestly don't remember. I wonder if there is a kind of existence on the far side of the autonomic. Or a different mode of autonomic where the great physical forces—space, acceleration, wind—increase their intensities, blotting out all else. Really, at that extreme, they might take over for processes normally ascendant in the brain and the circulatory system. If you still think that language is of a different order than, say, wind, you might choose to relate that last sentence to some experience you've had and discard the words after you've used up their metaphoricity. But of course, that would be a performance in and of itself as only doing so makes it so. And only incompletely at that. The fall comes when no one can explain certain effects and we have to find the courage to live them anyway.

I'll tell you what happened when I hit the ocean, but I have to consider carefully my mode of telling. I'm worried that the shock of "oceanic" language (after so many cold showers) might create even more antagonism between you and the membrane. Especially when, after a time, it spit us out. (Assuming you are not still "in" there.) But please tell me if you receive this. Even though everyone here in the city writes dozens of letters a day, the delivery system is most neglected. We're all rather nervous as a result. I can't give you directions, either. But perhaps you already know how to get here because you are here in some way my body has yet to discern.

P. S. (Phantom Script) Are you "mere words?" Please be real in any way you can.

Ψ Sorcerer Series I:
The Island Sorcerer (An Introduction) Ψ

> I am indeed convinced that the only way to assess correctly
> Deleuze's contributions to a theory of subjectivity is to read him
> the way he reads others: we must read him according to the series
> he creates, observe the ways in which these series converge and
> become compossible, and track down the ways in which they
> diverge and begin to resonate.
> —Constantin V. Boundas, "Serialization"

In "The Ends of Man," Derrida describes Sartre's humanism as centrally concerned with *the irreducible horizon and origin [of] . . . what was then called "human-reality.". . . Despite this alleged neutralization of metaphysical presuppositions, it must be recognized that the unity of man is never examined in and of itself* (1982, 115). Sartre's "reality" was that of human relationship: one's relationship to oneself and to others evidenced largely through the medium of emotions such as anxiety, anguish, love, pity, disgust, desire, terror, shame, grief, and occasionally joy. In both his fiction and his philosophical works, Sartre extrudes these emotions through multiple scenes of encounter in the café, the restaurant, the laboratory, the library, the scene of a conversation between friends, and scenes involving lovers, actual or would-be, all of which insistently, gothically, enact the scene of being seen by another: city scenes.

Central to Sartre's project is the concept of other-as-object or self-as-object to the other. In order to arrive at self-as-relation, Sartre casts the world of "ordinary" objects in the role of foil to more highly valued human worldings by which self and other are fractured and made. In doing so, he relieves "Man" of ontological, and hence in Sartrean terms, ethical responsibility for the nonhuman world. *The Other is in no way given to us as an object. . . . The objectivation of the Other, as we shall see, is a defense on the part of my being which, precisely by conferring on the Other a being for-me, frees me from my being-for the Other* (1956, 359). "Objectivation" frees one of the being that is being-for the Other. Objectivation enables the denial of the Look of the Other; it denies the constitutive relationship and authorizes oppression. In his philosophical novel, *Nausea,* Sartre speaks of a sickening viscosity that arises when one draws close to the other precisely because of the Other's gaze which is both constitutive and fracturing. This viscosity, this nausea, is relieved when one contemplates the world of ordinary objects, or when one becomes an object proper, giving up one's humanity. *I felt my body harden and the Nausea vanish. Suddenly: it was almost unbearable to become so hard, so brilliant. . . . I feel my body at rest like a precision machine* (22–23).

Nonhuman objects cannot look, they cannot give the lie to the unity or self-presence of the subject, they cannot participate in the dialectic of freedom and enslavement. If Sartre argues that self and other are cut into each other, and thereby in an intimate shaping relationship, this new relationship emerges only against the background of the *other* objects, which, unlike objectified Others, can be *known* and are now called upon to mark the limits of ethics, which are coextensive with the limits of the human. Sartre's humanism flickers on the edge of posthumanism; he critiques versions of the objectivation of the other that do not lead to consciousness of co-constitution and the limits of knowledge, but this insight is purchased at the expense of the nonhuman world. In the process of making ethics possible, he renders the distinction human/ nonhuman even stronger, and, in posthuman terms, reinforces exactly what underwrites the ethical dilemmas he seeks to correct.

Deleuze stages an exemplary foray into thinking past the Sartrean subject through a contemplation of Michel Tournier's novel *Friday,* a rewrite or "cover" of Daniel Defoe's *Robinson Crusoe.* Here, the man-on- a-desert-island is the focus of an experiment meant to induce the experience of a world without the orienting gridlines provided by relationships with other people (1990, 301–21). Constantin Boundas notes that, lacking others who normally serve as the horizon of normative perceptions, Robinson moves through a series of perceptual overloads and begins to lose his *personalogical and subjective coordinates* (111). Robinson encounters Friday, when he eventually enters, as *not an Other, but something wholly other* who Deleuze characterizes as *a bizarre object, sometimes as a strange accomplice...a mysterious phantasm* (317–16). The ordering function of the human Other has been decimated so that a new other can appear, one more akin to an object, or an accessory, or a nonhuman. This relationship with an otherwise-other provokes *instincts* that are *solar* and *androgynous* as opposed to the love of Earth and the desire for expenditures in the bodies of women. *"It seemed, indeed, that (Friday) belonged to an entirely different realm, wholly opposed to his master's order of earth and husbandry...."* It is for this reason that he is not even an object of desire for Robinson (317).

The dehumanized Friday is no longer the constitutive Other who guarantees that desire will find its proper object. Friday thus releases Robinson from the entire regime of sexual differentiation and the multiple compulsory sexualities based on sexual differentiation; he frees Robinson to redirect his sexuality toward the island itself, toward the cosmos (317). Such redirections of sexual energy away from other people and toward the divine or the cosmos are central to many spiritual traditions and to the sannyasins, yogins, priests, saints, sadhus, and shamans who inhabit them. For Deleuze, redirection is desirable, in part because of the fatal linking of human sociality to oppressive regimes of sexuality, gender, and humanist subjectivity. *The effects of the absence of Others are the real adventures of the spirit* (305). The cosmic urge of this experimental island-without-human-others moves like a line or a thread through the opposite end of Deleuze's experiment: a world utterly crowded with partial bodies, assemblages, conceptual personae, flows, desires, and intensities all in ceaseless movement. This end of the continuum restores a socius as a series of transversal, heterogeneous connections. But it is still a sociality unequipped to re-enter the café, the city street, or to revisit a meeting between lovers. These are branded and left to their old significations. This posthuman socius is still an island, propagating its own myths about the human monsters who live across the water.

Ψ Some Celibate Erotics ▼

Śiva: Permanently ithyphallic, yet perpetually chaste: how is one to
explain such a phenomenon?
— Wendy Doniger, *Śiva: The Erotic Ascetic*

Teaching stories from Indian spiritual traditions feature saints and *mahasiddhas* (great adepts) who cease referring to themselves in the first
person, using instead the third person or no person at all.

My guru encourages us to experience our reactions, qualities, and
emotions as belonging to a reservoir of energies, of becomings that flicker
inside an edge of belonging and no-belonging, of the personal and the
impersonal, the multiple and the One. Instructions: Replace "I am" with
"There is." *There is longing... There is cold... There is fear...* This seeming depersonalization brings, paradoxically, an enlarged sense of self that
participates in itself, with itself, within a shared world. *No notions such
as: "I am happy," "I am miserable" or "I am attached" (exist independently). They all clearly reside elsewhere, namely, (in that) which threads
through (all) the states of pleasure and the rest* (Dyczkowski 1992, 148).

The most famous Tantric mantra is a Möbius Sanskritic pair that inverts, one into another: *haṃsa-so'ham*. In practice, repeating one mantra
causes it to automatically convert to the other: She that I am, I am He.
(*Haṃsa* also means "swan," and so those who have reached a high level
of attainment are called *Paramahaṃsa* or Great Swan.) The mantra expresses the cosmos as a gendered relation, a dual/nondual modulation,
a sexual, expressive movement of folding and unfolding. The mantra

sensitizes the *sādhaka* (aspirant) to the larger, participatory context, a cosmic Self that not only includes the aspirant and all qualities (energies), but *is* the aspirant. She that I Am I Am He She that I Am He I Am I Am . . .

Deleuze and Guattari, in one of their most poignant passages, describe a celibate machine: a machine-body that succeeds the paranoiac machine-body of psychoanalysis. Sartre's human-turned-*precision-machine* is relieved of the nausea of subjectivity and, frighteningly, all ethical responsibility. This new machine, like Roquentin, the hero of *Nausea* and Robinson on the island, is also cured, however it accrues more positive, indeed ecstatic, connotations and achieves *a genuine consummation . . . a pleasure that can rightly be called autoerotic, or rather automatic: the nuptial celebration of a new alliance, a new birth, a radiant ecstasy, as though the eroticism of the machine liberated other forces* (1983, 18). This machine is contiguous with the body without organs, a body of *intensities, becomings, transitions,* liberated from the oppressive stratifications of the doxic organism and psychoanalytic master narratives (19). The mantra of this celibate machine is *I feel. There is a schizophrenic experience of intensive quantities in their pure state, to a point that is almost unbearable—a celibate misery and glory experienced to the fullest, like a cry suspended between life and death, an intense feeling of transition, states of pure, naked intensity stripped of all shape and form . . . an I **feel** at an even deeper level . . . an "I feel that I am becoming a woman," "that I am becoming a god," and so on* (18). For the schizophrenic, this *is a harrowing, emotionally overwhelming experience, which brings the schizo as close as possible to matter, to a burning, living center of matter* (19). Later, in *A Thousand Plateaus,* this harrowing, overwhelming experience is transmuted through the body and will of a **siddha:** a heroic, celibate adept with explicitly Tantric powers for extracting and transmitting energy. The longing of this Sorcerer is to achieve, through Tantric and Taoist technologies of self, the schizo's relationship to the *burning, living center.* Yearning for this *experience to the fullest,* the Sorcerer preserves himself as he passes through others, leaves them behind, and, as does Varela's selfless self, approaches this center alone.

Unlike for the Buddhist Varela, the Deleuzian center is not empty. The Sorcerer is a plenist, one who realizes a full world. Deleuze's affiliation with the plenist cosmologies of Spinoza and Leibniz has been widely discussed. However, this "fullness" also marks the classical distinction between Buddhist concepts of an empty self and Tantric nondual concepts of a full world-as-self. Approaching the center, Deleuze writes: *This is the central chamber, which one need no longer fear is empty since one fills it with oneself* (1988a, 123). Deleuze insists on the active stance: *one fills it*. There is no surrender into the world self. Deleuze-Sorcerer (and here I say "Deleuze" because I cannot help but find the Sorcerer more affiliated with Deleuze than with Guattari) expresses (extrudes) a line. This line moves, more visibly and less visibly, from a view of cosmogenesis that favors the singularity and pure individual expression, through a crowded middle stratum of proliferating multiplicity and zones of participation or involvement, toward one that favors a heroic, solo encounter of one with the One, with Being, with what Deleuze calls Life. Moving along this line, I move in and out of philosophy and desire, the impersonal, the ascetic, and the erotic, and the attempt to construct a rigorous cosmology out of positive difference and immanence intertwined with a yearning for consummation, an erotic/autoerotic return of the one to the One. I move from a philosophy of difference toward a figure who qualitatively distinguishes himself from others and literally separates himself in order to embark on a spiritually-flavored pilgrimage. I move from a view of cosmogenesis as expression, one uncannily in synch with Tantric cosmogenesis, toward a clinging to experience, a possession of it. This line, or series, an explicitly Tantric line, fails Tantra by favoring pure difference and relations of nonrelation, and, at the same time, it creates an opportunity for a more thorough Tantric intervention, one that can make difference tremble and bring posthumanism into the company of others.

*My teacher says in a satsang, a public discussion: The **vīra** [hero] has to do lots of practices, a million mantras, a hundred thousand **tapas** [austerities]. All this is to exhaust him to the point of surrender, to get him to relax. [giggle] The final practice for any **vīra** is always surrender. Ahhhhh...*

Ψ *Vīra* Action Ψ

Relationship or involvement cannot be understood in Deleuze and Guattari's writing without accounting for processes of individuation, for the becomings of a "special," molecular individual, and for the implication of all of these in an ethics of *becoming* that is in turn fatefully linked to a yearning for both freedom and a primal experience of Life. Scenes of heterogenetic involvement in Deleuze and Guattari actualize a Spinozan-Nietzschean ethics centered on increasing individual capacities *for affecting and being affected*. Each party, each individual participates in a zone of involvement *in order to* enfold the capacities or energies of others. However, this enfolding is never a merging: something is preserved untouched, furthering an ethics of individual becomings, of differentiation and power.

> Entry from *The Deleuze-Tantra Dictionary:*
> 1. capacity, *śakti*. *Śakti* is that power of consciousness to differentiate, to manifest a world. Differentiation is consciousness's *svarūpa* or essential nature. **Prakāśa** *[consciousness] alone exists for itself* **precisely** *by means of becoming other.* [For Abhinavagupta,] *the word* **śakti** *rarely has the personal sense of "goddess," but has the impersonal sense, "capacity"* (Alper 389 fn 25; fn19).

In his *Ethics,* Spinoza has famously written that *whatever so disposes the human body that it can be affected in a great many ways, or renders it capable of affecting external bodies in a great many ways, is useful to man* (221). These positive powers (for affecting and being affected) are instigated by joy. Spinoza defines joy as *that passion by which the mind passes to a greater perfection* (161) and *an emotion whereby the body's power of activity is increased or assisted* (222). Joy is *itself* the frictional movement of the body/mind to a more capacitated state, a state of greater activity, while pain is the decrease, the movement to a less capacitated state. Joy has several meanings or modes for Spinoza. The ethical person tends to progress along a continuum from passivity to activity, from passion to action, from joy to beatitude, but passion and passivity may also be ethically salutary.

Nietzsche also adopts, but in a very different manner, the notion of passive movements, or even incapacitated states, as positively generative. Nietzsche's *sick animal, serves as an interregnum in which Man suffers illness "rather like pregnancy"* or like *the wound itself which forces him to live* (1994, 64; 94). This pregnant, passive decomposition forms a bridge between animal and overman, promising the emergence of a human who wills himself beyond good and evil: a creative, active, guiltless, dancing Healthy new being (1978, 14–15; 118).

The becomings in the writings of Deleuze and Guattari, which are generally human becomings, advance through a greater and more consistent emphasis on active creation, more on controlled desire and active participation than on passive movements or on being affected in passive modes. Deleuze and Guattari's emphasis on active and often exuberant differentiation or creation lends posthumanist theory its strongest, most pervasive rhetorical flavor. Yet, for Deleuze, while heterogeneous couplings are the vectors for active creations (and decreations), a powerful ascetic urge fuses self-creation or becoming to self-command. Freedom is freedom to compose, to couple while withholding pleasure, to extract or concentrate capacities without losing control. This threat of loss of control is less acute with respect to more legibly "different" or "heterogeneous" couplings, and more acute with respect to human-human couplings.

Ψ The Wasp and the Orchid ▼

Deleuze and Guattari's couplings move in two directions, the cocreation of an interzone of "involvements" among heterogeneous entities and the preservation of a composing "X" or "X" zone that remains in charge and unaffected. Within the combining interzone, a philosophy of difference requires that no exchange, no multiplication, no imitation or repetition result in constellations or entities that are "the same." Individuations arise from preindividual processes of differentiation and produce more individuations; every movement results in fresh difference. Todd May has argued that the singularities or haecceities that make up the preindividual, nutrative plane of immanence *are, strictly speaking, place-holders for what lies beneath all qualities, which compose but do not themselves have qualities, are the positive differences that subtend all unities. For Deleuze, they exist—or better, subsist—beneath sense, language, concepts, bodies, consciousness, in short beneath all phenomena of experience. They are unexplained explainers in that they must be brought into play if we are to offer an account of the world that gives primacy to difference* (46). While I agree with May's assessment, I prefer, here, to accept Deleuze on his own terms. This will allow me to get at the ways in which a very personal commitment to figures of Sorcerers, and the general posthumanist predilection for asking questions in the singular, causes renditions of human-human relationships to proceed quite differently from other relationships that are allowed to "stand for" difference, for heterogeneity. This avoidance of merger—most intensely between human beings—underwrites the reinstatement of both a philosophically and culturally conservative notion of the self. I am heading toward an engagement with Deleuze and Guattari's productively contradictory figurations of hetero-genesis, and the resulting limitations of their ethics, in order to begin to conceptualize a posthumanism that capacitates or empowers without the need for ascetic separation, for celibate couplings.

Deleuze and Guattari's exemplary figures of heterogenesis are those of the wasp and the orchid. Brian Massumi describes this relation: *The wasp is an integral part of the orchid's reproductive system and morphology. The orchid's patterning "mimics" a wasp (their forms conjoin): the orchid is hermaphroditic and the wasp heterosexual (they conjoin reproductive systems); the wasp uses the orchid for food, and the orchid uses the wasp for fertilization (they conjoin alimentary and reproductive functions)* (1996, 165 fn30). And, from *A Thousand Plateaus: Wasp and orchid, as heterogeneous elements, form a rhizome. . . . There is neither imitation or resemblance, only an exploding of two heterogeneous series on the line of flight composed by a common rhizome. . . . Remy Chauvin expresses it well: "the **aparallel evolution** of two beings that have absolutely nothing to do with each other"* (10). What is at stake in the emphatic and emphatically approved **absolutely nothing to do with each other**? In citing Schérer and Hocquenghem's writings on wolf children, Deleuze and Guattari note that they *appeal to an objective zone of indetermination or uncertainty, "something shared or indiscernible," a proximity "that makes it impossible to say where the boundary between the human and animal lies"* (273). In *Difference and Repetition*, Deleuze describes this boundary as a *fringe of indetermination which surrounds individuals*. He gives the example of *two physical particles whose individuality can no longer be observed when their fields of individuation or domains of presence encroach upon one another* (258). An order of indistinguishability may play within blocks of becoming, but what demands, at the same time, that the wasp and the orchid have *absolutely nothing to do with each other*? What is it that must be preserved?

Over and over again, Deleuze and Guattari invoke the formula of becomings that do not "conjugate." *The line, or the block [of becoming], does not link the wasp to the orchid anymore than it conjugates or mixes them: it passes between them, carrying them away in a shared proximity in which the discernibility of points disappears* (1987, 293–94). *There is a block of becoming that snaps up the wasp and the orchid, but **from which no wasp-orchid can ever descend*** (238; emphasis mine). And of their formulation "becoming-animal": *It is clear that the human being does not "really" become an animal anymore than the animal "really" becomes something else* (238). The preservation of a zone in which something does not really become something else is not simply a matter of doxic organismic boundaries, which Deleuze and Guattari consistently acknowledge but seek to undermine and underlay with the less gridded body without organs (see 1987, 149–66). Nor is it a matter, in the case of human beings, of epistemic boundaries based on a closed cogito. With regard to the latter, and in contrast to systems theorists and also Derrida, Deleuze and Guattari are mostly uncompelled by the question of what we can know of each other. Their focus is on the exchange of ontogenetic, individuating powers. But neither is their emphatic and strict separation a requirement of their philosophy of difference.

In *Difference and Repetition,* Deleuze describes what he later comes to call the plane of immanence. Deleuze encourages us to think of the plane of immanence and the individuals related to it as *two scales of heterogeneous reality between which potentials are distributed.* The plane of immanence is a field of virtuality where "virtual" is not unreality but a reservoir of potential, a "preindividual" field of singularities ontogenetically available to, indeed composed of, processes of individuation. Deleuze goes on to say that *the act of individuation consists . . . in integrating the elements of the disparateness into a state of coupling which ensures its internal resonance. The individual thus finds itself attached to a pre-individual half which is not the impersonal within it so much as the reservoir of its singularities . . . the pre-individual field is a virtual-ideal field made up of differential relations* (246). The individual is always doubled, composed of actual and virtual, or potential aspects. Individuals, composed by the individuating processes of singularities, intersecting at boundaries and fringes, or later, neighborhoods, territories, and blocks of becoming, capacitating themselves by involuting or folding processes, are logically compelled to retain a pristine individuality or, as Deleuze says, *the whole of the philosophy of difference would be compromised. Individuation precedes differenciation . . . every differenciation presupposes a prior intense field of individuation* (247).

However, to state that the wasp and the orchid may have *absolutely nothing to do with each other,* or that there may be no *wasp-orchid,* is to give primacy to particular iterations of individuation, to delimited forms of differentiation. This *nothing to do with each other* is not a prohibition based on doxic organismic boundaries. While Deleuze and Guattari, and progressive posthumanist theorists in general, have few vocabularies for speaking of how humans might have *something* to do with each other, this "something" is given a rich specificity in the many iterations of the unnatural coupling of the wasp and the orchid who are consistently described as having a shared reproductive and alimentary system. Then, in terms of a philosophy of difference, a "wasp-orchid" is no less of an individuation than a wasp and an orchid. Difference is already built in "all the way down" as the irreducible ontological principle. In contrast to the movement of *différance,* which retains the structure interior/exterior only to make this distinction tremble, Deleuze and Guattari's individuations arrive via the creative movement of a pure, positive difference, one that differs internally from itself *autonomously.* This autonomy of differentiation constitutes a *univocity,* a differentiating without interruption, without exteriority. Differentiation is everywhere and immanent. It is this univocity, this "all-the-way-downness" of differentiation that guarantees Deleuze's philosophy of difference. Prepersonal processes of individuation always exceed any individual; the individual need not re-express these terms in any particular, delimited form. Individual, differentiating expression is always already *intrinsic.* By the same reasoning, a conserving concept of the composing individual as, in some crucial sense, *one* is not a requirement. The question of how we compose a world from the chaos of the plane of immanence does not require that the composer be organized under a concept that preserves a quality of *nothing to do with each other:* differentiation saturates regardless of what anything has to do with anything else. Difference is already guaranteed with or without the closed, composing individual, with or without "him."

Ψ Sorcerer Series II: The Yogi Sorcerer Ψ

Deleuze and Guattari's limitation on certain becomings between entities does not depend on organismic boundaries, nor on philosophical necessity. So what motivates it? To get at the urges that preserve figures of inviolable entities within the writings of Deleuze and Guattari, I turn to the Sorcerer, one of Deleuze and Guattari's most significant iterations of the composing individual. Of the Sorcerer they write: *Wherever there is multiplicity, you will also find an exceptional individual, and it is with that individual that an alliance must be made in order to become-animal.* While the path of becoming-animal is the path of the pack or contagion, the Sorcerer, like Ahab, *bypasses the pack or the school, operating directly through a monstrous alliance with the Unique, the Leviathan.* The Sorcerer is an *Anomalous*, a thermodynamic surprise who moves away from other particles (people), against the molar "rules" of becoming, and in the name of a revolutionary, creative power (1987, 243). This *Unique* is the plane of immanence, Deleuze and Guattari's diagrammatic concept for the prephilosophical, preindividual plane of hyperindividuations: *pure power* (Deleuze 1997b, 4). Contact with it requires that the Sorcerer leave his human contacts behind. At the same time, the Sorcerer retains the position of the pedagogue with whom other seekers on the path must ally themselves to facilitate their own becomings.

The involutionary processes or unnatural participations that fit the Sorcerer for self-mastery must preserve his composing integrity and increase his vitality. Involution is coupling, but a celibate coupling in the sense that it does not divert *essential* (nonsurplus) energies to others or invite uncontrolled leaks into oneself. *When we encounter a body that agrees with our nature, one whose relation compounds with ours, we may say that its power is added to ours; the passions that affect us are those of joy, and our power is increased or enhanced.... we "approach" the point of conversion, the point of transmutation that will establish our dominion, that will make us worthy of action, of active joys* (Deleuze 1988b, 27–28). Entering into *blocks of becomings* with others, absorbing the capacities of others, increases *our power*, establishes *our dominion*. To increase his power, the Sorcerer engages only in those couplings and only in such a way that preserves his integrity as a creative, and in some respects *closed*, individual. The liberation of desire is, finally, not Dionysian as Deleuze sometimes characterizes it (Deleuze 1994, 258), but an explicitly ascetic affair: an absorption and concentration of power in the body of the Sorcerer for the purposes of creative self-capacitation, creative individuation. The Sorcerer samples and extracts capacities that are within his *proximity*, but he never risks mergers that would necessitate relinquishment of the integrity of an unjoined composing individual.

> Entry from *The Deleuze-Tantra Dictionary:*
> 2. Sorcerer, *yogi:* The yogi gains access to *the **unmesa**, the reservoir of Divine potency* (Chatterjji xiii). *A yogi who has gained the higher levels of the cosmos and who is united with śakti [capacity, power] can create any kind of body he desires* (Flood 37).

The Sorcerer's exercise of self-control is linked to a desire for freedom and power, a desire to establish a *direct alliance* with the Unique, and to experience beatitude. In his last published essay "Immanence: A Life...," Deleuze describes this movement between the shackles of the personal and the finality of death as *utter beatitude* (4). This is an experience of the *between-moments the between life and death*—an abeyance of time. It is the atemporal cessation of the movements of joy, the cessation of movements *toward* perfection: it is the cessation of involution and a gaining access to the field of creating potential that is the plane of immanence. Freedom is the *controlled* freeing of affect from imposition and the concurrent ascendancy of a controlled composition by the anomalous who accesses individuations in their virtual state. *The thinker himself makes his individual differences from all manner of things: it is in this sense that he is laden with stones and diamonds, plants and even animals. The thinker, undoubtedly the thinker of eternal return, is the individual, the universal individual* (1994, 254). The Sorcerer becomes the universal individual in an explicitly Tantric mode: he trains himself to access the transformational energies of a potentially limitless virtual body, his body without organs. Deleuze and Guattari explicitly designate the BwO as the Tantric egg. *We treat the BwO as the full egg before the extension of the organism and the organization of the organs, before the formation of the strata; as the intense egg . . . The Tantric egg* (1987, 153). The *Tantric egg,* or what they elsewhere call the *cosmic egg,* refers within Tantra to the entire cosmos in potentia, to particular regions or expressive domains, and to the emanative aspect or principle of a human becoming. While the Tantric view of a human individuation in relation to the cosmos is often described as a relation of microcosm to macrocosm, it is more accurate to say that the individual and the cosmos or regions of it are modal expressions of each other. The *egg* designates a body of expressive capacities, or a body as the energy of expression. Deleuze and Guattari's description of the Tantric egg as *the extension of the organism and the organization of the organs, before the formation of the strata* is in exact alignment with Tantric cosmology.

> Entry from *The Deleuze-Tantra Dictionary:*
> 3. BwO, *Tantric Egg (aṇḍa): [Tantric] cosmologies divide the universe into broad "spheres" or "regions" designated by terms . . . which literally translate as "egg."* These eggs are both particularities and shared realities: *shared realities are fluid and transformable, becoming more of less coagulated at different levels of the cosmos* (Flood 121–22).

Ψ Sex Scene ▼

A key iteration of human-to-human coupling, described in *A Thousand Plateaus*, involves a man and a woman engaging in ritualized Taoist-Tantric sex. (I use a hyphen here as a short indicator of the long history of the interleaving of these traditions and to mark the proximity, within Deleuze and Guattari's text, of this passage to references to Tantra.) The particular scene invoked derives from Robert Van Gulik's *Sexual Life in Ancient China* (see Deleuze and Guattari 1987, 532 n14). In their rendition, Deleuze and Guattari emphasize the need for the male to retain his semen. In an appendix comparing Taoist sexual rituals with Indian and Buddhist Tantric rituals, Gulik notes that Indian Tantric texts were brought into China during the early part of the eighth century (350). The author takes great pains to "prove" that it was the Taoists who introduced the practice of *coitus reservatus* into Indian Tantra (354–56). This goes to show that the introduction of ejaculatory control is viewed as both a later development and also as progress, something to be claimed for one's own side.

Following Gulik, Deleuze and Guattari portray sexual yoga as a process of the male absorbing powers or capacities from a woman while withholding his own seminal emission. This absorption of capacity and concurrent transmutation of creative power is a charging, a powering up in anticipation of contact with the more chaotic and primordial creative field of the plane of immanence with the woman acting as a kind of battery pack for the male. The climax arrives, as it does for Robinson on his island, with an experience in which the adept gains access to a more authentic, prepersonal power: the differentiating engine of the world. Particularly for Deleuze, and in contrast to the Varela's empty self, any pedagogical-ethical purchase requires the preservation, not only of individuality as such, but of the self-laden particularity of an exceptional man.

Deleuze and Guattari write: *A great Japanese compilation of Chinese Taoist treatises was made in* A.D. *982–984. We see in it the formation of a circuit of intensities between female and male energy, with the woman playing the role of the innate or instinctive force (Yin) stolen by or transmitted to the man in such a way that the transmitted force of the man (Yang) in turn becomes innate, all the more innate: an augmentation of powers. The condition for this circulation and multiplication is that the man not ejaculate. It is not a question of experiencing desire as an internal lack, nor of delaying pleasure in order to produce a kind of externalizable surplus value, but instead of constituting an intensive body without organs* (1987, 157).

In their rendition of Gulik, Deleuze and Guattari refer processes of involution and capacitation, processes of a human male's becoming, to a version of ritual sexual yoga in which the role of the female is strictly limited to augmenting the *transmitted force* of the man, causing the man's force to become *all the more innate* (within him). The condition for this *augmentation of powers* is that the man withhold ejaculation. Augmentation is an exposure, an involution, but it is a celibate exposure in the sense that it redirects desire *away from* the scene of human-to-human relationality and toward an autocreative act.

The particular ways in which this rendition of sexual yoga appeals are telling. Such "celibacy" is indeed a feature of descriptions of Tantric sexual yoga. However, this nonreciprocal relation of nonrelation does not by any means delimit the Tantric repertoire, which often includes instructions pertaining to both male and female ejaculation and to the worship of female sexual and menstrual fluids (see Sinha 142). Of ejaculation, Somananda, one of the principle practitioners and philosophers of Kashmir Śaivism writes that *pure consciousness is perceived in the heart when semen is discharged* (Flood 283). In many central Tantric texts and in the teachings of the primary Tantric schools, the bliss of orgasm, with or without ejaculation, is considered a "path." Whether or not orgasm and/or ejaculation is a seen as a vector for *mokṣa* (self-forgetfulness), the worship of one's partner, and the dissolving of the ego into a larger self that includes one's partner, is paramount to the practice of sexual yoga. Writing of Kashmir Śaivism, which many scholars consider to be the paradigmatic form of Tantra, Gavin Flood notes that *desire is a means of gaining higher understanding and power, and through the path of orgasm the lover can become aware of the sound of the cosmos.... Orgasm itself can be seen as a symbolic form of the body of consciousness, and the expression of the joy of liberation* (284). The becoming *aware of the sound of the cosmos* is achieved through opening to influx within rituals of relationship. Achieved within the constraints of ritual, pleasure is a crucial mode of opening to the manifold by easing the boundedness of individuality.

▼ Becoming Woman, Becoming Yogini ▼

Throughout their later work, Deleuze and Guattari position "becoming-woman" as *the key to all other becomings*. Becoming-woman is a becoming-imperceptible, a becoming-indiscernible, a becoming-fugitive. The concept of becoming woman is also central to Tantra and informs its most significant practices. The concept is briefly referenced in Gulik's book, and he cites as his source the work of Arthur Avalon, the first scholar to introduce Tantra into Western academia and one who is noted for sanitizing and sublimizing the tradition in order to counteract the lurid aura bequeathed it by nineteenth-century colonialists (245; see also Urban 1999).

> Entry from *The Deleuze-Tantra Dictionary:*
> 4. Becoming-woman, *becoming woman: The ambition of every pious follower of the [Tantric] system is... to habituate himself to think that God is a woman. Thus the followers of the Śakti school justify their appellation by the belief that god is a woman and it ought to be the aim of all to become woman* (Bhandarkar 208).
> *Become a woman, brother, and then engage in this practice with a woman.* From "The Secrets of Sahaja Love," a nineteenth-century Tantric Bengali poem (Urban 2001, 128).

Tantra is populated by thousands of manifestations of the goddess figured as fully formed or partial personalities and expressing millions of aspects or capacities. Deleuze and Guattari deem that *to hide, to camouflage oneself, is a warrior function* (1987, 277). Here, pointedly cliché characteristics presumed-to-be-woman (imperceptibility, fugitivity) are transmitted or absorbed in such a manner that they transmute into usable minoritarian powers presumed-to-be man (camouflage, warrior). While Deleuze and Guattari often point out that women, too, must become-woman, the process seems to play out in such a way that men direct a process in which women transmute their "indiscernibility" into a warrior's ability to camouflage, and men absorb the becoming-indiscernible of woman in order to deepen the "innate" warrior within.

This becoming-active and transgressive of female capacities as they transmit to a man stands in stark contrast to most Indian Tantras and existing schools and lineages of Tantra that preserve a more original sense of the relationship between male and female principles. These principles, personified as *Śiva* and *Śakti,* nearly always figure the female or *Śakti* role as that of creative, active manifestation, while that of the male or *Śiva* is passive feeling-consciousness. In the Indian Tantric pantheon, Durga the warrior goddess is one of a group of ten goddesses known as the *Mahāvidyās.* David Kinsley writes in his study that *when the Mahāvidyās as individuals are shown with a male consort, they dominate him, standing on his supine body, assuming the "superior" position in sexual intercourse, or sitting on a throne or couch supported by male deities. . . . The Mahāvidyās, with a few exceptions, are fearsome. They dwell or are worshiped in cremation grounds, sit on corpses, wear garlands of severed heads or skulls, are naked and smeared with blood, and have disheveled hair. They tend to be rough, not soft, in nature. This fierce aspect overshadows their boon-conferring, indulgent nature* (63). The saint Ramakrishna described the nineteenth-century Tantric sect, the Kartābhajās as *a powerful but frightening group comprised largely of bitches* (Urban 2001, 9).

Deleuze and Guattari's interpretation and deployment of sexual yoga and Tantra generally misses the more profound minoritarian and antinomian urges present within the tradition. I will return to this. However, what interests me immediately is the way in which the relatively stricter controls brought to bear on contact between humans and the withholding of the threshold of uncontrolled contact reveal the nature of the investment in the *absolutely nothing to do with each other* and the moment, ambivalently longed for by Deleuze, when the rigors of celibate involvements might give way to beatitude.

Ψ English Tantra or the Imperceptible Man

As noted, the orchid's becoming-wasp and the wasp's becoming-orchid are given to us with relative specificity and richness of physical detail while becoming-woman is comprised of a few sketchy but central concepts such as *becoming-imperceptible*. Additionally, the wasp and the orchid may have *nothing to do with each other*, but they are still each figured as participants in a *block of becoming*. Becoming-woman, on the other hand, is accompanied by repeated prohibitions against considering such becomings as having anything to do with "real" women (Deleuze and Guattari 1987, 275–78). Here, the block of becoming forms between a "real" man and a woman-concept. As the move is made from nonhuman-nonhuman becomings to human-nonhuman becomings to human-human becomings, the celibate urge becomes more vexed and pressing.

> Entry from *The Deleuze-Tantra Dictionary:*
> 5. Becoming-imperceptible, *becoming imperceptible: Behaviour of a Kula Yogī: A Kula Yogī may dwell anywhere, disguise in any form, and remain unnoticed by everybody. . . . Yogīs in diverse guises, intent on the welfare of men, walk on the earth unrecognized by others. . . . The mode of Yogīs is not easily perceptible just as the starts and the planets of the sky in the presence of the Sun or Moon. . . . O Devi! The mode of the Yogīs is not seen like the movement of the birds in the skies and of aquatics in the water* (Rai, *The Kulārnava Tantra* 170–71).
>
> The **Sahaja** Man is imperceptible. He is manifest imperceptibly (Urban 2001, 125).

In an extraordinary passage, Deleuze and Guattari write: *Becoming-imperceptible means many things. . . . To go unnoticed is by no means easy.*

To be a stranger, even to one's doorman or neighbors. . . . Not everybody becoming everybody, . . . makes a becoming of everybody/everything. This requires much asceticism, much sobriety, much creative involution: an English elegance, and English fabric, blend in with the walls, eliminate the too-perceived, the too-much-to-be-perceived. . . . **becoming everbody/ everything**. . . *brings into play the cosmos with its molecular components. Becoming everybody/everything* **(tout le monde)** *is to world* **(faire monde)**, *to make a world* **(faire un monde)** . . . *and in this way enter the haecceity and impersonality of the creator. One is then like grass: one has made the world, everybody/everything, into a becoming* (1987, 279–80). Here, Deleuze and Guattari provide a gloss on practices regularly described in Tantric texts and scholarship where the specific language of involution and becoming everything develops out of an ontology that views all manifestations of the cosmos as real and modal with respect to each other. Sound, image, matter, flesh, consciousness, syllable, word, and gesture are ontologically related so that each serves as a portal to all the rest. "Becoming everything" is a matter of sensitization, of training so that one may interact with, use, and experience the everything one already is. Speaking of the Tantric yogi, Swami Lakshmanjoo, one of the foremost contemporary interpreters and practitioners of Kashmir Śaivism, writes: *For him, this universe is the embodiment of his collective energies* (10).

While it is outside of the scope of this project to compare Tantric cosmologies to those of Western philosophers such as Duns Scotus and Spinoza, it is clear that Deleuze's invocation of Tantra is of a piece with his other, more canonical philosophical commitments. Giorgio Agamben notes with respect to the cosmologies of Duns Scotus and others that *the passage from potentiality to act, from common form to singularity, is not an event accomplished once and for all, but an infinite series of modal oscillations. The individuation of a singular existence is not a punctual fact, but a* **linea generationis substantiae** *that varies in every direction according to a continual gradation of growth and remission, of appropriation and impropriation* (19). Comparatively, Harvey Alper writes that *[Abhinava] portrays Śiva-who-is-consciousness as being the embodiment of oppositions in the sense of being "unity within multiplicity" and* **vice versa**. *He describes this embodiment in terms of a "modal" theology. . . . What is ultimate for Abhinava is the totality of all relationships: the cos-*

mic process (382). Tantra's modal ontology expresses a commitment to relationships that do not respect, or a least potentially do not respect, hierarchies of class, caste, and of male and female. More profoundly though, *ontology* **is** relationship. *For [Abhinavagupta] there cannot be an absolute distinction between consciousness and matter, subject and object, cause and effect, or between the elements of any relationship whatsoever. Relationship as such is "internal" to, i.e., intrinsic to, ultimacy.... [Abhinava] highlights throughout the constant dynamic of world emergence and subsidence.... Abhinava postulates... a theology of constant movement that might be called a Śaiva "monism" of cosmic process* (375; 378). Ultimacy (god) is an overflowing becoming, is process rather than stasis. This process is described most often in terms of pulsation, vibration, and amazement. *The vibrating power of awareness (spandaśakti) is the bliss which is the wonder of the one compact mass of "I" consciousness embracing the endless cycles of creation and destruction* (Kṣemarāja, eleventh-century Kashmiri Śaivite quoted in Dyczkowski 1987, 84). The absence of a stable, ontological hierarchy and of a static, divine reference point keeps Tantric practices focused on the everyday lived world of multiple, heterogeneous relations. Tantra celebrates this overflowing, this surpassing of the bounded self by an inpassing, by the sheer baroque abundance of relationship: the ontogenic touch. Despite Deleuze and Guattari's admirable and sustained attempts to undermine the violent hierarchies that precipitate the humanist subject, their invocation of *an English elegance, an English fabric,* their ban on ejaculation, on expenditure, on forgetful exchange in the arms of the human other, their ban on "something to do with each other," feels, affectively, much more like "Brahminized" versions of Tantra motivated, in part, by the desire to retain cultural and political hegemony.

A Little English Kneeplay

[An outraged English visitor to India describes the Tantric ritual of *cakra-pūjā*, or indulgence in the forbidden five M's: *madya* (wine), *māmsa* (meat), *matsya* (fish), *mudrā* (fried cereals), *maithuna* (sexual union).]

She (the woman) partakes of the offerings, even of the spirituous liquors; and of the flesh though it should be that of the cow.... the spirituous liquors must be drank by measure; and the company while eating must put food into each other's mouths. The priest then—in the presence of all—behaves towards this female in a manner which decency forbids to be mentioned; after which the persons present repeat many times the name of some god, performing actions unutterably abominable and here, this most diabolical business closes (Ward 152).

Rather than a philosophical necessity, Deleuze and Guattari's invocation of nonejaculatory sexual yoga is an expression of a longing for contact with the impersonal plane of immanence. To become-imperceptible is to slip between particles, into zones of pure potential between life and death. This can only be achieved through self-control, through nonejaculatory coupling, and in the last instance, no coupling. *There is a schizophrenic experience of intensive quantities in their pure state, to a point that is almost unbearable—a celibate misery and glory experienced to the fullest, like a cry suspended between life and death, an intense feeling of transition, states of pure, naked intensity stripped of all shape and form . . . an I **feel** at an even deeper level . . . an "I feel that I am becoming a woman," "that I am becoming a god," and so on* (1983, 18). To "become everything/everyone" in an impersonal mode, to "make" everything into becomings, to limit and reduce the expressions of the becomings of the concepts of others, to exempt their spontaneous gifts, to control creation down to one's molecules is to desire to experience one's identity with the plane of immanence. This brush with a life of pure intensities, cleansed of all molar organizations, of the everyday, where "real" women and other entities have been "made into" occasions for one's own becomings, must, poignantly and paradoxically, be felt by "him," must be because *it must be*, because "he" so thoroughly desires it, so desperately yearns for it that he risks undermining his whole enterprise. This *between*, this nearing to death without passing through death, preserves both individuality per se and the personal self. Over the dissolvings of beatitude, this man prefers extremes of misery and glory, extremes of intensity that he does not in the end wish to surrender. Unbreached self-possession, a *yoked* individuality, even to the point of foregoing bliss, is the means by which the anomalous becomes the world: *I feel . . . I feel . . .*

*My guru and I discuss the prevalence of **vīra bhāva**, the heroic disposition, within the tradition. He admonishes me: You are building, as a real **vīra** will do, toward a big surrender of all this duality thinking and accomplishment stuff, this constant monitoring of the self experience in the guise of the SELF non-experience. Now! You must forget your experiences!*

ΨΨ *Vīra Bhāva* Kneeplay

The Sorcerer of *A Thousand Plateaus* is a *vīra*, a Tantric hero engaged in technologies of power. Resonating with Deleuze's encounter with Foucault in *The Fold*, the philosopher-Sorcerer writes of *a line of life that can no longer be gauged by relations between forces, one that carries man beyond terror... where one can live and in fact where Life exists **par excellence**.... Here one becomes a master of one's speed and, relatively speaking, a master of one's molecules and particular features* (Deleuze 1993, 122–23).

The Eight Siddhis (Powers) of the Accomplished Yogi:

aṇimā: the power to become minute
mahimā: the power to become infinitely large
laghimā: the power to become light (power of flight)
garimā: the power to become heavy
prapti: the power of extension of the body
prākāmya: the power to live underwater, to become invisible, to enter the
   body of another, to retain a youthful appearance
vashitvam: the power to bring oneself and others under subjection
ishatvam: the attainment of divine power (Sivananda 1986, 165–66)

Sorcerer Series III: Rheya ▼

At the end of Stanislaw Lem's 1961 novel *Solaris,* scientist Kris Kelvin abandons rationality and a perfect god. These have failed to provide knowledge of, or a means for, establishing communication with Solaris, the sentient ocean-planet that fills the view screen of the research station orbiting high above the ocean's kaleidoscopic surfaces. Lem marks the failure of these transcendent modes of understanding by sending Kelvin on a literal descent. He descends not to explore, but to "acquaint," to physically touch Solaris for the first time. Kelvin expresses bitter resignation at his fall into bodies, relationship, and time. Yet the touch comprises the high romantic scene of the novel. A flower grows from the ocean, forming a calyx to the shape of Kelvin's fingers. The ocean communicates its curiosity by emitting trembling waves through the stem to the cup and Kelvin's enfolded flesh. Almost. Kelvin's hand is gloved, and the ocean protects itself from complete contact by maintaining a micro-thin layer of air between the calyx and Kelvin's hand. Despite the hygienic conditions, Kelvin reports *I felt somehow changed. . . . I sat unseeing, and sank into a universe of inertia, glided down an irresistible slope and identified myself with the dumb, fluid colossus* (203).

From Plato to Burke to Kant, and most recently in fantasies about cyberspace, transcendence of human(ist) predicaments (imperfect knowledge, mortality, the burden of selfhood) works through the sublime: through charged and recharging narratives of decomposition and recomposition. Solaris is a wildly fecund, decomposing/recomposing dynamo that utterly confounds interpretation and repudiates sublimity while,

like Tantra, perpetrating a monstrous host of unwarranted, unauthorized encounters. The ocean's unstable, writhing topology consists of
gelatinous canyons, palpitating proboscises, polyps, *foul bubbling foam,*
greedy lips, geysers, tendrils, and a host of other sticky, simultaneously
intestinal and sexual forms. While the ocean produces this "organic"
profusion, it also throws up *monumental machines,* vast architectural
structures, deformed simulacra of the Earth scientists' instruments, and
even a horrifyingly enlarged "copy" of a human being that drifts below
its surface like a submerged continent. The scientists attempt to measure the ocean's activities, but their instruments record only *a profusion*
of signals—fragmentary indications of some outlandish activity, which
in fact defeated all attempts at analysis....Sometimes the instruments
almost exploded under the violence of the impulses, sometimes there was
total silence; it was impossible to obtain a repetition of any previously
observed phenomenon (21). Solaris is an ironic plane of immanence—a
plane of immanence with outrageous personality.

   Solaris works through a thoroughgoing critique of Western metaphysics
with its reliance on a transcendent *logos.* Lem implicates philosophical
and scientific idealism in colonialism and fantasies of transparent communication that demand accommodation of the alien to the human. In
the final pages of *Solaris,* Lem preserves the stereotypical primal scene
of transcendence—the meeting of the solitary male adventurer with a
chaotic, fertile, inhuman or suprahuman, oftentimes fluidic, oftentimes
female entity or substance. Typically, this touch, this brush with the
inhuman decomposes and then recomposes the hero who manifests
extrahuman capacities transferred during contact. However, unlike the
Sorcerer in Deleuze's narrative, in Lem's story, the human male *does not*
become more powerful. The glove and the calyx act as a kind of endgame
prophylactic: a continued withholding by the alien of the transcendent
moment, the continued reluctance of the human male to accept his limitations. Kelvin feels "somehow changed" and "identified" with the ocean,
yet this encroachment on his humanity provokes only bitterness and
resignation. *We all know that we are material creatures, subject to the*
laws of physiology and physics, and not even the power of all our feelings
combined can defeat those laws. All we can do is detest them (204).

   In a 1979 interview, Lem stated that the central concern in *Solaris* is
the freedom or non-freedom of the programmed mind (Parker 188). While
the ocean creates its multiforms, these do not remain under it's control.

The created becomes the creator; the forms generate their own forms, which are in turn decomposed by the ocean in a ceaseless froth of re-cycling (121). Humanist, technoscientific versions of creation, even if they happen to pass through decomposition or the sublime, always result in human control over human and nonhuman artifacts. In *Solaris,* the source of creativity cannot be fixed and seems to inhere as a generalized gestational/ingestational capacity, smeared over the surface of the ocean. The scientists are left to wonder if the creations of the ocean are the result of higher intelligence, unconscious outpourings, a mechanical process, or madness. Freedom, if it exists, issues from the blur of production/destruction; coherence/incoherence; signifying/asignifying, from *inside* these hyperdifferentiating, unclassifiable, ahuman, finally a-alien edges.

Throughout Lem's oeuvre the most fatal control program is the coer-cive force of gender imperatives that are nearly synonymous with the coerciveness of language itself. In a story which parallels Kelvin's descent, the ocean plucks memories out of his unconscious and fashions them into a simulacra of his suicided wife, Rheya. Rheya is Kelvin's "woman inside," the objective correlative of his humanist programming, of human-ist notions of the saving power of heterosexual love, of humanist dom-ination masquerading as paternalism, of humanist attachments to human couplings that would coerce the alien into *becoming human* as the con-dition for contact. Unlike Kelvin, the simulacra Rheya refuses these human becomings. Over the course of the novel, she wrests a measure of free-dom from the imprinting of her gender-stereotyped, human "original." She enters into the cycle of composition and decomposition: she learns to write, and she submits herself bodily to a "destabilizer" apparatus that has been specially designed to rid the space station of the creatures created by the ocean. This coupling of creation and destabilization coa-lesces at an indistinct membrane/edge where the undecidability of her ontology (Is she of human, alien, or technological origin?) and of con-trol (Who is writing, Rheya or the Ocean? Is the destabilization a sec-ond suicide?) continually restages a questioning of the problematic nature of any freedom she might enjoy. Like the ocean's other creations, Rheya too becomes a creator, but her freedom is always already compli-cated and compromised by the vexed question of her autonomy, by the encroachment of others—the original Rheya, Kelvin, the Ocean, and even Lem—on her creations, including her self-creation.

While Rheya is baroquely "peopled," baroquely subjectivized, she says, of her early attempt to write, *But I couldn't write anything. . . . I felt as if there was no body underneath my skin and there was something else instead* (143). Rheya initially feels that the "influence" of others has pushed out some remembered "I" that is now "missing." This influence may only be cured, she believes, by the "I" regaining control. But Rheya has no closure, even at the cellular or atomic levels. In her letter to Kelvin, delivered just after her destabilization and exit from the novel, a self-conscious "I" seems to concentrate, intensify, gain in power. In this complicated scene, her most intense moment of autonomous, creative personhood flips or transmutes into an event of cellular disintegration that depends on her status as a technological creation of another. *My Darling,* she writes to Kelvin of her request that another crew member train the deadly destabilizer on her and pull the trigger, *I was the one who asked him* (190). The success of her autonomous "decision" to destabilize hinges upon her status as a dependent, manufactured "thing." The creator becomes created again, or, rather, they fall into each other at such high speed, they blur.

Rheya's last act before destabilization is to incompletely cross out the letter's signature: *Rheya* (190). She refuses both the closure of a new name and the closing erasure of the old. What Rheya does, finally, is effect an unlinking of freedom from autonomy, of autonomy from the definitive ownership of a proper self. Rheya's freedom seems to issue instead from her willingness to hold herself open to multiple exposures, from her predication of her actions on the capacities that these exposures bring. She claims the "I" who makes these deadly arrangements, she attributes actions to herself, but she refuses to definitively own the various senses of herself, senses that are of uncertain meaning, origin, or that manifest through uncertain modes of transmission. These exposures are not limited by invariant or acquisitive possession; they risk becomings by a self that *has no container. Nothing is more distressing than a thought that escapes itself, than ideas that fly off, that disappear hardly formed, already eroded by forgetfulness or precipitated into others that we no longer master* (Deleuze and Guattari 1994, 201). While in search of the lost, "I," or more accurately, a zone of singular, irreducible "I-ness," the thought of being controlled, or out of control, of *being created,* horrified her. Yet in the end, she hardly distinguishes between composition and decomposition, between the activities or status of the creator and the created.

Rheya exposes herself, not to alterity as such, not to exteriority as such, not to the alien, which, now that the last zones of closure are opened, have become incomprehensible designations, but to *profligate (unceli-bate) modes of deferred belonging.* This situation is dramatized by Rheya's destabilization: she "throws" herself into the ocean. The ocean is hyperbolically *personal* even as its status as a person is entirely undecidable. It is imitative on a huge scale, although it is unlikely that Rheya will ever be able to categorize those simulacra, including herself, with any more success than the scientists. Rheya's "return" is a return to all the uncertainties and dangers of a relationship whose effects cannot be controlled or circumscribed. She enacts a form of multiplicity that relinquishes humanist notions of self-possession. This is a story of creativity, encounter, danger, and power, of power as *embrace.* In the end, Rheya bids her all-too-human companion, Kelvin, goodbye, writing: *You have been marvellous* (190).

Ψ Sorcerer Series IV: The Miracle of the Rogue

Deleuze and Guattari designate the celibate machine as the successor to the paranoiac machine and the miraculating machine. Machines are heterogeneous generators composed of partial objects, desires, concepts, imperatives, the social, the semiotic, the technical, the animal, and so on. The celibate machine is that assemblage that forms *a new alliance between the desiring-machines and the body without organs so as to give birth to a new humanity or a glorious organism* (1983, 17). The celibate machine is a Zarathustra machine, a Sorcerer machine that drives its devotees *as close as possible to matter, to a burning, living center of matter: . . . that unbearable point where the mind touches matter and lives its every intensity* (19–20). Of this moment, Deleuze writes: *Our essence is no longer kept in a state of involvement, we can no longer be cut off from our power: all that remains, indeed, is our power of understanding or action* (1992, 315). Something, our essence, is no longer involved, and it is involvement that *cuts us off from our power* just as the loss of seminal fluid in the body of a woman might literally sap the Sorcerer. Of the self-centeredness of this view, Keith Ansell Pearson writes: *The attempts of the human to destratify itself as an organism—which is the specific "ethical task" given to it in **Plateaus** . . . not only leave the social stratification of the animal [or others] exactly as it finds it but actually appears to require it for its own destratification and deterritorialization. I fail to see how these examples take us beyond the problem of human narcissism and solipsism* (186–87). In partial answer to this charge, and keeping with the pedagogical urges of the figure of the Sorcerer, Deleuze turns the celibate machine into a miraculating machine. The adept's solo triumph becomes the origin of anything that might bring an ethics of self-capacitation into relation with human others.

Writing of a near-death experience just months before his suicide, Deleuze imagines a miracle of sympathy. He recounts a scene from Dickens's *Our Mutual Friend. A good-for-nothing, universally scorned rogue is brought in dying, only for those caring for him to show a sort of ardent devotion and respect, an affection for the slightest sign of life in the dying man. Everyone is so anxious to save him that in the depths of his coma even the wretch feels something benign passing into him. But as he comes back to life his carers grow cold and all his coarseness and malevolence return. Between his life and death there is a moment which is now only that of a life playing with death. The life of the individual has given way to a life that is impersonal but singular nevertheless, and which releases a pure event freed from the accidents of inner and outer life; freed, in other words, from the subjectivity and objectivity of what happens: "Homo tantum" with which everyone sympathizes and attains a kind of beatitude* (1997b, 4). In this final, poignant, and anomalously human-to-human scenario, the move out of solipsism is achieved by a miraculating transmission of singular energy, an impersonal, pedagogical energy that induces care, sympathy, and then beatitude among those in proximity to the dying man. *The life of such an individuality effaces itself to the benefit of the singular life that is immanent to a man who no longer has a name and yet cannot be confused with anyone else. Singular essence, a life* ... (5). The threat of death miraculously precipitates ethical *behavior* through contact with a-life, a current from the plane of immanence channeled through the body of the anomalous teacher, be he wretch, Sorcerer, both, or more. This is ethics by conversion. *At the limit of this destruction, at midnight, the focal point, there is a transformation, a conversion from knowledge to creation, from savage negation to absolute affirmation, from painful interiority to joyful exteriority* (Hardt 51).

Responsibility by conversion, by miraculation, is the destiny of closure. Varelian compassion dawns. Deleuzian sympathy transmits. For Varela, the inaugural condition for ethical behavior is a compassion realized through solo contemplation that bridges the distance between one self-less self and another. The recognition that *there is no self in any* ... *actual experience* initially causes anxiety, but with practice, *a sense of warmth and inclusiveness dawns* (Varela, Thompson, and Rosch 247).

Eventually, *compassionate action can arise directly and spontaneously out of wisdom* (251). For Deleuze, ethical inspiration is tantamount to the transmission of an intensity, a singular capacitating leap at the limit near death. In Tantric and yogic traditions, the direct transmission of energy is the primary vehicle for instruction. In the beginning, a teacher might formally "give" a student transmission from eye-to-eye, from hand-to-hand, or through spoken or written words. More advanced practices include opening to transmissions from objects or simply from space. Sooner or later, the student realizes that transmission is not an event heralded by special or heroic circumstances: It is everywhere, intrinsic to the relational existence of everything, intrinsic to what we *are. You are just an environment. Allow energy to reveal itself. You want to live energetically, a rich life of sensation and connection. Physicality is a meeting place* (Dharmanidhi Sarasvati).

Ψ Heroes of Difference ▼

The emphasis on the exemplary figure within posthumanist discourses is part spontaneous consciousness, part anxiety about human-to-human violence, and part an affective investment in *autonomy* or freedom. Within posthumanist discourses, freedom is generated by autonomous processes of differentiation where differentiation is tantamount to negentropic creative production. Freedom equals freedom *from* coercion and freedom *to* change. For Varela, autonomy is creativity guaranteed by closure. *The notion of operational closure is . . . a way of specifying classes of processes that, in their very operation, turn back upon themselves to form autonomous networks.* **Such networks do not fall into the class of systems defined by external mechanisms of control** (Varela, Thompson, and Rosch 139–40; emphasis mine). Closure allows the creation of significance from the unique perspective of *an active autonomous self* (Varela 1999, 56–57). In a different neighborhood, a Deleuzian neighborhood, Brian Massumi defines autonomy as the *degree to which [affect] escapes confinement.* Affect is equated with autonomic intensities that roam dermally and synesthetically, transforming *the effects of one sensory mode into those of another* and leading to *nothing less than* **the perception of one's own vitality,** *one's sense of aliveness, of changeability (often signified as "freedom")* (1995, 96–97). Here autonomy begins with openness, or more exactly, with the ability to gather the fruits of openness. For Deleuze, as for Varela, this gathering capacity flows from solo practices that are literally or metaphorically yogic practices.

Despite the fact that autonomous processes of desire, of affect, of autopoietic systems, of the impersonal are on some level valued because they are seen as undermining the human self's presumptive sovereignty, the very act of formulating freedom as autonomous creation seems to precipitate individual human heroes out of the *insect continuum*. Deleuze invokes a line of flight, a rising, cracking trope opposed to submission and propagated with heroic valences. *There are lines of crack, which do not coincide with the lines of great segmentary cuts... we might say that a plate cracks* (Deleuze and Parnet 126). These cracks in the great grids of control are perpetrated by individuals, special individuals displaying *the progression of the soul of a dancer* (125). A dancer is one who defies gravity, one who escapes the weight of the everyday. The Deleuzian hero captures and manifests the heterogeneous potentials of more chaotic, hyperdifferentiated zones. Posthumanism is full of transforming and transformative figures who siphon, conduct, radiate, and escape as if the autonomy and creative generation so crucial to the operations of whatever is considered most basic (the plane of immanence, cellular autonoma, ontological forces, compositional principles) must precipitate, at the level of the person-entity, these autonomous figures.

Posthumanism's cyborgs, poets, insect hosts, multiples, queers, and engineers of self have been described by Rosi Braidotti as *counter-images of thought... no mere metaphorization... rather the cartographic commitment to constantly redrawing politically informed maps of the present* (1997, 167). Braidotti draws her cartographic inspiration from Fredric Jameson's call for a postmodern political strategy that would replace a presumed loss of sensitization to history with an intensified sensitization to spatiality (see Jameson 54), and from Deleuze and Guattari, who describe their *conceptual personae* as travelers, seeds, and carriers. *The figures... constitute the aspect through which the concept is created by and in consciousness, through successive minds* and *conceptual personae are... intercessors, crystals, or seeds of thought* (1994, 11; 69). Each of these conceptions of the figure as remedy, as a *constantly redrawing* center of creative activity, as the disseminating seeds of a philosopher's concepts, lend themselves to the heroic, which has always been shaped in the singular, healing, creative, seminal mold and exists in suspension with the posthumanist imperative to work against the sovereignty of that figure.

Returning to Steven Shaviro and his exhortation to *cultivate your inner housefly or cockroach, instead of your inner child,* these insects, hatching *alien eggs within your body,* seem to gestate against a mute background, one created by posthumanism's very reliance on concepts such as the alien or nonhuman or alter. Simply said, for these terms to do their work, to perform their antimetaphysical, anticolonialist acts, they must always be the envoys of difference *and at the same time open to possession*, to cultivation as aliens. The insect must remain insect as such. The nonhuman is doomed to hard labor as the nonhuman. The alter can invade, penetrate, and as Shaviro suggests, we might even ingest each other's DNA, but the other must steadfastly, even inside our guts, remain alter. In this sense, we take possession of alterity by ordering its meanings and functions. Sue Golding points toward this state of affairs when she writes that technologies of otherness are *the everyday strategies we use, unwittingly or no, to make all the we-selves into me-selves* (xiii). These strategies are *a corruption of the limit, whilst limiting none the less* (xiv).

While many of us have come to salutary and sophisticated understandings of the political importance of concepts of difference, we risk miring ourselves in another form of conservatism. What we "conserve" is the discipline of absolute distinction, the discipline of the cut, the discipline of the law of the unthinkable Same which always risks the return of precisely what it seeks to cure because it is still founded on opposition and exemption, the signal operational modes of humanism. This is why I believe posthumanism must work assiduously to both recover and discover for itself more complex understandings of difference. Rodolphe Gasché makes this point when he outlines extent uses of "difference" in cultural theory. These "forget" that difference as *a relation of opposition*, such as the relation difference/Sameness, or as simple distinction, are only kinds of difference. For instance, Aristotle, that magnanimous and tyrannic thinker of genus and species, defined *differentia* as *the realized genus itself, shared differently* (87). Importantly for my purposes, Gasché reminds us that the traits that are **minimally identical** among all the incommensurable senses of difference encapsulated in Derrida's term *différance*,—differing, dif-fering, deferring— guarantee that *différance as an infrastructure can never close upon itself. Not only is it structurally open, but it differs from and defers itself* (104; emphasis mine).

But what about the discipline of the nondeferral of the distinction self/other? What of the discipline of exteriority, of the alienized-interior? Derrida writes: *The other is not myself—and who has ever maintained that it is?* (1978, 110). Within posthumanist discourses, the other person is frighteningly the Same, unbreachably different, and untouchable on both grounds. Here, I return to the notion of the multiple. Current posthumanisms employ notions of the multiple and of performances of self to effect a seeming recovery from Althusserian views of the self as relentlessly constructed and oppressed by ideology. Despite the displacement of the humanist subject, there is, overall, a kind of active, possessive creative in-charge rhetorical flavor to posthuman renditions of the self as potentially multiple. The final sentence of Donna Haraway's essay "The Biopolitics of Postmodern Bodies" reads *anthropologists of possible selves, we are technicians of realizable futures* (230). Allucquère Rosanne Stone speaks of some forms of multiple personality as *useful examples of . . . a social mode ready to hand. Further, in the language of the programmers who already inhabit the frontiers of the technosocial, multiple personality is a mode that is already in place, fairly debugged in the current release* (43).

Posthumanism marks a transition from a view of the relationship between bodies, psyches, and language as coercive, to the assumption of capacities to construct and retool multiple selves out of cultural-linguistic materials and practices. But neither of these stances allows for the blurring of human self and other in a politically or ethically efficacious mode. The question of the separation or nonseparation of self and other becomes, Can we be more faithful to our acknowledgment of language's capacity for "self fashioning" and bodily creation? Can we, while acknowledging the spectacle of our porousness to language in oppressive contexts and elsewhere, while acknowledging the urgency of questions of responsibility and freedom, begin to reconsider our intrinsic dispossession, the breaching of our selves by effects that are not possessed and that *cannot* support an ethics that relies on any absolute cut between self and other? Can we evolve an ethics that remains faithful to a politics of justice, freedom, and nonviolence while making difference tremble?

Deleuze and Guattari (among others) name *drunkenness* as a generative mode of the prephilosophical. Posthumanism, thus far, has been too respectable, too reasonable, too committed to the coherent, especially to the coherency of difference. If we want to fundamentally alter our experience and conception of self, we must break the law of the other, the law of the alien, the irremediably unfamiliar, of exteriority (or interiority) as such. We need to get drunk with each other so we can become posthumanS.

▼ Third City Kneeplay:
The Wasp and the Orchid Cross a Letter Ψ

> The manifest world is made up of different vibrations, different combinations of sounds. . . . In the process of creating the world, the power of Consciousness manifests as these different sound syllables, which we know as the different letters of the alphabet. These letters are called *matrikas*. when it takes the form of the letters, supreme Consciousness is called *matrika shakti*, the power of letters.
>
> —Swami Muktananda, *I AM THAT*

. . . You have put food into my mouth. "Orchid."

I know why you insist on writing rather than meeting. Your little experiment! I haven't decided if you are cruel or if gratitude is due. We have obviously parted ways since our meeting in the membrane, and yet the orchid you sent lays so close against the insides, the undersides of my skin, the soft tissues. That fragrance, that petaled silk, that voluptuousness. I have never made love to a flower and now I will not be able to do anything else. Don't take this to mean that I concede anything with regard to your claims about the membrane. "It is everywhere!" you announced so sententiously. You obviously have a fondness for manifestos. But if what you say is true, why did I experience leaving it and entering the city as such a violence? Explain that, if you can, you who have never left!

Despite my protests, this flower-word you sent—orchid—is crawling around under my skin worse than the "real" flower ever did. Then, just to go along with you a little bit, could this particular mode of orchid be a skin-vibrating flower? I don't feel quite as welcoming to the proboscis.

Which is the only way, at the moment, I can experience your attribution (to me) of wasp. It's a wasp, yes, or the phantom of a wasp that keeps buzzing around my thighs, occasionally attaching itself. A kind of insect irony. The buzz of irony. The iron scent of orchid. Maybe that's what draws them so close, a third trajectory, a third word, iron. Remember the line "breasts sting like raspberries and milk"? Childish, but one is forced to live it in the flesh. If this is already true of words, I admit I'm a bit worried. What if you are right about the membrane intensifying these effects? What will be left of "me"? I have a change to report. Now the orchid has become "my" flower! Or, there you are, flowering between my thighs.

I told you my tale of abandonment, as you call it, in my last letter, which you apparently never received. If you are telling the truth, I will have enveloped a sharp line of anxiety that will sound its note during every interval between my writing and your reply.

The ocean did not envelop me, it played. It met me with a gentle concavity, the tenderest pocket. Falls terrify me. Heartbeat took up all the space. When it slowed, I realized that the ocean had picked up the sound and was playing it back like being in a womb, except after a time it had got hold of so many of my sounds, my body played a music I had never heard. I'd call it improvisational jazz, variations on a theme so distorted, at times, it seemed utterly strange. But then it returned, weirdly familiar. The ocean apparently has a sense of humor. The concert became rather synesthetic, accompanied by surface contortions, sculptures, light shows all formed from the ocean's "substance." What was the purpose of these displays? All I can say is that the ocean seemed to be possessed of a huge curiosity. I felt a quality of attention focused on me beyond self-interest, and yet the whole dance seemed to be about the two of us, about what could be done with the two of us. You can see why I was so bereft at leaving.

I'm lonely here in the city. Everyone works all the time. My neighbors don't like it if I drop by unexpectedly. They prefer planned meetings. Even then, certain topics seem to be taboo. The problems with the postal system, for instance. "Letters are so mundane," my neighbor told me yesterday. Funny, then, that the times I've knocked on her door, she always says, "Don't bother me, I'm reading my mail!"

The only reason I am going along with this separation (yes, I still insist on calling it that) is because you wrote *we will need a new language.*

I want one, of course. (Here, the word *want* will burst your skin . . . the page . . .) But will I feel less lonely when we speak the language of the membrane? When we are "together"? This will be my little experiment.

Signed,

your wasp-orchid

▼ Emanation/Expression ▼Ψ

The other is not myself—and who has ever maintained that it is?
—Jacques Derrida, *Writing and Difference*

In *Expressionism in Philosophy: Spinoza*, Deleuze distinguishes between emanation and immanation/expression. Beginning with Plotinus, Deleuze outlines the investments of emanationist cosmologies. *Emanation has in general a triadic form: giver, given and recipient. . . . The giver is above its gifts as it is above its products, participable through what it gives, but imparticipable in itself or as itself, thereby grounding participation* (171). This is a dualist concept of emanation based on the transcendence of god to his creations. *Plotinus also says that the One has "nothing in common" with the things that come from it* (172).

Deleuze contrasts this to immanationist cosmologies: *A cause is immanent, on the other hand, when its effect is "immanent" in the cause, rather than emanating from it. . . . From this viewpoint the distinction of essence between cause and effect can in no way be understood as a degradation. From the viewpoint of immanence the distinction of essence does not exclude, but rather implies an equality of being* (172). *Immanence for its part implies a pure ontology, a theory of Being in which Unity is only a property of substance and of what is. . . [being is] equally present in all beings. And the Cause appears as everywhere equally close: there is no remote causation. Beings are not defined by their rank in a hierarchy* (173). Deleuze then goes on to link immanence to a view of cosmogenesis as *expression. Participation no longer has its principle in an emanation*

whose source lies in a more or less distant One, but rather in the immedi-
ate and adequate expression of an absolute Being that comprises in it all
beings, and is explicated in the essence of each. Expression comprehends all
these aspects: complication, explication, inherence, implication.... From this
viewpoint the idea of expression accounts for the real activity of the partic-
ipate, and for the possibility of participation. It is in the idea of expression
that the new principle of immanence asserts itself. Expression appears as
the unity of the multiple, as the complication of the multiple, and as the
explication of the One God expresses **himself** *in the world; the world is the*
expression, the explication, of a God-Being or a One who is (175–76).

A series of terms convey the complexity of the Tantric cosmogonic
process: *sṛṣṭi* (expression, emanation); *unmeṣa* (unfolding, expansion,
opening out, expression); *ābhāsa* (emanation, manifestation, efferves-
cence); and *visarga* (flashing forth). Taken together, Tantric concepts of
cosmogenesis comport nearly exactly with Deleuze-Spinoza's explication of immanation/expression. The manifest world simultaneously *is* a
spontaneously multiplicitous, expressive divine and an expression *of* the
divine or consciousness/energy. There is only relative transcendence
folded inextricably into immanence. The emergence of the world *owes*
its reality to its emergence from the primary being... through an actual
transformation of the latter from the condition of cause to that of effect.
This being remains however unaffected by this transformation brought
about as a kind of sport by its overflowing bounty, its free and boundless
spontaneity (Padoux 81). The idea of cosmogenesis as sport or play is
one of the key notions that distinguishes Vedanta and Tantra. The
Tantric world body is often referred to as *the body of play* or *the play-*
house (Flood 86). Play *(līlā)* implies that cosmogenesis partakes of pleasure, aesthetics, spontaneity, personality, and a fascination with games of
disguise and revealing. A nonattached *bhā⁻va* (attitude) of play is central to any philosophical or practical engagement with Tantra. It may
seem, however, that the claim that *this being remains however unaffected,*
opens Tantric cosmology to a more standard, emanationist post-Platonic
interpretation by positing an outside that remains unaffected and from
which manifestations or expressions flow. The idea of an untouchable
beyond *does* appear in Tantric texts, particularly as propagated by stu-
dents and interpreters of Abhinavagupta following the eleventh-century
synthesis. However, there is a more nuanced and less Vedantically inflected

sense in which *remaining unaffected* does not partake of the static and dualist notions of transcendence critiqued by Deleuze.

Part of the problem lies in various levels of translation. It is just too easy to lose sight of the extent to which Tantric practices and attendant texts are built on paradox; it is too tempting to *decide*. Most often, and most profoundly, Tantra *does not decide, does not choose*, between transcendence and immanence, between oneness and multiplicity, between male and female. For instance, Gavin Flood, in his otherwise excellent encounter with the concept of body in Kashmir Śaivism, repeatedly notes "ambiguities" within the texts of Abhinavagupta. The instances are too numerous to cite. However, Flood often moves in the direction of attempting to explain or resolve ambiguity when the actual state of affairs is not ambiguity but a more constitutive ambi-valance or trembling meant to foil all attempts at resolution. Harvey Alper is one of the few interpreters of Abhinavagupta who honors and feels at ease maintaining the flickering paradoxes in Abhinava's work, paradoxes that emerge from Tantric practice and that are the true jewels of Tantra. Alper understands that Kashmir Śaivism is neither strictly absolutist nor idealist, as it is often described. He reads Abhinava's concept of ultimacy as one of constant expression, of becoming-multiple: a *world process* that *is* god. Sovereignty is *nothing but* the essential freedom *(svātantrya)* of the cosmos to become multiple. *To remain unaffected* then, does not mean to be external to one's creations, but to continue in one's essential nature: to abide in oneself in expressive multiplicity: to continue the play. As Alper points out, for Abhinava, externality is always *relative;* that is, given that every expression of the world Self is itself, externality can only arise in the context of its thorough imbrication with (not subordination to) immanence. *This cosmic process can be named as god and as consciousness. It is at once personal and impersonal. It transcends the ordinary distinctions between subject and object, mind and matter. Śiva-who-is-consciousness who is cause of the world cannot be "described" as material as opposed to ethereal, or* **vice versa.** *He is at once both and neither* (365).

And this returns us to Deleuze and posthumanism. So far, I have emphasized the similarities between Deleuze's gloss on expression/expression and Tantric emanation/expression, but there are significant departures and significant opportunities that emerge from these. Both

Deleuze and posthumanism *do decide:* they decide in favor of main-taining categories of difference, autonomy, and identity in ways that preserve, as I have argued, some of the figures and affective investments of humanism. Todd May identifies this problem with respect to Deleuze, who wants to think ontology as difference all the way down. May writes that *where the primacy is given to difference the thought becomes incoher-ent. . . . If meaning were merely the product of difference, there would be no meaning, only noises unrelated to each other. In order for meaning to occur, identity must exist within difference, or better, each must exist within the other. . . . To put the matter baldly, a thought of pure difference is not a thought at all* (46). At the same time, Deleuze longs for an unmedi-ated experience of the univocity of being, longs for it as an individual who can have or possess experiences, most pressingly, a moment of feverish contact with an ontogenic fire. Alain Badiou notes in his pre-cise and sobering textual encounter with Deleuze, the *enthusiastic vibra-tion* that attends Deleuze's invocations of *the One-All—that forms the supreme destination of thought and to which thought is accordingly conse-crated* (1999a, 11). He goes on to say that *thinking* [for Deleuze] *consists precisely in ascetically attaining that point where the individual is **trans-fixed** by the impersonal exteriority that is equally his or her authentic being* (13; emphasis mine).

Transfixed is a felicitous word here as it holds all the meanings and effects that distinguish Tantric expression/emanation/immanence from Deleuzian expression/immanence, those that result from the transfix-ing of categories of univocity and multiplicity so that each may be con-tained and possessed through the experience of the Sorcerer. The Deleuz-ian experience of both univocity *and* multiplicity is filtered through one human part and never results in self-dispossession. This contrasts starkly with the Tantric notion of the adept's experience, which is not radical, impersonal, or possessed by one. Describing those who become established in a fuller sensitivity to nonduality, my guru says: *Nondual-ity [in duality] is ordinary, perfectly ordinary. And yet everything is com-pletely different. The individual ego does not go away, but it is no longer a source of attachment. It becomes what it is: an expression, a field of expressions and potential expressions of an immanent divine.*

Or as my *paramaguru* (my guru's guru) puts it: *[A sannyasin] should become such a perfect artist that he does nothing; events happen through him* (Saraswati 115).

▼ Three Bodies Ψ

1. The sensation body: I am sad. I am hungry. I am happy and so on.
2. The energy body/the BwO: a body of variable energetic qualities, intensities, and speeds.
3. The emanation body: a body of expression and value.

Three Bodies Practice: Project three bodies as modes of each other. Roll up the sensation and the energy bodies into the emanation body. Experience yourself as the world: the moving expressive creation.

Everything is a body. The body expresses everything. The body is a city, a cosmopolis. *Oh, how wondrous are the habits of the human body— Calcutta!* (Urban 2001, 137).

▼ Three Bodies: Exposition in Preparation for the Avatar Body Ψ

The body expresses, contains all. The body is a city. Within Tantric cosmology, everything is a body, a multipli-CITY: individual entities, bodies of emotion, the body of consciousness. The cosmos comprises thousands of gradations of bodies. Bodies are more or less condensed, more or less expanded, continually undergoing processes of involution and evolution: folding and unfolding, continually becoming. Human beings and all entities are *expressions* of this undecidably shared body: we, along with everything else, are zones of encounter, of touch, of the event, and of chance. We are simultaneously particular and infinite. Our human bodies are modal expressions of cosmic bodies of energy and consciousness. This creates, as Gavin Flood notes, *variability of the boundaries of the concepts of body, person and world* (42). This variability, or *infinite event of the person,* delivers us to an entirely different disposition with regard to the question of responsibility. Viewed from a nonlocal, oceanic perspective, *individuals* are not responsible. Tantrics do not believe in karma in the sense of an individual, identifiable trail of actions that must be worked through by one person or to which one person is accountable. Karma is *a force which is trans-individual. . . . every act is the result of the karma of many people* (Flood 173). Actions are smeared across an infinite field. However, from a wave perspective, you and I *are* relatively individuated expressions. The very fact of our relative locatability means that we have certain capacities for experiencing and expressing the results of and our responses to trans-individual actions. We are responsible *to* these capacities, recognizing that acting from a relative location in an individuated body gives us the opportunity to transform ourselves, and thus *everything*.

Ψ Avatar and Expression ▼

The word "avatar" comes from the Sanskrit "*avatāra*" and means, most generally, a down-coming of the divine into human or animal form. Hindu divines, such as Vishnu and his consort, Lakshmi, choose to incarnate in order to perform tasks, in order to establish pedagogical relationships with human beings, and as a means to experience play in duality. In the classical Indian tradition, beginning with the Upanishads and thoroughly immanent to India's class and caste system, the avatar is a being who participates in human life yet remains distinct in both an evolutionary and an ontological sense. He or she takes on human or animal characteristics, including, in some cases, mortality. The avatar exemplifies how to live in this world in order to eventually transcend it. Despite human appearances and behaviors, the classical Hindu avatar is not a representative or envoy or performance of some aspect of a person in the contemporary sense: he or she is a divine. As Geoffrey Parrinder points out in his influential study, *Avatar and Incarnation,* the proliferation of avatar personalities and the personalization of the divine was a reaction against invocations of "divinity without qualities" in earlier, Vedic texts (14). While remaining apart, the historical purpose of Hindu avatars is to bring the divine into an expressive, often loving and protective, reciprocal relation with mortal humanity.

Within Tantra, a view of cosmogenesis founded on expression/emanation impacts the more determinedly dualist concept of avatar inhabiting post-Vedic Indian cultures and cosmologies. Tantra does not distinguish, ontologically, between the human, the material, the animal, the psychic, or the divine, but works along baroquely conceived gradations from subtle to gross, expanded to contracted, involuted to evoluted, static to kinetic, active to passive. It addresses its rituals and practices to a baroque variety of cosmic expressions or manifestations. Along these gradations, absolute staticity is never achieved. Khanna: *there never was a "first," nor will there ever be a "last" cosmos, nor will there ever be a period at which the universe will have reached a static phase of total disintegration or total integration* (77). Instead of changelessness, one finds never-ending pulsation and vibration (Flood 32–43; Padoux 82–83). Duality, as an expression or mode of nonduality, is a matter of kinetic polarities that *stretch* from radical potential or virtuality to material manifestation or actualization. As discussed, Tantric cosmologies view reality, that is, everything including deities, rocks, humans, words, sounds, images, gestures, powers, and personalities, as ontologically related, *modal* expressions of a single, heterogeneous real. Avatar refers to circulating, active modalities or expressions of reality that are present everywhere in potentia. The overarching aim of Tantric practice is to involute expressions such as sound, image, gesture, powers, and personality and, in doing so, learn to transit from one modality to another, accessing the intrinsic relatedness of everything.

While the advent of avatar manifestations within traditional Hinduisms provided a vector for personalized relationality between people and the divine, Tantra is a worldview and a set of techniques for relationality *all the way down*. On every level, from daily practice to metaphysics to cosmogony, the desire for relation and the pleasure of relation is the prime motivating or moving force. The written Tantras centralize practices, cosmogony, and ritual around different cosmogonic persona, mainly *Śakti, Śiva,* and their expressions. Generalizing from several different kinds of accounts, a spontaneous desire for manifold relationships manifests a multiplicitous world. Latter-day interpreters, for instance, the twentieth-century Kashmiri Tantric scholar/practitioner Swami Lakshmanjoo, tend to emphasize a doxic concept of divine will *(icchā śakti)* as the explanans for the manifest world (CD1). However, the Tantras themselves have a much more complex and ambi-valent notion of cosmogonic desire that constantly moves inside an edge of compulsion, will, sexual desire, experimentation, self-expression, and a spontaneous, free, overflowing. Barely containing these tensions, the eleventh-century Kashmiri Śaivite Kṣemarāja writes that the creation is a *brilliant throbbing consciousness* (quoted in Muller-Ortega 85).

At the level of human relations, this complex sense of desire permeates Tantric practice and symbolism. As the motive force of cosmic differentiation, desire is also the vector for proliferating the relationships that constitute individual practices of self-capacitation. Yet pleasure, or bliss, a temporary state of forgetful merging with others, is a crucial aspect of recapitulating and participating in the rhythm of creation. Describing the state of god consciousness attained by yogins involved in *maithuna* or sexual yoga, the *Kulārnava Tantra* states: *Just as the enjoyment of drinking milk mixed with sugar can be derived by a person who drinks it, in the same manner pleasure of this state is beyond description and can only be experienced. . . . The Supreme Pleasure of Divine Impulse experienced in this state cannot be described even by intelligent persons through concentration* (Rai 155). Here, the motive force of creation on a cosmic scale is described as *Divine Impulse*. This is a common locution, and it emphasizes the pulsing, spontaneous upsurging of creation rather than a more sanitized notion of will. Yogins accessing this state of becoming through the vehicle of their bodies experience this as pleasure. Across the entire range of Tantric traditions, pleasure in relationship and the desire for creative manifestation are inextricable.

Ψ The Difference Difference

Bearing an uncanny resemblance to Deleuzian-Spinozan invocations of differentiation or creation, Tantric ontogeny establishes itself through a series of modal relationships between sound, syllable, word, image, objects, animals, human bodies, gestures, and capacities or creative energies where manifestation results from spontaneous desire. However, unlike in Deleuze, for whom the substrata of individual relations, the singularities or haecceities, must be presumed to have no intrinsic relation to each other in order to support a cosmogenesis based on pure difference, Tantric individual modalities or expressivities are based on the premise that matter, consciousness, and energy are copresent, differing expressions of each other, extant in varying intensities within individuated manifestations of creation and without absolute delimitation. In some incalculable sense, a body *is* sound, a word *is* image, a gesture made by a student *is* a goddess or a partial personality of a goddess. These modal expressivities touch *all the way down*.

The Tantric concept of difference agrees with deconstructionist concepts of difference as it assumes the nonidentity of individual expressions or modes to themselves. However, this nonidentity to self stands in contrast, not only to Deleuzian invocations of difference, but also to the general thrust of deconstructionist thought. Tantric nonidentity to self is not predicated on a relation of nonrelation. Relations of nonrelation are central to postwar, antifascist views of the person as they both unseat the *fascist within* and salvage an opening for freedom. These include the relation of nonrelation between signifier and signified, between self and other, and for Deleuze, between individual manifestations of univocity. Tantra, on the other hand, is a practice of relationality that ultimately suspends terms such as self and other, interiority and exteriority. It ultimately holds difference in suspension within a nonlocal unity that is also subjected to *différance*. This means a retention of the primacy of the relation as the fault line along which identity is deferred, with, at the same time, an openness to blurrings of self and other that occur under a different philosophical, affective regime: a regime of pleasure and capacitating porosity rather than trauma.

Tantra views the human body as the most appropriate vehicle for sensitizing the practitioner to the creative, differentiating power of a nonstatic reality and for making that power more available to human beings in their everyday lives. Tantric practices are a taking of the world into the body of the practitioner, a re-embodiment that sensitizes the practitioner to the correspondences between her and everything else. In this sense, Tantra is a *local practice* of *nonlocality,* a local sensitization and opening to the influx and influence of differentiated manifestations of a univocal desire that is itself a world in potentia.

Within Tantric cosmogony, a nonstatic yet unified state of feeling/consciousness *(Śiva),* indissolubly linked to creative potential *(Śakti)* expresses itself into a vast multiplicity. Conversely, the *sādhaka,* or student, travels through the vast multiplicity by establishing relationships between herself and the world in order to experience the pleasure of a nonduality that is nevertheless a process of differentiation. The experience of nonduality is valued precisely because it signifies access to a less constrained experience of multiplicity. Bounded individual life is not contrasted to oceanic oneness or individual ascension to unmediated knowledge, but to an enlarged "self" that becomes and can utilize the manifold (Flood 113). *Life and its manifold processes are not an inert, even, state of oneness; what justifies existence is variety, contradiction, change and multiplicity. Tantra shows a preference for a dynamic concept of cosmic unity which implies a harmony of all differentiations and paradoxes. . . . The ultimate consummation for the **sādhaka** lies in his absorbing this vision of unity in diversity* (Khanna 60).

Tantra comprises a set of practices of relationality or contact that hold, perhaps even more rigorously than those discussed here thus far, to procedures of nonexemption, that is, procedures and practices founded on concepts of self and other that are themselves always deferred and that never discompose *différance* into simple distinction. Traversed by the manifold, manifesting a creation that expresses itself *as* me through ontogenically related modalities of sound, word, image, flesh, capacity, thought, emotion, personality, and so on, I am capable of expressing many bodies, many selves or partial selves that are never statically identical to my "self," that come to me from an outside, from an other or others where "outside" and "other" always defer and differ, inarticulably from any static concepts of outside and other and self. As an ontologically modal expression, "I" *am* this relation to the manifold that is also "me," but at the same time, distinct. Distinctions exist along a continuum that *yokes* "im-personalities" such as vibration, movement, intensity, sound, and syllable to personalities such as anger, generosity, and love.

▼Ψ Avatar Bodies, an Invitation Ψ▼

Perhaps for social reasons, Tantra's central concern both practically, and in it's complex linguistic ontology, is to break through prohibitions on touch. There is excess and surpassing, but surpassing is a surfeit of in-passing to which one becomes sensitized through practices of attention and active passivity. The aim of Tantric practice is to become adept at relationship, to proliferate relationship, baroquely, until one cannot articulate the difference between oneself and another, oneself and the world. In the most general and profound sense, Tantra is a set of techniques for local sensitization to nonlocal reality, conceived as a fabric, a weaving, a Tantra in which every thread touches every other thread. The *bound person,* one who is not sensitized to his or her relational participation in cosmic reality, is *relatively powerless because he is so particularized or individualized.* A more adept person is aware of having a shared body that *by the very nature of its being manifest . . . must contain differentiation and therefore multiplicity in some sense. . . . the higher the shared reality, the less constraint* (Flood 111). Tantric emanations, then, are not down comings, but the comings and goings of a reality from which no touch is exempt. This state of nonstatic relationship which "I" *am,* this thoroughfare, this nexus of relationality is the avatar body. Here, the conjunction "avatar" and "body" signals a shift away from the concept of avatar as a representational envoy of a relation between that which is essentially separated and toward a concept of avatar as expressive of a general *condition* of entanglement.

I want to invite a Tantric concept of expression to begin to alter concepts of avatar as these are nearly always figured as representations, as simulacra whose potential detachment from or uncertain inhabitation of an original gives rise to a great deal of anxiety of contact. Avatars are always claimed by those who invent them or by those whom they inhabit. Deleuze and Guattari's *conceptual personae* are avatars, signed by the philosopher's who invent them: Plato/Socrates, Nietzsche/Zarathustra, and so on. *Conceptual personae carry out the movements that describe the author's plane of immanence, and they play a part in the very creation of the author's concepts* (1994, 63). Similar claims are made upon avatars who come to inhabit us when Derrida writes: *I have the experience of "myself" as a multiplicity of places, images, imagos, there are others in me* (Derrida and Düttmann 1997, 13). These others in me must both *be* me and, in a different register, maintain their integrity as unalterably other; they may not be a confusing or confused in-between. Tantric expressions, on the other hand, are always shared, always *confused:* they are capacities that circulate and that may be accessed but never absolutely claimed. They have personality, yet are not determinedly personal or impersonal. They can never be "radically alien." The concept of expression opens zones of individual closure up to saturation by uncertain belongings, uncertain relations. If I think, it is because the cosmos manifests the capacity for thought. If I feel, it is because the cosmos manifests a capacity for emotion. If I wound, it is because the cosmos wounds.

Ψ *Itara* and *Avatāra* ▼

Tantric expression does not recognize a hierarchy of sacred and profane, real and illusory, but only a nonlocal, localizable reality of ontogenic
effects. This comports in significant ways with the Derridean concept of
iteration. As Derrida notes in "Signature Event Context": *iterability—
(**iter,** again, probably comes from **itara, other** in Sanskrit)* (1988, 7). *Avatāra,
itāra,* other, iteration. These will be the crucial and related terms as we
proceed. Iterability is, according to Derrida's well-known formulation,
the capacity of writing, in the largest sense, for acting in the absence of
a specific sender or receiver. The citational capacity of writing interrupts the authority of identity, assignation, and signature by preventing
the stabilization of these around a single meaning and instead initiating
a wayward chain of "authorities," a chain of significations. *Every sign,
linguistic or nonlinguistic, spoken or written... can be **cited,** put between
quotation marks; in so doing it can break with every given context, engendering an infinity of new contexts in a manner which is absolutely illim-
itable. This does not imply that the mark is valid outside of a context, but
on the contrary that there are only contexts without any center or absolute
anchoring* (12). In other words, a mark does not function *outside* of a
world (context), but is capable, as Derrida puts it, of functioning as *a
sort of machine which is productive* within any context, in the *radical
absence of every empirically **determined** receiver in general* (8; emphasis
mine). Derrida's concept of iterability is generalizable, valid *not only for
all orders of "signs" and for all languages in general, but moreover, beyond
semio-linguistic communication, for the entire field of what philosophy*

would call experience, even the experience of being: the above mentioned *"presence"* (9).

Tantric expressions take up the entire field of iterability as Derrida describes it, including semio-linguistic units, sound, vibration, gesture, emotion, communicable capacities, image, and *the experience of being.* These circulate from context to context, multiply signed but not definitively owned, in relation, but precisely due the unbounded proliferation of relationality that traces, that tracks through everything not identical to themselves. This is articulated in the well-known locution from the *Viśvasāra Tantra: What is here, is elsewhere. What is not here, is nowhere* (Woodroffe 24).

Derrida's concept of iteration is central to why I believe posthumanism would benefit from renewing its interest in and commitment to deconstruction. I want to point us away from the sorts of limits on relationality I have begun to outline here and to push through to what Derrida has tentatively called *postdeconstruction.* "Postdeconstruction" *could be* a nomination which inaugurates a letting go of the ideological work that we have called upon an Other-as-such to perform in favor of a more pervasive notion of iterability, one in which there are *gradations* of quasi-presences and quasi-absences that are never identical to themselves, disallowing the *as such* and its disciplinary distinctions even with respect to the categories "self" and "other."

▼ Tantric Bodies ▼

Tantra describes itself most consistently as a science, a practice of self-realization, and a practical way of life. It is particularly rigorous with respect to formulating practices that awaken the student to the active participation of the body in a creation process that operates through differentiation. Within Tantra, the body is the nexus that allows the practitioner to experience all of the differentiated expressions of which the cosmos is capable: there is no body *as such*. As Vicky Kirby has so eloquently argued, many progressive theorists still treat the body as a surface for inscription, leaving a biological residue of the unable to be thought, an inarticulable beyond language or writing in the most general sense that is held hostage to the violence of culture (151). In the work of Levinas, whose thinking of responsibility is central to Derrida's work, and in that of Deleuze, the body serves as ground for the inauguration of the necessary conditions for ethics. In Levinas, the body anticipates and grounds ethical responsibility due to its capacity for radically passive wounding. This anticipation is presubjective and sensorial. Oppositely, in Deleuze, active, heroic asceticisms work to contravene oppressive regimes of the organism, creating a less tyrannized BwO through directed processes of involution that, despite infoldings, keep the other at bay. In my antinomian version, postdeconstruction means learning to recognize the body's incorporations, including those occasioned by trauma and pleasure, as *participatory capacities*. In Derrida's reading of Levinas, the body must remain passive in order to maintain the concept of an other who wounds, who scores, who marks, making subjectivity possible, but without itself being subjected to appropriation. This is, as we shall see, an otherness outside *différance*. However, by acknowledging the body's active participation in worldmaking, "self" and "other" become an undecidable relation where "undecidable" signals the untenability of setting limits on iteration and thus on maintaining a concept of alterity *as such*.

Looking ahead, Tantric active passivity, a state of alert receptivity that encourages the body's participations in opening the self to the world, does not distinguish between the personal and the impersonal, nor does it motivate itself primarily with the affects of anxiety and horror auto-toxicus that have understandably characterized formulations of ethical relations between humans since World War II. Without at all denigrating this response, I invite you to consider whether capacities for joyful participation, joyful intimacy, the joyful inpassing of self and other could be made available for an ethics that could also be considered antifascist in the broadest sense.

▼▼ Fourth City Kneeplay

... When I was a child, my mother often took me to the museum. She told me about a game she and my father played during the early days of their courtship. Sitting on the steps of the museum, they made up stories about the passersby, about what kind of jobs they did, their relationships, or other, more lurid narratives. The point of the game was to catch people out in being predictable and then to turn banality into a form of entertainment. It was a way of creating an otherworld where the cliché was deformed, deferred by imagination or perhaps mockery. Most kinds of mockery have their innocence, their utopian longing. Here is my version of the game: Fixing a certain unfocused, yet receptive gaze on my chosen subject, I carefully shape my body posture to hers. I let my forehead, cheeks, lips, eyes assume her expressions, my shoulders match her exact tilt and slump. And so on, down to the degree of heaviness in the legs resting on stone steps. I settle in. I breathe her breath. I fall into gestural and rhythmic unison with her. I let the flesh direct until I begin to feel emotions, a movement of discomfort in my body. Discomfort blossoms into shame, a tiredness in the chest, a shallow breath born of shame. Anger wrapped in the belly. A resolve at the lip. These are expressions of the body/psyche that connect, not just us, but other animals, too. To whom do these expressions belong? Which part of them is "me"? Are they personal or impersonal? The language of light, the language of the eye (me looking at her), the language of the skin, muscle, joints, organs, bone, the language of shame, anger, resolve, the language of this tenderness, this protectiveness, this fear I now feel wrapped around "you" in "me," the language I am writing to you here. Instead of translation, mediation, the cut, the fold into myriad surfaces, what if I spoke of an avatar body, of capacities, of emanations that differ, defer even their differences? Then, this shame would be the emanation, the avatar of the shame aspect of you in me, belonging neither to you or me, shared incompletely, incoherently, where my contribution is the making of gestures that will proliferate this vexed correspondence. I absorb without claiming ownership. I invite your signature, and countless others, on me, in me.

Perhaps this constitutes, mainly, a change in outlook, yet one that is difficult to promote, if not forbidden. Levinas's self-as-hostage-to-the-other devotes itself to an impersonal other, an other before any others. Is my absorption of you, even with uncertain ownership, always appropriation in the way we have meant it? I am thinking of something like ontogenic kinship. And the desire to sensitize myself to it. The pleasure of it. Is this potency, this desire, this pleasure the yoke, or does the yoke = the saying "I"? Then, could "I" become a vehicle of desire for the manifold inflected humanly? Yoke, shelter, thoroughfare, debtor, diner.

I can't figure out where "we" are . . .

▼ Eating, Well . . .

In the opening pages of *A Thousand Plateaus,* Deleuze and Guattari proffer one of their exceptionally rare discussions of their collaboration. *The two of us wrote* **Anti-Oedipus** *together. Since each of us was several, there was already quite a crowd. Here we have made use of everything that came within range. . . . To reach, not the point where one no longer says I, but the point where it is no longer of any importance whether one says I. We are no longer ourselves. Each will know his own. We have been aided, inspired, multiplied* (3). The coauthors offer this statement by way of acknowledging their effects on each other, but also the effects of the "crowd," those who inhabit each of us and write with us, alongside us, for us. Yet in a strange and tense pairing, they seemingly must say, *We are no longer ourselves. Each will know his own.* This is, perhaps, the most succinct expression of the ethical situation of the posthumanist subject: to no longer be oneself, yet to unfailingly recognize one's possessions. In the ethical series that runs from Spinoza to Nietzsche to Deleuze and much of posthumanism, to know one's "own" is the necessary condition for a directorial creative self-capacitation. In the series that runs from Levinas to Derrida and his interlocutors, a certain closure on being none other than oneself is the necessary condition for responsibility. Yet, in his "conversation" with Jean-Luc Nancy, "'Eating Well,' or the Calculation of the Subject," Derrida calls for a new sense of responsibility. *I would say that it is in the relation to the "yes" or to the Zusage presupposed in every question that one must seek a new (postdeconstructive) determination of the responsibility of the "subject"* (105).

Here, and elsewhere, Derrida picks up the theme in Levinas of hospitality as an affirmation, a "yes" that is always a response and a reception of the other, before the "I." This is why *hospitality thus precedes property* (1999a, 45). It is the interruption of one's self by a sensibility to the other that is self as other, a paradox or a Möbius, as Levinas is well aware. But as Derrida notes, ethics must always engage politics and law, to which I would add a transversal term: sociality (1999a, 115). So, in "Eating Well" he writes that *the question will come back to determining the best, most respectful, most grateful, and also most giving way of relating to the other and of relating the other to the self* (114). When considering ethics, it is not possible or desirable to remain within the domain of philosophy. Knowing that one will eat, the question becomes: how may one eat hospitably?

ΨΨ Eating Animals

In "Eating Well," Derrida writes that the eating of flesh constitutes the signal act of a sacrificial form of a *carno-phallogocentric* humanism which *installs the virile [flesh/other-eating] figure at the determinative center of the subject* while all others, women, animals, must defer to, be eaten by, him (114). This is true, Derrida notes, even in discourses, such as those of Heidegger and Levinas, that *disrupt... a certain traditional humanism. In spite of the differences separating them, they nonetheless remain profound humanisms to the extent that they do not sacrifice sacrifice* (113). Later, Derrida expands on the precise forms of this unsacrificed sacrifice: the sacrifice of men naming animals, of constituting the category "animal" (*Animal is a word that men have given themselves the right to give* [2002, 400]) and the actual killing of animals. Derrida then places under the purview of genocide what he reckons as two centuries of the accelerating production, killing, and engineering of animals: *No one can deny the **unprecedented** proportions of this subjection of the animal.... No one can deny seriously, or for very long, that men do all they can in order to dissimulate this cruelty or to hide it from themselves, in order to organize on a global scale the forgetting or misunderstanding of this violence that some would compare to the worst cases of genocide (there are also animal genocides)* (394). Nothing constitutes the human or the humanism of Derrida's principle tutors, including Emmanuel Levinas, more than this *second original sin* whereby what is proper to man is *his **superiority** over what is called animal life. This last superiority, infinite and par excellence, has as its property the fact of being at one and the* *same time **unconditional** and **sacrificial*** (410; 389). Pointing toward an altered relationship to animals that may delicately, tentatively, and, acknowledging a certain utopianism, finally usher in the *posthuman*, Derrida writes: *I move from the "ends of man," that is the confines of man, to "the crossing of borders" between man and animal. Crossing borders or the ends of man I come or surrender to the animal—to the animal in itself, to the animal in me and the animal at unease with itself, to the man about which Nietzsche said (I no longer remember where) something to the effect that it was an as yet undetermined animal, an animal lacking in itself [e.g. without possession of a name]. . . . Since time, since so long ago, hence since all of time and for what remains of it to come we would therefore be in passage toward surrendering to the promise of that animal at unease with itself* (372).

Yet, in "Eating Well," Derrida says, in coincidence with the inaugural moment of the posthuman, *if the limit between the living and the non-living now seems to be as unsure, at least as an oppositional limit, as that between "man" and "animal," and if, in the (symbolic or real) experience of the "eat-speak-interiorize," the ethical frontier no longer rigourously passes between the "Thou shalt not kill"(man, thy neighbour) . . . but rather between several infinitely different modes of the conception-appropriation-assimilation of the other, then, as concerns the "Good" **(Bien)** of every morality, the question will come back to determining the best, most respectful, most grateful, and so most giving way of relating to the other and of relating the other to the self* (114). This "relating" is an unavoidable eating of and *with* others. *One never eats entirely on one's own: this constitutes the rule underlying the statement, "One must eat well." It is a rule offering infinite hospitality* (115).

Derrida's acknowledgment of the unavoidable introjection and assimilation of the other demands, most pressingly demands, the work of otherness. We eat in company, we eat each other, we are eaten, but these are meals that, in their digestive *failure*, comprise the necessary condition for ethics, for justice, for a responsibility that is openness to the other. This failure of appropriation has been the condition for ethics since the genocides of World War II, what Derrida terms, here and elsewhere, *the worst* (104). *Something of this call of the other must remain nonreappropriable, nonsubjectivable, and in a certain way nonidentifiable, a sheer supposition, so as to remain **other**, a **singular** call to response or to responsibility. . . . This obligation to protect the other's otherness is* *not merely a theoretical imperative* (110–11). The supposition of the other's otherness *is* hospitality: it is "eating well" by allowing the trace, the track of exteriority to inhabit us in some crucial sense untouched, unharmed, and yet active. In this respect, the other remains as the vector of the effect of otherness in me, the trace of *différance,* itself unsubjected to *différance.* I protect the other from the violence that, through both necessity and sheer supposition, I will or invite the other to do to my *self* in order to protect her from me by assuring that I am always in a state of *trembling.* Even though I must eat, even though every act of hospitality, of responsibility, of eating well, presumes violence, *something* remains. This remainder is indeconstructible. It is not a thing, but an act. As Derrida says *it is what deconstruction performs* through a commitment, an openness to being exceeded (1997a, 19–29). Yet, between remorse and hospitality, between the criminal and the host, arises a suspicion of an overdetermining yoking, a possibly untenable assumption of control that slips in just as I am surrendering, just as I am forfeiting control.

▼ Vegetarians, Brahmins Ψ

Derrida says of the formal structure of sacrifice, of eating the other and its relationship to humanism and sacrificial carnal-phallogocentrism: *What is still to come or what remains buried in an almost inaccessible memory is the thinking of a responsibility that does not stop at this determination of the neighbor, at the dominant [sacrificial] schema of this determination.* An *ethnology* of originary religious domains from which such sacrificial schema developed would *in particular have to spend quite some time in the complex history of Hinduist culture, which perhaps represents the most subtle and decisive confirmation of this schema. Does it not, precisely, set in opposition the political hierarchy—or the exercise of power—and the religious hierarchy, the latter prohibiting, the former allowing itself, indeed imposing upon itself the eating of meat?* (Derrida and Nancy 116). Here, Derrida refers to the socially differentiated diets of the *varna,* the Hindu class system that evolved an entire social structure around two kinds of sacrifice: the "impure" sacrifice of animals and other human beings and "pure" self-sacrifice or asceticism.

Brian K. Smith, in his seminal essay, "Eaters, Food, and Social Hierarchy in Ancient India," notes that ancient Vedic culture divided everyone and everything into eaters and food. Each class "ate" the next one down the food chain from Brahmins to *Kṣatriya* warriors to the *Vaiśyas* or commoners, who were *sometimes directly equated with animals* (188). *Food may circulate from the cosmic point of view, but from a hierarchical social perspective it flows (or should flow) only in one direction: from the exploited to the exploiter, from the other to the self* (185). According to the

Vedas, the Brahmins were the only class not to be eaten due to their relation to the violent sacrifice of animals and eating of divine food during
ritual. Again, the constituting of a class called "animal," and the killing
of members of that class, defines a socio-political-religious order. Ritual
sacrificial power was considered, by the Brahminic class, as superior to
the military might of the *Kṣatriya*. The organizing principle here is the
tension between two kinds of aggressive powers. *The Brahmins, in other
words, displayed their ritual as war by other means, indeed, by superior
means.... Brahmin claims to supremacy... were not those of a "spiritual"
over and against a "temporal" power* (195).

Still, as Smith argues, the ritual wooden sword in practice did not
yield the same effects as the deadly weapons of the *Kṣatriya*. The "solution" for the Brahminic class, beginning in about the sixth century BCE
was to change the terms of contest from those of ritual versus military
power to that of purity versus impurity. It was at this juncture that veg-
etarianism and the doctrine of *ahiṃsā* or nonviolence began to find its
way into Brahminic culture. *A new type of opposition between men was
introduced. It was no longer a matter of courage and fear, domination and
servitude; it was instead an opposition between the pure and the impure
and a hierarchy of castes* (Francis Zimmerman, quoted in Smith 197).
But sacrifice was not abandoned, instead it proliferated, disseminated
through practices identified with sacrifice such as asceticism, renunciation, and so on. These practices became associated with a decarnalized,
purified virility that still maintained men of a certain class or caste at
the center of a sacrificial structure in which self-sacrifice and abstinence
is equated with social and spiritual superiority, with power over others.
It is this self-sacrificial tradition, the renunciation of flesh and impurity
that grants some men power over others, to which Tantra responds
with a "third" mode of eating.

▼ Tantra's Third Way ▼

The limit cases of Tantra's mode of eating are the rituals of *pañca-makāra* (the five Ms) and *cakrapūjā* (circle worship). *Pañca-makāra* is an indulgence in the five Ms: meat *(māṃsa),* fish *(matsya),* fried cereal *(mudra),* wine *(madya),* and sexual intercourse *(maithuna).* While this baroquely complex ritual is rarely practiced these days, it is still widely cited as expressive of the core values of Tantra. Before eating forbidden foods or performing forbidden acts, the participant first undergoes a long period of training by a guru in order to rid him or herself of hatred, doubt, fear, shame, backbiting, conformity, arrogance, and status consciousness (Mookerjee 185). The *cakrapūjā* ritual is undertaken in a group setting with a guru presiding. According to the *Kulārnava Tantra,* one of the primary sources for the description of the ritual, *exuberance, supreme Bliss, increase of knowledge, playing on flute and Vina, poetry, weeping, orations, falling down and rising up, yawing and walking—all these actions, O Devi! are assumed to be like Yogic practices. . . . Excited by passion, treating other men as their own beloveds the ladies take their shelter. . . . Intoxicated men embrace men. . . . Yogīs take food from each others' vessels and putting drinking pots on their heads dance around. Filling wine in their mouth they make ladies drink it from their mouth itself. Put pungent things in their mouths and then transfer them to the mouth of their beloveds. . . . Devoid of mental perversions when there is exhilaration then a superior Yogī obtains to Devatābhāva* [god consciousness] (Rai 150–53).

The elements involved in these rituals have many layers of meaning. The preparation, the components of the rituals, and the group setting in which class and caste distinctions are deliberately trespassed, all speak in opposition to the purist, hierarchical culture of post-Vedic Brahminism. Indeed, the ritual of the five Tantric "sacraments" is a subversion of a normative Hindu sacrament, the *Pañcagavāya* or "five pure products of the Brahman's cow" (White 1992, 77). On the level of Tantric philosophy, the *pañca-makāra* enacts three crucial tenets. First, that no material, no act, no sensation is inherently pure or impure. Thus, the eating of "bad" foods demonstrates that, approached with the right attitude, anything can propitiate liberatory results. Second, the ritual is a self-surrender, but a surrender through indulgence, a surrender *to,* not a surrender *of.* Here it must be noted that in its post-Vedic context, the eating of animal flesh during the *pañca-makāra* signifies a becoming-animal just as the sharing of food and sexual and/or menstrual fluids effects a transmutation of self into other, or, more accurately, the dissolution of these categories. The surrender to "contamination," to intoxication marks a profound surrender to relationship, to the experience of one's self within relationship brought to such intensity that the self as a unitary, bounded entity dissolves. *Maithuna* and the *cakrapūjā* recapitulate the creation and promote an experience of the local bodies of practitioners as an expression of the manifold body that is the cosmos. Third, the rituals celebrate the nonhierarchical manifold *as the inpassing of everything in everything else* as indexed by the eating of everything by everyone. All substances may pass through, *as all people may pass through.* The direction to make love with strangers, with the spouses of others, and with those of different classes and castes declares that a general state of inpassing is the state of creation.

At the height of the *cakrapūjā*, practitioners call out, "*Who are you, who am I, who are these people around, why have we come here, why are we sitting here, is it a garden or our own home?*" (Rai 152). This is *prauḍhanta-ullāsa*, a state in which one experiences the end of pride, the end of separation. However, the loosening grip on selfhood is achieved for brief periods of time only. This "weak transcendence" is one aspect of the movement in and out of greater and lesser duality. Here, transcendence does not connote transcendence of the world, the body, or its falsity. Nor does it remain within the Levinasian prescription for subjectivity figured as a nonreciprocal interruption by an other who remains unalterably other. It is, instead, a surrender of self into another, into becoming another in order to enlarge the self. The body, which is not one's "own," involves itself with a modally differentiated, nonlocal body. This state of heightened involvement affirms a creative potential that is thoroughly grounded in the recognition and experience of the relationships we always already make and of which we are made.

The five elements are dissolved and mingled with the earth. [Just consider] the whole expanse of all things, all forms, all types—which belongs to me? and to which do I belong? Both these ideas are equally useless (Urban 2001, 82).

▼ The Responsibility of the (Postdeconstructive) Subject Ψ

In "Eating Well" Derrida writes, *It is in the relation to the "yes" or to the Zusage [pledge] presupposed in every question that one must seek a new (postdeconstructive) determination of the responsibility of the "subject"* (105). Simon Critchley comprehends the "yes" or the pledge within Levinas's purview as a *sensible* openness or vulnerability to the other, a presubjective passivity to which one cannot say no. Responsibility is *response-ability,* a preintentional sensibility to the other, a sensibility to which one is hostage. Returning to the insect theme, Critchley writes, characterizing Levinas, that *"the other is like a parasite that gets under my skin"* (33). Critchley states, quite succinctly, the deconstructionist and posthumanist imperative: *It is* **qua** *alien that the human being comes into its own, and what is proper to the subject is its expropriation by the other. . . . I must never be indifferent to the demand that the other places upon me, a demand that presupposes that I must be me and no one else. The deconstruction of the subject facilitates a novel account of the ethical subject qua me, without identity, an idiot, a creature, a hostage to the other* (37). Here, Critchley precisely locates, within deconstruction, the point that carries the greatest ethical burden. I am interrupted by alterity, by the other, by finitude. I am intrinsically dislocated. At the same time, I must be accountable, me and no one else. In my accountability, even as a multiplicity, I must be, in some sense not yet described, *closed:* the *one* who answers.

Responding to Derrida's formulation of the postdeconstructive subject that would *no longer include the figure of the mastery of self, of ade-*

quation to self, center and origin of the world, etc. . . . but which would define the subject rather as the finite experience of nonidentity to self, as the underivable interpellation inasmuch as it comes from the other, from the trace of the other (Derrida and Nancy 103), Critchley offers two proposals. First, he proposes that, through *renewed and persistent deconstruction,* we avoid any determination of the subject (39). Second, he proposes that in the wake of a version of Heidegger inflected by Levinas, we conceive of the human being nonsubjectively, as open to Being before intention, before theory: a subject infinitely subjected, passively and *sensibly* subjected to exteriority (41). In his more recent work, Derrida has described or proposed two concurrent and interdependent modes of susceptibility to the other, one of which is more precisely a susceptibility or subjection to an insusceptibility, a subjection to what cannot be assimilated.

▼ Love and Justice ▼

The first mode, a susceptibility to being essentially changed by the other, for instance, in love, is also the domain of the discourse of human rights, of property, and of a proper relation to oneself that is constituted by its capacity for disturbance. Derrida says of love, *I would want it that the other, precisely in the experience of love, disturbs or effects my property, my own proper relation to myself* (1997a, 25). In another, related register, he writes of one of his many invocations of the qualifier "perhaps": *The perhaps does not only condition the possibility of the coming of some**one**, but the coming of a plurality of some**ones**, the possibility for me to be more or less than one. The polarity of subject and object reduces the perhaps, there is no perhaps in the subject-object correlation. The perhaps implies that others are plural singularities, and that on my side too there are pluralities of singularities—this isn't simply a formal way of putting it, I have the experience of "myself" as a multiplicity of places, images, imagos, there are others in me, I have experience mourning where the other is in me, there is more than one other, we are numerous in ourselves* (Derrida and Düttmann 13). The operational mode of this susceptibility is iteration: the recontextualization, the rereading of emanation, an assimilation of something "other." *Iterability requires the origin to repeat itself originarily, to alter itself so as to have the value of origin, that is, to conserve itself* (Derrida 1992, 43). In the act of maintaining my "self," or perhaps here we should return to Critchley's *sense of self,* I become other than what I was so that both the other in me and my former sense of self change. I eat; I iterate. I am changed; I conserve myself, via appropriation, differently.

While iterability is in one sense an assimilation, an *eating* that makes everything other, including my "self"—something, some X, *remains*. What remains is indeconstructible, noniterable. This remaining lies outside deconstruction. It is, according to Derrida, the possibility of deconstruction. Derrida's name for this indeconstructible X is the unalterably other, the unassimilable, responsibility, and foremost: *justice*. Justice is distinguished from the discourse of property, and *from love, and even morals and the usual sense of ethics. Justice is something which exceeds the deconstructible, it is indeconstructible, it is what deconstruction should perform* (1997a, 26–27). In the most profound sense, justice is the structure of relationship as such. Because the other is always, in some sense, absent, always to come, always coming, Derrida has called this structure of relationship as such *messianic*. Relationship to the other, that is, all relationship, requires a leap of faith toward a future, toward a coming, an arriving. This second mode of susceptibility is a constitutive susceptibility or openness to the *absolutely different singularity* (1994a, 68). It is a constitutive relation of openness to nonrelation, to the radically, unalterably other that persists, that *remains*. The undisturbable and more primary aspect of my "proper" relation to myself, or the relation that inaugurates my self, is one of nonrelation to the unassimilable. This relation, I believe Derrida would say, is an originary undisturbable disturbance. It is not a disturbance *of* something pre-existing, but a disturbance that inaugurates.

I want to put pressure on this distinction between love and justice by focusing on Derrida's invocation of *experience* as the term of relation of both the other-in-love and the messianic structure of relationality in general. This will open up a necessarily and perhaps unpardonably short intervention into the deconstructionist and posthumanist reliance on concepts of the absolute or the radically other. My purpose in this initial approach will be to create the conditions that will make it possible to consider a postdeconstructive responsibility of the subject that does not rely on the radically unassimilable. I realize, however, that deconstruction *is* openness to the constitutive encounter with an unassimilable exterior, an unsubjectivable X. In a sense, then, I am traveling through deconstruction to "betray" deconstruction and thus remain more faithful to it.

Experience ▼

Derrida equates the event, the other, the singular, and justice with experience, that is, relationship as such. The event *is a name for the aspect of what happens that we will never manage either to eliminate or to deny. . . . It is another name for experience, which is always experience of the other* (1994a, 32). David Wood argues, with respect to Derrida's increasingly frequent recourse to experience, that *the return of the centrality of experience to philosophy has made possible a reconfiguration of the ethical. Experience regained no longer shelters within conceptuality, or within the classical conception of the subject, but plots their limits, and in time breaks open each and every complacent demarcation* (117). This is a sense of experience based not on *having* experiences, but on *excession.* Excession, a process of exceeding, is both a going out or forth and a motion *out of place.* This sense of experience as being premised, conditioned, and constituted by an ongoing excession, an ongoing exceeding, an ongoing dragging me from my place, an ongoing emanating away from myself is also, at the same time and from another perspective, a process of something excessing, going forth, toward me from an exterior: a coming I cannot fully assimilate, one that calls me to experience, to the possibility of a world, just before subjectivity. Derrida says of this presubjectival event, *It's immediate. For instance, I must answer the call of the other: it's something which has to be absolute, unconditional and immediate, that is, foreign to any process. Now, of course, if I want to be responsible to the "I must," then in the name of this just response I have to engage myself in a process; that is, to take into account conditions, strategy, and rhetoric and so on* (1999b, 72).

Foreign to any process: foreign to subjectivation, to conditions, to strategy, to rhetoric, to deconstruction, to iteration. Derrida bases his claim for the possibility of this radical alterity, the indeconstructible, with reference to what Merleau-Ponty and others have called the *Nullpunkt* or zero-point (see Merleau-Ponty 1968, 248–51; 1962, 403–25). This *zero-point of space and time . . . is what I mean when I say "I," and in this place "you" cannot be, it's irreplaceable. I can't be in your zero-point* (1999b, 71). In another iteration of this claim, Derrida seems less sure. *I can have no direct access to what the other lives in him or herself, that is something which remains absolutely inaccessible for me, **at least** in the form of intuition. Now, **this quasi-evidence**—that what you live on your side I cannot share, that here and now I occupy this absolute zero-point, and that yours is infinitely different from mine—is . . . the condition for a relation to the other, for being responsible for and to the other* (Derrida and Düttmann 13; emphasis mine). Derrida's *at least* leaves open the possibility, as we shall see, that knowledges *other than* cognitive, Husserlian *intuition* might provide accessibility to the other. The *quasi* leaves an opening that interrupts the *irreplaceable* and the *absolute.* I would go further and say that Derrida's own equation of the absolutely other, the remainder, and the event that makes relationship possible, that *is* relationship, contravenes the possibility of an absolutely other, an unassimilable, indeconstructible alterity.

If experience as such is a constitutive encounter with the unassimilable, then what lives most pressingly at this *zero-point* is a strange movement, a strange imbrication of the most urgently, intensely *familiar* and the other: the intense familiarity of otherness. Because the encounter with the other is experience, before subjectivity, before process, then this familiarity is not personal in the usual sense of the word. Nor is it an impersonal exteriority that transfixes. It is an event of the personal. Another name for this familiarity may be recognition before cognition: a reception. To answer a call, the call of the other that beckons and inaugurates experience, something must be received or *heard.* If this hearing is not a process, not a rhetoric, not an iteration, not a strategy, I must be prepared for the other, for otherness: I must be ready to receive before receiving. This "fit," this immediacy is *intrinsic* to the situation of two, coming from everywhere and nowhere: undecidably belonging both to "me" and to the "other," who therefore in some way *cannot be distinct,* even if that indistinction is minimal. This new sense of experience must be simultaneously distinction and indistinction or nothing would inaugurate, nothing would be heard. I can only be constitutively, presubjectively, and immediately open to that in which I have some minimal involvement, to that in which I am involved *in advance:* the always already assimilated. This general state of assimilation, or *nonlocality* may perhaps never be articulated because it is a Möbius *context,* never definitively interior or exterior. My very readiness is a *knowledge* in advance of cognition, in advance of cognitive intuition, that contravenes the radicality, the absoluteness of the other. *Both* alterity and "self" tremble in this suspension that is relationality, that is experience.

At the *zero-point,* I am continually plunged into excession, continually exceeded by something I can't fully grasp but which is most intimate, most familiar to me, to which I answer and in which I necessarily *participate.* What could be more intimate than this sensation of being continually made away with, this continual movement of something approaching and of this grasping toward, this tendency to answer that is "me"? This is the moment when subjectivity breaks down, when I experience the irresolvable entanglement of in/distinction that inaugurates and conditions subjectivity. And I can, if I am attentive, access this sensibility, this familiarity at the breakdown of subjectivity at any moment. Dharmanidhi Sarasvati: *This immediacy, this flowing presence that we are, cannot be articulated other than in retrospect. You cannot articulate your self in it, and it is your self coming from everywhere.*

Derrida writes, *Responsibility is not my property, I cannot reappropriate it, and **that** is the place of justice: the relation to the other* (1997a, 27). Returning to the distinction Derrida makes between love and justice: there is no end to the disturbance of the proper relation, of property or properties. The relation of nonrelation takes on a different meaning, that is, not a relation to that which is *absolutely different,* but a relation to an undecidable distinction, a relation to an immediacy *prior to* the decidability of the question, Is it this or that? Me or other? This is what I would want Derrida to mean when he says, as he often does, that deconstruction is *intrinsic.* The task of a postdeconstruction then, would be to sensitize ourselves to this intrinsic entanglement of $2 + n$.

▼ Intuition, Perhaps

Derrida's absolutely other is *something which remains absolutely inaccessible for me,* **at least** *in the form of intuition.* Following Levinas, Derrida writes that *being affected by the other is always a trauma, which is not simply wounding in the bad sense—which it is as well. It is something which affects me in my body, in my integrity; if the other doesn't transform me in an essential way then it isn't the other* (Derrida and Düttmann 15). This repeats the problematic gesture of so much of post–World War II progressive theory as it is inhabited by the bodies of the radically wounded victims of genocide. The starving, incarcerated, cut-up, burned bodies of Auschwitz cannot be rescued from their vulnerability, which is already incontrovertible: they must, it seems, be rescued *to* vulnerability, *to* violence. An inevitable, intolerable susceptibility to violence can only be partially redeemed by making it *serve.* Yet this being held hostage to violence disallows the body's participation as anything other than non-participation; the body acts only insofar as it is acted upon. The other achieves its radicality, its stability *within me* as definitively other *in opposition to* a passively transforming body. The untenability of maintaining this passivity becomes most articulable precisely at the scene of trauma. Here, the body's capacities for constructing narrative, compensating, intensifying, deintensifying, transmuting, and so on allow the traumatic event to survive as an iteration, an avatar emanation that is multiply signed, uncertainly possessed, hybridized, deformed, reformed, repeated, and circulated in uncalculable, undecidable ways. Deconstruction tends to see these events as modes of *being affected* and not as the body's capacities for affecting. However, if the body were granted active, positive contributory, constitutive powers, then the status of the unalterably other within me or without would become undecidable: there could be no radically unassimilable, as the body is *always eating*, even before intuition, before subjectivity.

The alternative is not the forgetting of difference, or of *différance*, but a change in syntax that intensifies and continues the work of deconstruction. The syntax of deconstruction has been that of the interruption, the space, the rupture, of the *fort/da*. This is a syntax that breaks into an interior but preserves a more definitive exterior even as that exterior lies within: it is a syntax of effraction, of burglary. The preceding discussion suggests that the intrinsic undecidability of distinction and indistinction constitutes relationship as such. This requires a syntax that trembles all the way down, a syntax of vibration, of the break that pulses so rapidly it blurs, a syntax of stretching and oscillation. Gerhard Richter writes in *Walter Benjamin and the Corpus of Autobiography*, *What makes the corporeal self an unusable concept for fascist purposes, or any politics that relies on stable meanings and transparent essences, is precisely that it cannot be reduced to a single, determinable moment of signification, not even a negation. A negation too, as a gesture of nihilism, could be coopted by a politics of single stable meanings. It is only in the moment of the undecidable, when negations and affirmations perpetually trade places and when we are confronted with an object or text that we do not know how to read and arrest for good, that the ethico-political significance of what refuses to be a stable concept may emerge for us* (172–73). Rather than interruption, rupture, the unalterable, the radical, it is *vibration*, the perpetual trading of places, that puts me in suspension with you. The avatar emanations of our bodies enfold each other as rapidly shifting quasi-presences, quasi-absences. Between an untenable radical alterity and the impossible full intuitive experience of your experience, between absolute separation and standing in your place, there is the loom of emanations that, through engagement with multiple contexts that are active and engendering, can never stabilize but *stretch* from estranged familiarities to familiar estrangements.

While I agree with Derrida's and Critchley's claim that any postdeconstructive formulation of the responsibility of the subject must go through deconstruction and persist in it, I nonetheless propose that we have not gone through far enough if we still hold to the usual terms under which both sense of self and the calculability of the subject can appear and stand responsible. Derrida imagines that such a postdeconstructive determination may fall outside of the purview of *philosophical discursivity* (Derrida and Nancy 104). What falls outside, what is nonphilosophy in the sense of a philosophical outrage, is openness to the question of the deferred difference between self and other, the holding in suspension of the whole question of otherness so that we might experiment (here, in this text) with sensitizing ourselves to nonphilosophical wellsprings that would perhaps allow this suspension to find its way back into philosophy. Avoiding, as Critchley proposes, any determination of the subject, can we also avoid any determination of the other?

Alain Badiou has written: *Our philosophers, taking on the burden of the century and, when it comes down to it, all of the centuries since Plato, have decided to* **plead guilty** (1999b, 28). This stance is exemplified by Philippe Lacoue-Labarthe when he writes that *in the Auschwitz apocalypse, it was nothing less than the West, in its essence, that revealed itself—and that continues, ever since, to reveal itself* (35). Derrida has called nonphilosophy—the appeal to empiricism and the recourse to prephilosophical experience and nonphilosophical genres—philosophy's *death and wellspring* (1978, 79). During the last fifty years of thinking about the conditions for ethics, for avoiding the worst, both deconstruction and posthumanism have designated certain prephilosophical states wellsprings, while others have been cordoned off or rejected outright. The privileged terms are the presubjective, the apsychological, the nonhuman, the alien, anything that might move us away from the horror of the mystic unities of the fascist state and the oppressive narratives of the heteronormative family. I want to point out here, however, that the humanist horror of falling into materiality or animality finds its shadowy double in the deconstructionist, posthumanist horror of falling into others. For this reason, other states, other wellsprings have been undervalued or cordoned off: pleasure, the cosensorious experience of being inhabited by others, by their personalities, their words, their gestures, their emotions, their aspirations, their talents, their skills, their aesthetics, or even of being inhabited, in the present, by persons presumed dead, for instance by ancestors or the imprints of collective histories.

Posthumanism is generally better than deconstruction at thinking about the positive capacities of bodies even as, in some of its iterations, it seeks to bring the body under the control of a change artist or a sorcerer.

Deconstruction is better at thinking about dependency and responsibility. I believe that paying attention to those states, those events that confuse self and other, that make otherness, and thus singularity, and thus possession tremble, opens us to an expanded and more integrated sense of both capacitation and responsibility. Holding fast to Simon Critchley's proposal that the subject remain undetermined through persistent application of deconstruction, I want to begin to develop a different sense of capacitation, of enfolding or involution or involvement that does not hold self and other prophylactically apart, but that suspends both self and alterity. This different sense of capacitation is unsusceptible to the assignment of zero-points of responsibility, but stretches responsibility across a sticky field of quasi-absences, quasi-presences. Every iteration of capacity vibrates, oscillates "within" and "without." To enfold a capacity is to hold in trust something of a differentially shared, nonlocal reality. Capacity and responsibility are everywhere, smeared into each other, in suspension, indissoluble.

▼ A Tantra for Posthumanism Ψ

Tantra: a written scripture, usually in dialogic form and comprised largely of instructions for practice; a text with exoteric and esoteric content; a direct transmission to initiates of an oral tradition.

1. *Bhāva*

State of being; existence; emotion; feeling; attitude; becoming or a state of flux; a feeling of absorption or identification; a spiritual attitude.

—John Grimes, *A Concise Dictionary of Indian Philosophy*

For Levinas, as well as Derrida, love is that against which "higher" values of hospitality and justice are measured. Hospitality, Derrida notes, is distinguished by Levinas from love (1999a, 41). Because of its relationship to need, love does not fulfill the condition of hospitality that is a *disinterested* welcoming and sheltering of the other. *Love remains a relation with the Other that turns into need, and this need still presupposes the total, transcendent exteriority of the other, of the beloved. But love also goes beyond the beloved* (Levinas 1969, 254). This *beyond* is the domain of the needy self and of a transubstantiation. *Voluptuosity transfigures the subject himself, who henceforth owes his identity not to his initiative of power, but to the passivity of the love received. He is passion and trouble, constant **initiation** into a mystery rather than **initiative**. . . . The amorous subjectivity is transubstantiation itself* (270–71).

This is the closest that Levinas, the philosopher of no contact par excellence, gets to an evocation of a deep and active touch, and he relates this amorous subjectivity to a notion of avatar. *He will be other than himself while remaining **himself**, but not across a residue common to the former and the new avatar* (272–73). In other words, there is not a residue of a former self transported to a new avatar, but only the recommencing of a new avatar: a self without original, a transubstantiating fecundity, a series of initiations, not initiatives. This relation that maintains the otherness of the other but needily seeks a transubstantiation of self, constitutes, according to Levinas, *the originality of the erotic which is, in this sense, **the equivocal** par excellence* (155). Thirteen years later, Levinas clarifies the distinction between hospitality or responsibility and love. *The identity of the subject comes from the impossibility of escaping responsibility, from the taking charge of the other. . . . I am not a transubstantiation, a changing from one substance into another, I do not shut myself up in another identity, I do not rest in a new avatar. As signification, proximity, saying, separation, I do not fuse with anything* (1998, 14). In order to *take charge,* disinterestedly, I must be me and no one else. Despite the fact that the body's radical openness to wounding initiates me into relations with the other, hospitality demands that my response to this entanglement must be initiative rather than initiation, unequivocally. Levinas's invocation of love, of Eros, of voluptuosity precisely contrasts to hospitality at the presumed disjunction of transubstantiation or *fusing* and responsibility. This is the same fracture line within systems theory and Deleuzian-inspired, posthumanist ethics that requires unfused individuality as a condition of ethical self-capacitation. But there is another attitude, another affect, another wellspring, another destination, another *bhāva* that enfolds both hospitality and love, both responsibility and self-capacitation.

2. I Am Speaking of Devotion *(Bhakti)*

July 19, 2002

I miss you. I've noticed that as missing goes, this episode feels rather objectless or not based on lack, e.g. on missing something identifiable. It's kind of a free-form, nonconcept missing. Which makes me want to conclude that it's a higher grade of missing. (Insert self-ironizing smile.) When I go into it, there's a space. No, I think I should be more grandiose: an expanse. We are the expanse. (Toto, too.) Confession: I'm writing this on a laptop in the San Leandro Bayfair Mall food court while I wait for my car to be repaired at the 76 station down the street. The owner, Al, has a Masters in Mechanical Engineering from San Francisco State. He paid for it by working three jobs and not eating or sleeping much right after he arrived here from Mexico. He's in his fifties now and has never taken a vacation. Al is the one who told me I could go to the mall's food court and write or read without anyone bothering me because it's one of those dying malls. So there's bound to be a tone shift.

When we were doing transmission, not THE transmission. Nothing wrong with that. I'm just getting a new timing belt. Uh, when we were doing transmission, I knew you were writing yourself into me, not just giving me a little energetic assistance. I knew you wanted me to be carrying you around. Now I keep seeing your face on my face. This is not face-to-face. This is not the face of the other. This is my/your face. I keep getting this feeling that I am you, or vice versa. Not completely, of course. I just have to do a little half turn, a little fan fold, a little shift, and there you are. I can't say how. Or how I knew in that moment, several of those moments, that you wanted this. And I "said," "well, okay." Surrendered. Like the vampire at the door, you have to invite him in. And you want to be that reckless, to feel your blood changing through contact. Without this promise of contamination, no one would care anything about vampires. Or gurus.

Not that I think of you as a vampire, although I admit to feeling some fear as I have known you so briefly in the ordinary sense. At some point, articulating the fear, the words *getting your energy fingerprints all over me* flowed through. Later I thought of a *Star Trek* episode in which the android Data tries to describe what missing someone is like for him. He's not programmed for ordinary emotions, but he does experience the inscription of others in his system. He finally comes up with this: "My neural pathways have grown accustomed to your neural pathways." Today, after I had already sent you that somewhat enigmatic e-mail, I came up with this: my heart signature misses your heart signature.

Then, you were so pleased when I asked for your picture and we exchanged various gifts of flowers and malas and small services freely rendered.

I need to say more about the expanse: I see god more easily now. Because of you. In you.

But how could I miss god?

Why not? Tantra teaches us that God misses god, right? Intransitive longing expanding into the expanse. God *wants* to miss god. God, Śiva consciousness, Śakti, con-energy, whatever you want to call it/us, multiplies and forgets itself deliberately simply for the pleasure of re-meeting itself. Where am I? Here I am!! (Reality as a game of peek-a-boo-I-see-you.)

After a few hours, I got tired of the food court and went back to the garage. Al pulled up a chair so I could write while he and Mike worked on my car. He put the chair right next to a lift where a Toyota Camry had its axles off and various cables dangling. I told Al I was writing him into my book. Here's another confession: Al did not say I could work peacefully in the mall because it was "dying." I added that on my own. But when I came back to the garage, he said, "Yeah, it's one of those dying malls." So who is writing this book? And am I ever "on my own"? You know the answer already.

Devotion enfolds both hospitality and love, both responsibility and self-capacitation. It suffers less from the neediness of love. It sustains itself via an unbridgeable distance. It presumes that the other transcends me: I follow behind. As a pedagogical relation, devotion engenders a reciprocal responsibility, a fierce hospitality, fierce gratitude, fierce attention. At the same time, and while maintaining a kind of distance, devotion indulges in ecstatic moments of transfiguring transubstantiation and the confusion of self/other boundaries. The proposed affectional *bhāva* or attitude of the avatar body, then, is devotion, an equivocal, trembling concatenation of hospitality and love, of distance, respect, and nonstatic merging. However, such an attitude skirts dangerously close to the charismatic devotions, the charismatic mergers that are, in part, the engines of fascism. What distinguishes posthuman devotion is precisely what it can borrow from Tantra: an indiscriminateness with respect to its "objects." I become increasingly attentive to the nonstatic states of passing and inpassing that derive from deliberate ritualization. In other words, posthuman devotion recirculates humanist or fascist devotions with indiscrimination and *awareness:* a nonheroic, unconditional hospitality, an indiscriminate, noncharismatic, and deliberate offering that can never resolve into static sameness or absolute difference.

Devotion is the *bhāva* that sensitizes me to my constitutive inability to maintain either self or absolute otherness; it sensitizes me to the deferral of possession and to the way in which this disarticulated state of weak transcendence and the capacitations it brings arrive along a vector of fierce hospitality. I cannot be devoted to you unless we relate along a line of estrangement, unless I am "gazing up." A *bhāva* of devotion does not simply arise; it must be cultivated through a gestural practice, through fostering a culture of devotion. *Here are the nine means of cultivating Bhakti. Śri Rama says to Sabari:* "**Herein, the culture of devotion is the first means**" (Sivananda 1957, 82; emphasis mine). Cultivating a *bhāva* of devotion *begets and fosters* estrangement and, simultaneously, weak transcendence (porosity), hence the trembling of interior and exterior, self and other, male and female, personality and impersonality, flesh and sound, sound and image. The elastic polarities estrangement and familiarity take on a particular cast when operating in the realm of devotion. Devotion is a *breath before breathing,* a readiness. It is a saying of becoming, not Sorcerer, but student or disciple.

Devotion connotes porosity between disparities. That sentence tells you that we are outside of the realm of the autopoietic imperative where linkage or zones of involvement guard against the ontogenic leaking of one closed individualism into another. Devotion opens an unmaintainable channel. This channel is a momentary psychosensory dedifferentiation during which I cannot articulate you as other or me as me. Through repetition (ritual), the trace of this surpassing becomes available to me, becomes an accessible capacity *here* in this body, *now*. With this formulation of weak transcendence as capacity, I want to mark yet another displacement. Levinas moved transcendence out of the superluminal realm into the domain of the Other who exceeds me as the *idea* of the infinite. His conception of the sensorial body as an ethical body was limited to the body's capacity for wounding. What I am calling weak transcendence is an interval of psychosensory dedifferentiation experienced pleasurably on the skin, in the organs, the breath. These terms, "weak transcendence" and "dedifferentiation" emphasize what happens in more reciprocal relations of contact and explicitly avoid the postwar language of deterritorialization that commonly designates liberation from a coercive organization, a coercive relationship. Reversing the Levinasian trajectory of passivity transiting toward *taking charge,* devotion is *an initiative that opens to initiation,* to transmission, to chance, to the influx without exemption.

3. Discipleship *(Dīkṣā)*

My taking up of devotion is the attitude of the interlocutor, the foil, the one by the dying man's bedside, the student, the nonphilosopher, the woman, the disciple, the queer, each of whom suffer from greater specificity, greater *locality,* greater personality than the male Sorcerer. Writing about Sartre, Chris Kraus says: *It's inconceivable to him that female pain can be impersonal* (2000, 113). She goes on to compare Aldous Huxley and the philosopher-activist Simone Weil, each of whom *longed to attain a state of decreation,* Huxley through drugs, Weil through anorexia. *Huxley . . . is a distinguished and credentialed thinker, and so we take him at his word. Yet why do Weil's interpreters look for hidden clues when she argues similarly, for a state of decreation? She hates herself, she can't get fucked, she's ugly. If she finds it difficult to eat, it must be that she's refusing food, as anorexics do, as an oblique manipulation . . . Anything a female person says or does is open to interpretation* (116). Kraus wants to rescue female body practices, female asceticisms like anorexia, a "girls" desire to leave the body, a "girls" sadness for an ethics of global import, for the impersonal. I want to reclaim personality, the local manifestation, the baroque expression for a possible posthuman ethics in such a way that personality and the nonlocal are always in a state of trembling saturation.

In contrast with the more typical posthuman figure or conceptual personae—the philosopher, the poet, the engineer—the disciple seeks a weak or transitory transcendence of self/other boundaries. The disciple's body relates to the other as to a teacher. Ritual preparation invites leakage, invites transubstantiation and the absorption of the other's expressions in such a way that intensifies pleasure in the relationship. You cannot be a disciple of an abstraction; a disciple is the student, the follower, the beneficiary of a teacher here, now. The devotional gesture is knowledge and transubstantiation without *full intuition.* Again, this is a stretching, a vibration without pause, without arrest, without a *zero-point,* without renunciation.

Everything about our relation is partial. Because I follow you, look to you, attend and observe you, cultivate devotion toward you, I intensify my estrangement from you. But this incessant observation, attention, listening at the same time renders me porous to you in the way that children are porous so that I become more and more what I revere, so that my devotion to you becomes self-devotion. Your words are recalibrating my speech. Your histories—their affects and images—are adhesions, pulling movements from my body, inserting themselves in what formerly were stories I considered my own. My body is stirring with the minutiae of your most characteristic gestures. I am eating the food, the words you placed in my mouth. I am loving these flavors in ways that are indistinguishable from my love for you. Your music is in my throat, the music that came from thousands of others. Your name is on it, along with theirs, and now mine, these trembling, tender, dying attributions.

In the realm of difference, in the realm of your inviolable otherness, or even in the realm of "self-esteem," these involutions might be called fetishization, assimilation, codependency. But between the directorial self-capacitation that demands I do not really become you and the radical passivity that demands you transcend me as absolute otherness, the vehicle of devotion connotes both active porosity and active passivity. Cixous: We need *an active passivity capable of bearing transition and transference* (47). Posthumanism is good at bearing transition, but we have done less well with transference because of the association of transference with colonization and murder. Cixous goes on to say that *an ideal marionette would begin to move under the touch of something that would go through the body. It would be the impulse that music gives to the body* (47). The devoted avatar body as ideal marionette moves, gives itself over to being moved *under the touch* of emanation. Devotion: I place myself under your touch, so that I become the impulse of your music in my body, so that I capture your music in the midst of hospitality, so that you see me doing this and are honored. My body, my text, this text is your thoroughfare: hospitable, observant, grateful, *hungry*. Even if it hurts, and it will hurt, *I have resolved to be capacitated, even by those capacitations that incapacitate me.* The ethics of devotion is a pledge, a "yes" to seeking capacitation in everything you emanate.

4. Iteration *(Japa)*

I am what you give me and what I am doing with your gift: a reception, a ritual rather than a reading. Baudrillard writes: *Hospitality represents a reciprocal, ritualized and theatrical dimension. Whom are we to receive, and how are we to receive them? What rules should we follow here? For we exist solely to be received and to receive (not to be known and recognized)*

(142). This is the crux of the problem when Derrida says *the other is not myself—and who has ever maintained that it is?* (1978, 110). To say the other is myself has always meant, in the West, to have a first-person experience of the other's first-person experience, not to receive, but to know as you know. The being-here of the absent other *no longer belongs to knowledge. At least,* Derrida writes another time, *at least to that which one thinks one knows by the name of knowledge* (1994b, 6; emphasis mine). This *at least* reverberates through every presumably *irrefutable* argument that closes the "I" around a perspectival *zero-point.* I am inculcated into the *experience* of knowledges that never attain to the level of any incontrovertible *zero-point* of self-knowledge or self-recognition. These are knowledges I neither *own,* nor knowledges owned *by an "I."* Which "I" closes around the kinetic-knowledge of my mother's characteristic attitude of examining her hands while speaking and inducing in me a mother sense when *"I"* find myself enacting an iteration of these (her) ritual gestures? Which "I" closes around the sense-knowledge when the African American doctor, his Japanese nurse, and their Jewish patient (me) breathe in, together, the sharp smell of burning flesh under a cauterizing knife as it cuts into my right breast? Which "I" closes around the feeling-knowledge when my body rushes ahead of any "I" in response to expressions of terror, naked suffering, grief *because it already "knows" every trauma in advance, always?*

What I experience, these knowledges, carry histories and futurities beyond anything I could definitively own, beyond any closure in the name of a singular perspective. I am seized physically, psychically, literally. And my words, my gestures, my emotions disseminate: I seize myself, I seize others. I receive. I emanate. I transubstantiate. I express. The question becomes: How can I accede to expression, to iteration in the largest sense? This is tantamount to asking, how can I sensitize myself to the thoroughfare of relations I am, to this avatar body? *I might ask whether my mother is, even now, truly absent from my body, as if dead and gone from the moment of my birth/breach from her.... Or is "s/he," differently and still, articulating herself/me* **here** *in the tissue of a becoming that exceeds us both?* (Kirby 96).

Hospitality as reception—reception of an iteration, an expression—intensifies the undecidability of the question "Who?" It is this intensification that activates the question of the relationship of self-capacitation to responsibility. Performing rituals of reception, I increase my capacities at the same time that I undermine my sense of unity and self-possession in favor of an intensified and enlarged sense of "self" as nonlocal, partially present, partially absent, entangled with you, and not able to stop at you, not able to know if there is a stop, an envelope. If, as I am arguing, experience, and even *the experience of being,* to use Derrida's phrasing, has this characteristic of ritualism, of iterability, without exemption, what might be the rituals appropriate to sensitizing the avatar body to this movable feast?

5. Transindividualism *(Nyāsa)*

Madeleine Biardeau terms Tantra an amplification *ad delirium* (140). Tantric delirium is a baroque and pleasurable indulgence in expression: sound, word, image, emotion, character, and *personality.* These are devotions, honed through obsessive involvements that burst cognition and amount to a ritualized flooding: cognitive, sensory, kinetic, affective flooding. Tantra is a practice, not of the line, the cut, the rupture, the interruption, the anomalous, but of the elastic, the watery, the Möbius, the stretch, the rolling landscape, the vibration, the flow. In his gorgeous essay, "Strange Gourmet," Joseph Litvak finds in Proust a queer and adolescent sophistication whose yearning is to transfigure the waste of this world into a magical otherworld through incessant observation and deformation of what is not supposed to matter: gossip, gesture, intonation, bitchiness, style. Tantra also looks where it is not supposed to look, eats what it is not supposed to eat, and refuses to recognize the illusory as illusory, the trash as trash, the insignificant as insignificant, the immoral as immoral. It is a queer antiheroic heroism.

Tantra turns the body into a palimpsested landscape of associated colors, sounds, syllables, words, images, flora, animals, goddesses, and emotions. But nowhere is the Tantric baroque more in evidence than in its invocation of the feminine. The goddess, Śakti, manifests or emanates into thousands of expressive aspects. These expressions are other goddesses or aspects of goddesses with their own complex iconographies and personalities and hundreds of names. *The Supreme Goddess is the source of countless "energies," female deities who are principally her emanations, or her partial archetypal images* (Khanna 56–57). Ritual consists of the repetitious *placing or laying down (nyāsa)* of these personality and other expressions on the body of the *sādhaka.* This is a practice of identification that, through a literal assault of iteration, renders porous the boundaries of the body-psyche, effecting an absorption, and simultaneously an awakening, of capacities (Flood 270).

Severo Sarduy writes that *we might well ask if in essence the baroque is not merely an immense hyperbole in which the axes of nature... have been broken, erased. ... In the classics, the distance between figure and meaning, between signifier and signified, is always limited; the baroque enlarges that break between the two poles of the sign* (1989, 46). That *break,* however, is only the making room, the breaking *into* the face-to-faceness of the sign, between the figure and "its" alter ego with a grotesquely proliferating dissemination of figures, a thickening arc of simulation/ stimulation that *is* the nonlocal, localizable movement of *différance* in the midst/mist of bodies, words, and thought. Thickening works via infusion, a more intimate and risky venture than folding, which only contacts surfaces. Folding, I still know what belongs to me even as I change shape to accommodate what comes from elsewhere. Infusion borders on the problematics of penetration, substitution, and addiction, skirting dangerously close to those rhetorics and yearnings as they have motivated the West's founding narratives of transcendence. Yet as an infusional cosmology without hierarchy, without the division between the real and the illusory, between the One and the simulacra, Tantra makes of penetration and substitution the general, everyday mode of the real, circumventing the rhetorics of rising and falling, of immortality. This is transcendence *brought down* to the level of technique, a way of life, a style of shared existence.

Transindividual attitudes or gestures disturb the heroic condition of One. *Nyāsa,* the laying down of expressions on the body, or laying down the words of others in this text, proceeds through a process of *casting or imprinting.* This process is the invocation and welcoming of a de/forming relationship with expressions of the goddess performed through gestures of touching parts of the body while reciting mantras. Touching says "here," while making a depression, a mark. At the same time, it *seals,* it holds something in, something that is subject to moving from hand to hand, subject to traveling. Sealing is an invitation addressed to the ontogenic effects of expression/emanation. The effects of *nyāsa* can be contrasted with those techniques associated with the axiom that *each will know his belongings.* Making an impression, a mark, invites every part of the body/text to open to deforming influence, to a baroque plethora of transindividual imprints that flood the prophylactic gap between the self and everything else.

Mantra for a postdeconstructive avatar:
You are my body, too...

6. Enjoyment, Intoxication *(Bhoga)*

Sarduy, avid student of Tantric Buddhism, writer of Tantric novels of transubstantiation, queer, says this about mild states of intoxication: *The prose of beeromania has yet to be written. I'm not speaking, of course, about the self-absorbed, chronic alcoholism already studied in the vast, complementary literatures of Repression and Medicine, but about the benign albeit compulsive celebration that aspires only to the state of "happiness," to momentary irresponsibility, to a letting go, around the brief noon hour, of the weight of one's self, of the punctual watchfulness of the Other in the omnipresent shape of the Law* (1995, 11–12). Speaking of the drinking of wine during the *pañcha-makāra*, the *Kulārnava Tantra* states: *Not intoxication, not disorderly functioning of the senses, but a withdrawal from external, petty preoccupations and a relaxation **into the folds** of a lighter and larger consciousness that sees and feels less constrictedly* (Rai 48–49; emphasis mine). How can we drink each other in sips, in ways that are weak transcendences, (small) abrogations of the law, the law that you remain you and I remain me and that we, at the same time, watch over each other as twin Abels over twin Cains? How can I receive you, hospitably, while indulging in you? During sexual yoga, couples lock at the mouth, breathing, so that the breath circulates through both bodies causing a state of mild hypoxia and a sensation of skin dissolving into a diffuse energy field. This *knowledge* of dedifferentiation then becomes available for the purpose of inviting the manifold, inviting the effects of emanation on the avatar body.

Of his appearance in drag, Sarduy asks: *Am I simulating? What? Whom? My mother, a woman, my father's wife? Woman? Or rather: the ideal woman, the essence, which is to say, the model and the copy have struck up a relationship of impossible correspondence and nothing is conceivable as long as there is an effort to make one of the terms **be** and image of the other: **to make what is the same what it is not.** In order for everything to signify it is necessary to accept that I am not inhabited by duality but by an **intensity of simulation** that constitutes its own end, outside of* *whatever it imitates: what is simulated? Simulation* (1989, 2). Simulation, particularly queer simulation, is not a copy of an original, but an intensification of a simulation that causes the presumed identity of all prior simulations to mutate. I witness your simulation of my simulation and I am no longer myself. You have entered into my simulation with my simulation emanating from you. Sarduy relates intensity of simulation to writing, and particularly to scholarship. *Ultimately, in literary criticism it would be useful to abandon boring, diachronic sequence, and return to the original meaning of the word* **text**—*textile, tissue*—, ... *A text that repeats itself, quotes itself without limits, plagiarizes itself; a tapestry that unravels so as to spin other signs, a stroma that varies its motifs infinitely... a system of communicating vessels* (54).

If I imagine posthumanist, postdeconstructive ritual intoxications such as the Tantric five Ms, such as indulgences in the intensity of simulation, simulations that intensify the question "Who?" they would be intoxications with each other's words, each other's texts. I would breathe, drink in your words and recirculate them in an operation that was both devotional and estranged from your "self," creating an uncanny sensation of familiarity. The intensification of the porosity of texts would continually ask about, inquire after, experiment with the relations of (not *relations between*) word and flesh, seeking out the manifold expressions of these entanglements, not just those of violence or desire. The categories "text" and "flesh" would be drawn together, undecidably. If I became sensitized to the knowledges emerging from the humble conversations of flesh and words, every node of contact would be a city, then further on, an ocean of washes and rubbings. I could, perhaps, discern the waning of intensity of these expressive selves, both me and not me, but I could not entirely envelop them, control them.

Every event of word/flesh is a ritual indulgence in appropriation, in "mis"-use, the central taboos with respect to both human relations and academic writing. Sarduy overloads his words with the words of others, he recontextualizes them, decontextualizes, and even deforms. Such deformations are both transvestisms and transubstantiations. Sarduy compares these works of transvestism to the *autoplastic* art of insects whose bodies become their environments. *Animal mimesis... represents more than an unbridled desire for waste, for dangerous luxury, for chromatic magnificence, a need to display colors, arabesques, filigrees, transparencies, and textures, even if they serve no purpose. ... we will have to accept, as we* *project this desire for the **baroque** onto human conduct, that the transvestite merely confirms how "in the natural world there exists a law of pure disguise, an indisputable, clearly proven practice that consists in managing to pass for someone else* (1989, 95).

Sarduy is inspired, in part, by William Burroughs's fold in method, employed, among other places, in *Cities of the Red Night.* Sarduy translates "fold" as "dub" *(doblar),* which in Spanish carries the double meaning of both "to fold" and of cinematic dubbing, "to lay down" a voice (1989, 52n). Timothy Murphy points out that in the earlier "cut-up" *Nova* trilogy, Burroughs saw revolution as *simple rupture,* a negative breaking of the reality script, a negation of history without positive content (171). In Burroughs's later work, the positive *magic* of writing is more explicitly thematized (174). This *magic* is a textual intoxication that merges and deforms identities (of sentences, of characters) with an eye to capacitation and, ultimately, an immortality wrought through vital disseminations that are never static.

Burroughs constructs narrative with folded-in, semantically reorganized or remixed paragraphs from his own text. This tweaked iteration through shifting contexts provokes the sensation that the uncannily familiar words have come from elsewhere entirely, from outside the text. The reader encounters a weird situation in which Burroughs manages to pass, undecidably, *for both himself and for someone else.* By donning, as a decontextualizing transvestite, his own clothing, he creates a difference that is sensibly porous to identity and an other who is sensibly porous to self. In places, the mix is remixed, or twice folded, as paragraphs following directly upon one another recontextualize and recirculate deformed but recognizable semantic units. The object is not utter confusion but extension via differential repetition that ratchets from context to context, picking up significations along the way. The increase in signification of ratcheting textual units corresponds with the accumulation of capacities or powers by the characters, powers such as a sudden knowledge of fluent Spanish or the topology of rural Mexico (1981, 149). Such porous ratcheting expresses and enacts a hope for an enlargement of life that constantly risks death. Sarduy: *You resort to this intoxication, I told myself, because you feel that God denies you true intoxication, true euphoria. . . . Another beer* (1995, 11). In this sense, Burroughs's method is reincarnation as iteration, always a letter, a repetition through changing contexts, always the quasi-arrival of a quasi-nonarrival because of the ways in which the changed and the same confuse each other. Burroughs: *The means of suicide haunts their position.... To be reborn at all makes your condition almost hopeless* (1987, 114).

Date: Sun, 09 Jan 2000
From: Chris Kraus
To: Ann Weinstone
Subject: membrane

Dear Ann,

There's this great cut-up trick that William Burroughs and Brion Gysin invented in their book, *The Third Mind*. (Well actually they didn't invent it . . . they resuscitated it from the Dadaists.) Sitting around in hotel rooms in London, they devised the "fold in" technique to penetrate any text's true intention. Try it: it works. Take any page of any book or newspaper and fold it three times in on itself. The resulting compression of words conveys the text's secret message. (Although the random result is not absolute—as Burroughs confessed once, "it's *my* random.")

But I think you are talking about something quite different: the ability of texts – yours and mine?—to enter and penetrate *each other*. When we met last October in San Francisco, we agreed to embark on this kind of experiment. And of course I was flattered: I still see myself as some kind of punk, you were a Ph.D. candidate at Stanford. What I read of your text was very intriguing: the way you can range from a highly proficient synthesis of big philosophical texts, to the utterly lyrical. But I'd like to suggest something else (and this certainly isn't original)—the way that writing can be a performance, a form of direct address, thinking in real time in front of the reader. Being able to do this—segueing back and forth between the trivial stuff of the moment and really high thought—is what certain female artists have most to offer. It is the Art of Conversation, and I think it could be an answer to the absence of human-to-human relationships you lament in the texts that comprise "posthuman theory."

Jill Johnston did this in her early art writing, until it made her so crazy she stopped. Eileen Myles does it too (I think partly she learned it from Jill), and it was what made Kathy Acker's first writings so fierce and so open they became indisputable. Those books went straight to my heart, because I believed her. There was her "I," and it was talking to *you.* In *Algeria* she writes: "Whenever a cock enters me every night three nights in a row, I ask myself regardless of who the cock belongs to should I let my SELF depend on this person or should I remain a closed entity. I say: I'm beginning to love you I don't want to see you again. The man thinks I'm crazy so he wants nothing to do with me." How many girls haven't felt this? "THE IMPORTANCE OF SEX/BECAUSE IT BREAKS THE RATIONAL MIND". . . and then she starts writing about Algerian torture. Charles Olsen of course proposed this as theory—that "poetry should be a direct exchange of energy between writer and reader"—but it took late-twentieth-century girls to make it a practice. Because we have nothing to lose and we aren't afraid to admit that the actual facts of our lives are often so drekky. Kathy's rants, her leaps between trash-gossip and depression and high theoretical thought were proof that life had a point, that someone could actually *move* between things. (Asked once if she sought to "move" her audiences, the actress Ruth Maleczech said: *Yeah, from one place to another.*) Kathy took the "personism" of New York School writing and radicalized it. If her life was chaotic, she never used "grace" to escape. Because Kathy was very ambitious, she cannibalized certain French theories then fashionable, without ever distancing theory from its roots in real life: desire and sex, ambition, career, and plenty of gossip. As she got older, it became increasingly harder for her to do this. When you're young, the facts of your life are often more sordid, but much less embarrassing. A life that's invested in becomes harder to treat as *material.* But she tried to maintain this, this unspoken challenge of any philosophy, Who is speaking to Whom?

Dear Ann, I am believing in the deceptive humbleness of conversation. Love, Chris

Dear Chris,

I like the idea that the Art of Conversation might be an art of conversion, of moving among the modalities of one's life from *high* theory to gossip. Then there are Acker's conversions of other people's texts, another kind of conversation as transubstantiation. I'm thinking of how Acker dedicates *Empire of the Senseless,* her "cover" of William Gibson's *Neuromancer,* to her tattooist. Conversation-as-tattoo interrupts conversation's humanist signification as a rational, measured commerce between autonomous individuals and becomes an exposure, a giving oneself over to the question "Who?" Paradoxically, textual tattooing, covering, deforming all of these vigorous actions presume reciprocity and chance. You have to let the other "body" *in*. The tattooist tattooed. The initiator initiated. Interlocutors become *intralocutors*.

I remember our conversation about *Avatar Bodies* and particularly what you said about my way of overloading my text with other people's words. Yes, I have been experimenting with rituals of intoxication. In addition to my usual overloading, I've stopped producing any marginal text in hopes of engendering a sensation of immersion, a mild hypoxia that comes from breathing another's exhalations without rest. I think I told you that I once wrote a novel with no paragraphs or punctuation other than periods. This is the chastised version of that project. Then, I want to invite the words of others to intersect mine without the requisite doses of qualifying interpretation. Trinh Minh-Ha generously writes: *You and i are close, we intertwine. You may stand on the other side of the hill once in a while, but you may also be me, while remaining what you are and what i am not* (90). Applied to texts, this sense of undecidable proximity, even to the point of *you being me,* is close to a strategy of making my words more explicitly a space of reception and less emphatically a space of interpretation. I want to acknowledge the ways in which my speaking is always intoxicated, belonging definitively neither to me nor to my interlocutors. Another way of saying this is that I am trying to circle back, to induce a sense of porosity that is not a threat (because it is also a devotion) and that does not demand that the speech of others do the work of the other as such. I want to make explicit my longing that you might feel honored when I say, "See what I'm doing with your words—see what your words are doing to me."

In line with what you say about conversation (and conversions), I have become promiscuous with respect to sources, including conversations, found text, CD jacket writings, encyclopedia entries, stories, letters, and, most importantly, with respect to the influences that drive me to care about what I care about, and to write anything at all. My eighteen-year-long engagement with Tantra is one of the "sources" I am attempting to bring into my scholarship. This means a difficult and risky exposure of my own intellectual, emotional, and yes, spiritual genealogy, a kind of continual coming out that performs the fact that none of us here in academia are "properly" distinguished either as scholars or from the rest of the world or from each other.

By the way, I was reminded of this even more when, after ten years, I reread Sarduy's astounding essay, *Written on a Body.* In the section "Writing without Limits" he says: *Add fictional characters, mine or another's, to criticism. Mix genres. Have a possible reader chime in* (55). Chris, you wrote that my idea of asking others to participate, via letters, is *a great conceptual coup.* Perhaps a *great conceptual burglary* would be more accurate. Actually, I have no idea which is more accurate.

Love, Ann

(Sent via ground mail)

7. Gesture *(Mudrā)*

(from mud = "joy" + ra = "to give")
—John Grimes, *A Concise Dictionary of Indian Philosophy*

Tantric practice works, in part, through the adoption of hand gestures that are held in place while meditating. A form of *nyāsa*, *mudrās* are invitations, both an opening to the manifold and an involution of energy. They are formalizations of a willing porosity, the opening of the mouth. *Mudrās are eating well.* I initiate a gesture, summoning the body's capacities for active absorption, then I hold myself in an attitude of waiting for what may arrive. *Deeply exploring what mudrās are invokes within us a greater appreciation of the world as an ongoing energetic exchange. Mudrās solicit us to experience the world not as divided by self-other boundaries* (Miller 5).

Soliciting unbounded exchange, offering oneself up for transformation: the *mudrā* picks up the dice, lingers in the interval after the throw. A *mudrā* for posthumanism would be a specific gesture that intensifies and makes more available one's capacity for hosting where hosting fully participates in a process of becoming. A language gesture, perhaps. One of the meanings of *mudrā* is "stamp." Invoking a *mudrā,* I become a letter sent out. Language, written language, spoken language, silent language. Words, letters, syllables, vibrations baroquely named, occupy the center of Tantric cosmogony. Every body is a series of letters in all senses. Language is not only mediative, not only communicative; it is an active agent/reagent: material, psychic, energetic, capable of producing its effects in the absence of any determined interlocutor, in the absence of *initiative.* Your expressions are letters sent to re-embody me in all their modalities. This is why Tantra is also about death, but it is the death that accrues to the amorous procedure, to the 2 + n, not the anomalous. The *mudrā* is a deliberately staged, ritual opening to the influx and inpassing of becoming: *an indulgence with awareness.* As an opening to chance influx, it is both discriminating and nondiscriminating just as participants in the *cakrapūjā* engage in sex with randomly chosen partners but impose upon those relations the precision of prescribed gestures. The making of gestures of willing porosity are postal gestures.

▼Ψ Fifth City Kneeplay:
Solaris in Your Eyes

The first attempts at contact were by means of specially designed electronic apparatus. The ocean itself took an active part in these operations by modeling the instruments. All this, however, remained somewhat obscure. What exactly did the ocean's participation consist of? It modified certain elements in the submerged instruments, as a result of which the normal discharge frequency was completely disrupted and the recording instruments registered a profusion of signals—fragmentary indications of some outlandish activity.
—Stanislaw Lem, *Solaris*

I dreamt I saw Solaris in your eyes. You sat writing at an old wooden desk beneath a window with pale sunlight and dust motes drifting through the shaft. You looked up at me, and in your eyes were all the words we have exchanged, and all the words yet to be exchanged, an ocean roiling with color, an unbridled volume of contour, texture, shape, an energy not quite bound or unbound, inside the edge, virtual and actual, potential and manifest, a point of intensity, an intense emanation, and, at the same moment, a thoroughfare, a passage, a gateway, the sheerest membrane. I would touch you and we both would scatter to a world. I am longing to do this. With you.

I have never loved you so much as I do since having this dream. I mean it. Even though it was "only a dream" and this is "only a letter." And this is only a book. Even though we are not "the same," we are both in uncertain relation to these words. My flesh is folding, feasting. I can't hold anything back, especially as committing to this avatar writing/reading we grow more sensitive to the trembling of our possessions, our distinctions. We interrupt each other with the movement of these words, then I am this weave of interruptions, this texture and a pulling together, a concentration and an unraveling, a streaming. This is the zone I want to learn to inhabit. With you.

To increase my sensitivity to these suspensions, these differences and their deferrals, I adopt an attitude of devotion. This is to adopt the attitude of the student, the attitude of the receptive as opposed to the hero or renunciate, as opposed to the poet, the sorcerer, the engineer, or even the apprentice to an exceptional master. Edward Said thinks back longingly to a time when the absence of mechanical or electronic means available to the scholars, authors, and thinkers . . . imposed a heroic regimen of discipleship and work the likes of which has all but disappeared (288). I want to answer that without the authority of the hand, the authorizing touch, the heroic imprimatur of humanist transmission, I can begin, finally, to account and be accounted for. This is a nonexemptive practice of discipleship, a dedicated alertness to the impure thoroughfare of gesture, affect, image, word; an eagerness for the surprise of your unauthorized, unwarranted touch; and a determination to apprentice myself to the capacitations of both labor and ease, both pleasure and trauma, even to "the worst."

I was rereading *The Crying of Lot 49*, that novel of surprise postings. Remember Oedipa Maas and her famous line taken by so many as the mantra of postmodernism? *Shall I project a world?* Well, it's followed by a caveat, a caveat that no one in their world-projecting fervor ever quotes: *If not project then **at least** flash some arrow on the dome to skitter among constellations and trace out your Dragon, Whale, Southern Cross. Anything might help* (Pynchon 82). At least. Not a particularly heroic project that tracing, that at least. This is my skittering arrow, my little flash, a trace that wants to learn your most surprising shapes. At least.

Ψ Epistlirium ▼

[Worldwide,] 20 trillion e-mails were sent in 1996. Two years later, in 1998, over 78 trillion messages were dispatched. By 2003, the total should skyrocket to 452 trillion.
>—Nancy Konish, "So You Can't Keep Up with Your E-Mail? Check This Out."

E-mail is so lame.
>—Rich Doyle, a humble conversation

I never did this over e-mail.
>—Dharmanidhi Sarasvati on sending me a mantra via e-mail

I visited the Stanford library the other day. In the humanities reading room is a collection of three hundred books on "digital culture." The books issue from domains ranging from media studies to cultural theory to sociology, philosophy, and linguistics. I searched the index and relevant sections of every book in the collection and could not locate a single extended discussion of e-mail. This result jibes with observations I have made during the past two years and is also registered by Naomi Baron, a linguist with a longstanding interest in electronic writing. Baron is one of the few scholars who does approach the topic of e-mail in a sustained manner. She notes that most studies of electronic "dialogue" focus on mailing lists, Usenet groups, multi-user gaming or social environments, chat rooms, and organizations. While arguing that distinctions are fuzzy between what she calls *one-to-one dialogues* and *one-to-many dialogues,* she also states, rather offhandedly, that *one-to-many dialogues are not technically e-mail* (1998a, 146). I am struck by this comment as it points toward the affiliation, socially and technically, of e-mail with older forms of the letter. Given the affiliations of posthumanism, it seems probable that the exemption of discussions of e-mail from discourses of posthumanism relates to the proximity of e-mail to less recent postal culture generally, and to the association of humanist scholarship with letters and attendant values such as reflection, communication, and friendship. But it is just this proximity, acting within an altered technical and sociocultural milieu, that renders e-mail a viable point of departure for welcoming a posthumanist ethics to come.

Letter from William Burroughs to Allen Ginsberg, June 4, 1952: *Incidentally I was not thinking in terms of **transcendence** but in terms of actual* ***change.*** *Some new and **useable** techniques* (Burroughs 1993, 129).

▼ Every Relation but One:
Part II Ψ

While Baron's characterization of the extent literature on computer-mediated communication (CMC) pertains mainly to the fields of linguistics and psychology, her comments apply as well to discourses that explicitly invoke the posthuman. Theorists of the posthuman write about science-fictional and technoscientific iterations of virtual reality, about hypertext and the fate of print media, about MUDs, MOOs, listservs, and other cybersocial domains, about "networked" selves, about virtual surgery, reproductive technologies, life preservation, cyborg anthropology, virtual gaming, and even user relationships to ATM machines. E-mail accounts for the highest volume of Internet use, and, at the time of this writing, half of U.S. households regularly write e-mail. While e-mail garners an occasional mention, I have not been able to locate a single author writing under the rubric of posthumanism who deems e-mail to be a topic worthy of sustained cultural or political consideration. The closer one gets to the *humble conversation,* the more attenuated, or perhaps tentative, is the posthuman interest.

Announcements of the death of print culture and the apotheosis of the image suffer from near total amnesia where (what I do not believe it would be inflated to call) the new epistolary culture is concerned. Even authors working under the general rubric of media studies, including those who have recently published works on electronic media that purport to be comprehensive analyses, eschew the topic of e-mail. For instance, Jay David Bolter and Richard Grusin's recent survey of processes of remediation in new media, that is, of the ways in which newer media always refer to and enfold their immediate predecessors, contains only one passing reference to e-mail. This is despite the fact that the authors patiently move through a series of specific media such as computer games, virtual reality, the World Wide Web, film, and digital art. The few texts that do approach the topic have thus far focused on what *cannot* be done in e-mail mediums and remind us of e-mail's limitations: its impoverished poetics, the presumptive "forgetting" of bodies and the natural world, and the loss of some more primary connection this entails (see Amato; Baty). What I intend to do here, however, is to open a consideration of the technical and social disposition of e-mail and the rhetorical field within which it operates. These include, in some fashion, imprints of the history of postal systems and letter writing in the West and their relationship to humanism and humanistic disciplines. I want to explore the modes of relationship that are *enabled* by these structures and histories. I believe that the domain of e-mail is a salutary one for the project of staging an encounter between a posthumanist ethics of capacitation and a postdeconstructive determination of responsibility.

My discussion hinges on four claims. First, that the complex disposition of e-mail undermines the heroic, renunciate figures of both posthumanism and the postal system. With regard to the postal system, I am limiting my domain to the history and relationship of the U.S. postal system to the advent of e-mail. Second, that e-mail enacts a different relationship to sacrifice than did letter-writing cultures that went before. As discussed, sacrifice is at the heart of the constitution of humanism. Third, that the social and technical disposition of e-mail is potentially capacitating and draws attention to the undecidable encounter of bodies and text, flesh and word: those encounters that hold in suspension distinctions between self and other. Fourth, that there are specific and salutary consequences of this undecidability for humanistic scholarship and disciplines.

Some of my remarks will pertain to e-mail in general, but the main trajectory of my discussion will be to propose the adoption, via e-mail, of a posthuman devotional attitude *(bhāva)* and a posthuman devotional gesture or *mudrā.* A devotional gesture is one that gazes up, maintaining a distance, an estrangement, at the same time that, through a willing porosity, through the sensitization to chance influx, it disarticulates the self-other distinction, engendering weak transcendences, undecidable intimacies, and uncanny familiarity. The devotional gesture I propose here is the daily, diaristic practice of writing to strangers.

Ψ Hard to Say

It's hard to say anything interesting about e-mail.
—Alan Sondheim, *a humble conversation*

Several specific orientations pertaining to the social and technical disposition of e-mail form the basis for my discussion. In outlining these, I
exclude, for instance, e-mail sent during the course of running a business or "junk" e-mail. I focus primarily on the e-mail that is most problematic for posthumanism and for the relationship of the humanities to
the letter: e-mail sent between friends, lovers, and colleagues.

1. *E-mail is an emerging mode of writing.* The phrase "between
friends, lovers, and colleagues" already points toward the emergent
properties of e-mail. Every linguistic study of e-mail notes that humor,
personal observation, and personal disclosure regularly appear in even
introductory or formal e-mail correspondence. As Naomi Baron has
argued, e-mail is a *creolizing modality,* one in which older modes of communication drawn from speech and letter-writing cultures are evolving into something new. Baron lists among the emergent properties of
e-mail: the tolerance of error; the expanded stylistic range and mixing
of genres within e-mail; the informality of address; the potential for
confusion as to the ownership of written text due to modes of e-mail
cutting, pasting, and word play; and, importantly, the relative ease of and
opportunity for access between strangers that e-mail enables (1998a,
161–65; 1998b, 49–52). Communications sent via Instant Messenger, for

example, circulate nearly exclusively among those who have already had some other form of contact.

2. *E-mail affiliates with the letter.* E-mail is more closely affiliated with the letter than other forms of CMC. E-mail, like the letter, is generally a one-to-one communication. Judging from its omission in discussions of CMC, e-mail may be assumed to be more closely affiliated, culturally, with "old" rather than with "new" electronic forms of communication. E-mail is still more often referred to as "mail" or "letters" than other forms of CMC. E-mail software encourages the retention of more "letter" features than many other forms of CMC, e.g. Instant Messenger, chat, MUDs (multi-user dungeons), or MOOs (MUDs, object oriented). The archiving of personal e-mail is left up to the interlocutors. There is no supervision of personal e-mail content as there often is with other forms of CMC. The advent of e-mail is related to the history and future of the postal service in ways that other forms of CMC are not.

3. *E-mail affiliates with the "virtual."* While e-mail affiliates with the letter, it also partakes of discourses of the virtual and cyberspace in uncertain ways. More than the paper letter and other forms of CMC, e-mail provokes tensions between rhetorics of delay, loss, and disconnection and rhetorics of the virtual that promise personal power, immortality, and instantaneity. This is especially true where e-mail correspondences between "strangers" are concerned. The uncertain "reality" status and authority of such relations is exacerbated by the fact that nothing has passed from hand to hand.

4. *E-mail enables committed, "broadband" relationships.* Compared to other modes of CMC, and more like the letter, e-mail is most likely to be the platform for extended relationships that encompass a broad range of interlocutors' lives and concerns. Listservs, Usenet groups, chat rooms, and MOOs generally have specific themes and purposes. People may move in and out of these CMC situations with relative ease and in some cases, anonymity. However, the relative nonanonymity of e-mail as compared to discussion groups or chat rooms, places e-mail within a social disposition of greater responsibility for one's interactions. For instance, participants in electronic discussion groups who agree to communicate "back channel," are effectively declaring a deeper commitment to each other. As Bolter and Grusin note, the *networked self is constantly making and breaking connections, declaring allegiances and interests and renouncing them* (232). Participants in group discussions may "lurk,"

without ever committing to explicit interaction, while those who have become more central to a group discussion may experience departures as traumatic split ups. In the main, however, it is relatively easy to come and go with little explanation and few consequences. Within chat rooms, the commitment to others is most attenuated as people come and go under assumed names and sometimes elaborate invented characters. While these might be seen as salutary and capacitating experiences of "multiplicity," the attenuation in these realms of sustained entanglement and sustained experiences of the intractability of others, may actually enhance a sense of sovereignty by other means.

5. *E-mail enables diaristic writing.* Compared to other modes of CMC, and in resonance with some periods of letter-writing culture among Western literate classes, e-mail enables a "return" to daily writing that serves as a mode of ongoing relationship and self-accounting. An entire genre of Web-based diaristic writing, or Weblogs ("blogs") has emerged in the past few years. While "bloggers" do constitute communities, most blogs remain defacto one-way communications, read more as short stories than as letters inviting response.

The near total absence of discussions of e-mail within progressive posthumanist discourses may be usefully placed in the context of the relationship of the letter to humanism and humanistic scholarship. As I have argued, progressive posthumanism generally prefers the scene of the human/technology join or approaches human relations with a great deal of tentativeness, watchful distrust, or even paranoia due to the history of violence, racism, colonialism, and genocide attributed to humanistic concepts of relationality. E-mail, insofar as it is usually structured as a one-on-one relation, lends itself to association with paper letter writing. It invokes an "older," humanistic set of values such as reflection, friendship, conversation, and, more so than group forms of Internet communication, demands nonanonymity. Then, the study and publication of letter collections and letter writing has been a mainstay of twentieth-century humanistic scholarship. Most of this scholarship, until recently, has concerned the friendships of literary men. In his book, *Humanism,* Tony Davies argues that *friendship—rather than allegiance to a shared ideological or intellectual programme—remains . . . the ideal humanist relationship, finding its model in the private letters and **de amicitia** of Cicero* (76). Derrida has noted that, in the West, the friend, by which he means the elite friend, the primary friend, the one who is,

to the exclusion of all others capable of friendship, belongs to *a famil-
ial, fraternalist and thus **androcentric** configuration of politics* (1997b,
viii). These relations gave rise, in the eighteenth century, to idioms such
as *the commonwealth of letters* and *the republic of letters* that analogized
the affiliation of those involved in literary pursuits to an enlightened,
and thus exclusive, nation-entity.

More recent critical work has focused on letter writing as performance, as transvestism, as transgression, as a vector for the crossing of
boundaries, geographic and cultural, and as a nexus for tensions between
the public and private, absence and presence, and governmentality and
spontaneity. Despite the shift in focus to questions and issues that should
be of interest to posthumanists, and despite the relative ubiquity of e-mail
usage in comparison to that of other technologies favored in the writings of posthumanist theorists, the association of letters with lettered
humanism appears to be a fatal one. Relatedly, letter writing, throughout its history in the West, has been associated with the simultaneously
governmental and effete, with pedagogical and regulatory Latinate letter-
writing manuals, with the teaching and transmittal of forms of proper
public conduct, and, as we shall see, with the establishment of national
myths of the new American republic structured around the overcoming
of "barbarism" by "civilization." Today, employers monitor their employees' e-mail, and e-mail confiscated from corporate and government
computers serves as evidence in court proceedings. Given this evolving
history, it is plausible that letter writing signifies as a regulatory practice
on several different levels, a characterization that, thus far, seems to have
outweighed the potential for letter writing, and its history, to figure as a
mode of circumvention of, or intervention in, regulatory institutions
such as the family. As a friend of mine once exclaimed when I mentioned
that I was writing about e-mail: *E-mail is nothing but surveillance.*

Ψ The Postal Age ΨΨ

Two contemporary theorists have taken letter writing to be paradigmatically and/or practically related to questions of progressive politics and ethics: Derrida and Foucault. Both are relevant to my purposes here. As various people have remarked, Derrida's entire oeuvre may be, and likely should be, read as a meditation on the post, on postality, and particularly on electronic communication (see Poster, 99–128; Ulmer 3–29; 125–53). While it would be impracticable to reprise even a fraction of this postal thinking, Derrida has argued that the letter is paradigmatic with respect to all writing broadly conceived. He means this in two senses. First, logocentrism, or what Derrida calls the *postal age*, is based on the presumption of the uncontestable identity of senders and receivers and on the authority of the signature. The identity of god, *logos*, the father, truth, and being—of identity as such—founds logocentrism and destines or commands all others to arrive at their single, proper places, their proper names (1987, 62–63; 422–36). The subject is subject to a law of address, a law of correspondence. However, in his influential response to Lacan's reading of Poe's, *The Purloined Letter*, Derrida argues that any letter might go astray, that a letter can always not arrive at its destination. *Not that the letter never arrives at its destination, but it belongs to the structure of the letter to be capable, always, of not arriving. . . . Here dissemination threatens the law of the signifier* (1987, 444). The constitutive structure of the letter, of the signifier, the necessity for its dissemination, its passage through unknown hands, the certainty that it will be read differently in multiple contexts, that it may never arrive, that is it always *capable* of not arriving, threatens identity as such and the entire power structure of Western thought. This trembling, occasioned by the letter thought paradigmatically, is related to the intractability of the other, to the interruption of a certain conception of identity by the other, and thus to the condition for ethics in progressive thought since World War II. Despite my necessarily brief recital, one can at least get a sense here of how Derrida's entire engagement with metaphysics, violence, and logocentrism is bound to the letter. Looking ahead, in *Archive Fever,* Derrida relates the institutionalization of power, memory, and forgetting to the creation of archives. Here he makes what is probably the only extant claim for the significance of e-mail as inaugurating an *archival earthquake* that is *on the way to transforming the entire public and private space of humanity, and first of all the limit between the private, the secret (private or public), and the public or the phenomenal. . . . The technical structure of the archiving archive also determines the structure of the* **archivable** *content even in its very coming into existence and in its relationship to the future. The archivization produces as much as it records the event. . . . what is no longer archived in the same way is no longer lived in the same way* (16–18). Questions about the relationship of e-mail to the technical disposition of the letter and about what kind of archive, if any, e-mail constitutes will frame the remainder of my discussion.

Foucault invokes letter writing in the third volume of *The History of Sexuality,* and in some of his other late writings, as an example of a technology of self. Citing, among others, the letters of Seneca and the homoerotic correspondence between Marcus Aurelius and his tutor, Fronto, Foucault's purpose is to draw out the possibility of ethical practices that focus on self-examination, the body, everyday experience, questions of the pedagogical relation, control, sexuality, dependency, and autonomy. These would seem to be of interest to posthumanist theorists. Yet while the general notion of technologies of self is implicitly or explicitly invoked in much posthumanist theory, the cause of provoking interest in the topic of letter writing is most likely harmed by Foucault's rather brief but pivotal discussions.

Foucault positions letter writing as tending toward self-containment and the relative quiet of self-consultation, toward *enjoyment without desire* (1986, 68). Theorists of the posthuman prefer the relatively autonomous movements of desire, those that exceed the subject in a salutary manner. Pleasure survives, when it survives, at human/technology boundaries. Here, the relaxation of vigilance with respect to difference that pleasure brings may be enjoyed with less frightening consequences (see Haraway 1985, 66). For Foucault, letters facilitate a mobile, ratcheting relationship of the self to the self based upon the contemplation of understandings developed within daily relations to others. Letter writing is an aesthetic practice, a mode of self-styling that bears little relation to the apprehensive watchfulness of much progressive posthumanist theory. Foucault's use of letter writing is in the service of a vigilance, but it is a vigilance that cultivates the small encounter, the detail, the daily, and a meticulousness with respect to self-knowledge and pleasure in oneself and others in the hope that these will lead away from the proscribed, the already categorized. *The problem is not to discover in oneself the truth of sex but rather to use sexuality henceforth to arrive at a multiplicity of relationships.... The development towards which the problem of homosexuality tends is the one of friendship* (1989, 308).

Watchful but not traumatized. It is this openness to the ethical efficacy of friendship that gives Foucault's invocation of letter writing its humanistic scent. Elsewhere, I have argued that e-mail serves as the banned *homo*erotic of posthumanist discourse. Here, "homo" plays on Homo sapiens, homogeneous, the Same, and the fear of difference being forgotten or attenuated (Weinstone 1997a). It also resonates with the *commonwealth of letters,* as this has, until recently, comprised largely homoerotic or homosocial activities between men, particularly as humanistic endeavor has pivoted on the relation between an older male pedagogue and a younger male student (see Barkan 48–49). Foucault asks, however, *What relations, through homosexuality, can be established, invented, multiplied and modulated?* (1989, 308). If e-mail, like the profession of letters, is, in some yet-to-be-determined sense, also "homo," I want to ask how this resonance with humanistic professions is rendered otherwise by the social and technical disposition of e-mail. Can e-mail serve otherwise, that is, can e-mail disseminate relations, multiply and invent under a different regime than that of androcentric identity, exclusivity, violence, and exemption? This is tantamount to asking: Can posthumanism talk about friendship?

Ψ (Post) Heroism Ψ

A certain heroism accrues to the post. Anything "post" seems to axiomatically connote an overcoming or a surpassing and, despite underminings of Enlightenment epistemological conceits, a heroism of knowing better even if to know better is only to know one's own aporias. To return to my remarks about pleasure made at the beginning of this *episode,* contemporary post heroisms often ride on a certain asceticism with respect to pleasure: a heroism of unmasking and continually re-marking scenes of trauma; a heroism of vigilance, watchfulness, self-policing, and warning off. As such, the structure of post heroism, of post vigilance is delay, the delay of immanent violence, of longings for presence, of the forgetting of difference, of even momentary human mergings that, despite all warnings, punctuate our days. Yet delay joins, in well-worn Möbius style, vigilance to desire. Foucault's preference for pleasure may be understood as an attempt to modify and moderate the philosophical and political play of vigilance, desire, delay, and, as he saw it, appeals to repression or lack. *I cannot bear the word **desire**; even if you use it differently, I cannot keep myself from thinking or living that desire = lack, or that desire is repressed* (Foucault, in conversation as reported by Deleuze 1997a, 189). Foucault's invocation of pleasure with respect to technologies of self suggests an ethics that passes through the erotic, tending *toward* renunciation, but without arriving at renunciation, without the *purification procedures* that characterize the play of vigilance and desire (1985, 251–54).

While Foucault's invocation of ethics and its relationship to letter writing in imperial Rome is largely suggestive, the general tendency of his thinking is toward stylized, ritualized experimentation within relations to oneself and others. Stylization and ritual *regulate* but do not prohibit experimentation with the production of a shared history. This production comes as the result of the daily, diaristic writing and reading of letters that provide a framework and vector for modifying one's ethical self within a practice that intensifies and problematizes social relations. Although Foucault does not say so explicitly, the lesson he appears to draw from the Roman example is one that does not focus on communication per se, but on a shared work. *Around the care of the self, there developed an entire activity of speaking and writing in which the work of oneself on oneself and communication with others were linked together. . . . it constituted, not an exercise in solitude, but a true social practice* (1986, 51). Interestingly, Foucault positions the advent of Christian diary writing as a move to a focus on *the notion of the struggle of the soul* (1988, 30), using this change in the genre of written self-examination to index a shift in modes of subjectivation away from the social relation and toward the heroic and solitary relation with god. In contrast, Foucault's ethical persona par excellence is the artisan, and not the artist, the tinkerer and not the engineer, the householder and not the holy man.

As discussed previously, within progressive posthumanist discourses and their sources, the heroic affect, the heroic tone emanates from scenes of the creative becomings of cyborgs, poets, and engineers, to name but a few. However, it may be that the posthuman heroic issues most intensely from the association of these figures with renunciation: the renunciation of the unitary, sovereign self, the renunciation of coherency, the renunciation of certain forms of contact, each of which are also pleasures taken otherwise. For instance, Judith Halberstam and Ira Livingston write in their introduction to *Posthuman Bodies: The posthuman repudiates the psychoanalytical and so the posthuman is also postpsychic, beyond any therapy that attempts to rectify the disorder and illogic of desires with health, purity and stability. . . . Posthumanities embrace a radical impurity that includes the pure without privileging it. Extrafamilial desire exposes the family as a magic trick pulled by science and sustained by social science. Mommy and daddy are not sexy, and the Freudian family sitcom isn't funny anymore* (13). The engines of the posthuman heroic here are repudiation, exposure, and the "embrace" of disorders of desire, which, when pushed, may lead to a kind of Nietzschean-Deleuzian joy that is ahuman, intense and outside the range of enjoyment of more humble communions that are not "radical." Yet there are satisfactions, pleasures along the way: the indulgences in a theory of renunciation is itself pleasurable, especially when one considers renunciation as a surpassing.

While Halberstam and Livingston's indulgence in posthuman pleasure is not very sub-rosa, even in the bitterest moments of renunciation, pleasure is the supplement. Sociologist and systems theorist Niklas Luhmann, in one of his starkest descriptions of the individual as a circular, self-referential system, claims that human *motives, then, are to be thought of as filling the inner void, the empty circularity of pure autopoiesis.* He goes on to admonish, *But beware: this is not a nice theory, neither a theory of perfection nor even of the perfectibility of the human race. It is not a theory of healthy states. Autopoietic systems reproduce themselves; they continue their preproduction or not. This makes them individuals. And there is nothing more to say* (1990, 119). A kind of heroism accrues to the one who dares to make such an announcement and to those who dare to take up such a rigorously renunciatory view. This theory that is not "nice," functions as the ultimate demystification. Those who subscribe to it, promulgate it, indulge in the pleasure of having the last word, the pleasure of the trump. This may be the pleasure of all sciences and systems of thought which indulge in the "nothing more." We are "nothing more" than code, algorithms, autopoietic systems, and so on. Recalling Barthes and the suspensions engendered by pleasure, one can see the persistence of pleasure in repudiation, exposure, renunciation, the "nothing more," and further on, in narratives of the posthuman self's congress with the alien, the inhuman, the impersonal and so on. Pleasure continually interrupts renunciation by throwing into question my relationship to the unalterably alien or inhuman and by interrupting the work that these disciplinary boundaries are supposed to do. *One of the last initiations occurs when the sannyasin realizes that there is nothing to be renounced. He will renounce renunciation* (Satyananda Saraswati 83–84).

Ψ Post Heroism Ψ

Multiple forms of heroism and asceticism have also structured the North American postal system since its codification by the second U.S. Congress in the Postal Act of 1792. The heroic character and mission of the new republic sallied forth along with its mail, or especially with its mail as conveyed by several figures: the postrider, the postmaster, and the postal bureaucracy itself. The postal system was widely thought of as pushing forward the leading edge of civilization through technical innovation and cultural conquest. Physician Benjamin Rush, writing in his 1787 "Address to the People of the United States," proclaimed that *for the purpose of diffusing knowledge, as well as extending the living principle of government to every part of the united states—every state—city—county—village—and township in the union should be tied together by means of the post-office. This is the true non-electric wire of government. It is the only means of conveying heat and light to every individual in the federal commonwealth* (10). The postal bureaucracy was nearly synonymous with the heroic overcoming of the republic, one that would surpass the empires of Greece and Rome because of its superior mode of communication. For many commentators, the advent of the U.S. postal system presented an opportunity to repeat one of the central gestures of all Western humanisms: the incorporation into a national or intellectual mythos of an imagined Greco-Roman past (John 9; 14). In his 1843 polemic, "The Post-Office System as an Element of Modern Civilization," minister Leonard Bacon boasted that: *No ancient government, even of the most cultivated or powerful nations, had any such thing as what we call a post-office department. Neither Egypt when her Pharaohs built the pyra-mids, or when her Ptolemies made Alexandria the emporium of the world—nor Greece . . . nor Rome.* Bacon even goes so far as to fault the mode of transit of the Apostolic epistles on the grounds that they could not be routed through a post office (10). Because the early postal system was so variously associated with revolution, electricity, superior knowledge, a new prosthetics of self, both collective and individual, and the creation of a new public sphere, Richard R. John, in his admirable account of the history and significance of the early U.S. postal system, writes: *It would hardly be an exaggeration to say that by midcentury a rhetoric of the bureaucratic sublime—with its curious mingling of pity and terror, wonder and dread—had firmly established itself as a dominant motif in popular discussions of the postal system in the press* (11).

The heroism of the post has been the heroism of conquest: the con-quest of barbarism and the "frontier," the conquest-by-acquisition of an American-style aristocratism concentrated in the figure of the post-master, and the conquest of distance by speed concentrated in the figure of the postrider. As John notes, the postmasters of the eighteenth and nineteenth centuries were leading political figures, comprising a kind of new American gentleman class, embodying *the distinctive combination of moral rectitude, personal modesty, . . . good breeding, financial indepen-dence, personal tact, and, very often, a certain flair for literary exposition* (129). The postmaster symbolized the new republic's surpassing of its former ruler by combining bureaucratic and technical prowess with cultural sophistication. However, it is the postrider, and particularly the Pony Express rider who survives as the bearer of whatever remains of postal heroism, a heroism linked to the conquest of distance by speed and the risk of human life.

The Pony Express was the brainchild of William Russell, an entrepre-neur who hoped to win a government contract for transporting mail. In contrast to, or perhaps in concert with, its endurance as an emblem of something inimitably American, the Express was primarily a staged publicity stunt. It ran for only eighteen months beginning in April 1860 and carried letters, many of them commemorative, between Missouri and Sacramento, California, with the route from New York to Missouri being covered by train, and from Sacramento to San Francisco by steamer. The riders set off astride race horses and sported silver spurs and flow-ery costumes that played on an imagined figure of derring-do. Once

out of the public eye, this getup was exchanged for a *regular horse and...
trappings* (Visscher 33). When the first Pony Express rider reached San
Francisco, he paraded down Montgomery Street, and news reporters
noted that the band played "See the Conquering Hero Comes" (Biggs
9). As with the postmaster, the Pony Express rider conveyed not only
letters, but moral rectitude, streaking a line of civilizing effects: Pony
Express riders swore oaths, eschewing drink, profane language, fighting
and pledging honesty and fidelity (Biggs 3). In May 1861, Russell failed
to win the desired government contract, and he sold the whole circus
show to Wells, Fargo and Co. The Pony Express soon went out of business, however, when the transcontinental telegraph began operation in
the same year. Writing of the Pony Express in 1956, one commentator
notes the stunt's *exceedingly short* life, but then advises *discover, if you
can, an average man and ask him how long he believes the Pony Express
operated. The answer will likely be interesting* (Biggs 13).

Post Ψ Post

It would seem, at the outset, that e-mail inaugurates a post postality in several respects. As I have discussed it, "post" connotes various heroisms: heroisms of surpassing, of renunciation, and, in complex ways, filiation, the *coming after* humanism, after modernism, after psychoanalysis, after structuralism, and even more impossibly, after deconstruction. The heroism of the North American postal system is also one of renunciation and filiation, that of the new bureaucracy coming after, but implicating itself in empire: British, Greek, and Roman, and the association of this with the literal *coming sooner* of the mail. In a sense, progressive posthumanism connotes the attempt to send otherwise, to detach the diffusion of self, the effects of speed, and the sociopolitical significance of technology from the individual as conqueror, from uninterrupted self-presence, from empire, and from governmentality. Thus, the post-human heroic works to intervene in the postal heroic. To pose the question of "post postality," then, would be to inquire into the heroic structure of the post in all of the senses I have outlined. Post postality would, in Foucauldian fashion, tend toward the renunciation of heroism, which for posthumanism means it would also, paradoxically, tend toward the renunciation of renunciation. In Tantric fashion, it would exempt nothing, including the impure boundary confusions of the human-to-human touch. Post postality would work *through* the histories, fears, desires, contacts, and forms that it seeks to alter but with which it is filiated. One of these forms is the letter.

E-mail tends toward the nonheroic and the nonfigural, both with respect to older forms of the post and the heroisms and figurations of posthumanism. E-mail precipitates no postriders, no masters, no wizards, no gurus. While wizards and gurus populate the Internet and online communities, there is no *figure* of e-mail. Interestingly, corporate attempts to construct a figure of wireless communications in recent television advertisements invariably focus on a solo *sending* subject, one who is in command of his or her autonomous emanations, but who need not suffer the anxiety of awaiting response. E-mail cannot serve this figure. The Internet is often spoken of in ways reminiscent of the postal sublime of yore, and discussions of a "new public sphere" center on the World Wide Web. E-mail, on the other hand, uneasily carries the burden of association with the personal letter and the private, even when it is being written in a business setting, and, at the same time, the burden of a new vulnerability to dissemination, wholesale viral incursion, and legal seizure. Unlike users of the paper post delivery system, most users of e-mail have little idea of the mode of its delivery. Clearly, though, the mail no longer passes from hand to hand. The domain of the hand-to-hand, as in *hand-to-hand* combat, allowed the paper post to fall under the protection of the postrider, the postmaster, or simply the mail carrier, who must still swear oaths, who must still warrant the intention to perform heroic sacrifice in order to insure delivery. The decentralized mode of electronic mail delivery and its passage from machine to machine rather than from hand to hand renders it unsusceptible to the ministrations of the heroic, human figure. As one CNN reporter advised during a recent, international virus scare, *There's nothing much you can do except not open your mail.*

The heroic figures of the post during the first century of mail delivery in the United States, that is the postmaster, the postrider, and the postal system itself, coalesced around the problematics of space and time, of literal distances crossed, of lands and people conquered, of speed and technologies of speed, of distance from the British Empire, of both the assimilation and reconstruction of European cultural icons, and especially of a view of progress that took its mark from an imagined Greco-Roman past. The cyborg is the most familiar figure of posthumanism, but there are many others, some of which I have discussed here: the Sorcerer, the poet, the engineer, and the figure of the posthuman as insect host or assemblage. Perhaps e-mail confounds posthumanism as a figure of e-mail could not be *one*. The association of e-mail with letters, and thus with friendship and the whole range of rhetorics of the brother, the double, and soul merging, renders e-mail dangerous ground with respect to maintaining a politics grounded in legible difference. William Decker, in *Epistolary Practices: Letter Writing in America before Telecommunications*, notes that *pre-electronic correspondences make frequent reference to a provisional contiguity of body and soul: a contiguity of inscribing hand to letter sheet, which receives and bears a text whereby one soul speaks to another by virtue of the artifact's eventual contiguity with the addressee's body and (hence) soul* (15). Heterogeneity, the substance and the vector of the figure in posthumanism, is threatened by the traditional rhetoric and forms of letter writing that lead into and in fact infect e-mail. But this threat becomes something other when I consider the specific technical and social disposition of e-mail as it lends itself to the intensification of social relations that decidedly contravene the commands and effects of *the* letter.

Ψ The Sacrificial Structure of the Post

The history of the letter is one marked by famous fires; certainly
there have been significant burnings about which little or nothing
is known.

—William Decker, *Epistolary Practices*

The hero must pass through trials. The same may be said of the letter,
and of friendship. Renunciation, purification, and asceticism are vectors of sacrifice and participate in what Derrida calls *the immanent
pleasure of virtue* (1997b, 23). The postmaster manifested the virtues,
the abstemiousness, of a reconstituted British aristocrat. The postrider
swore off alcohol and other inebriates. And while promoting involvements that capacitate individuals or urge a constitutive responsibility
for others, both posthumanism and deconstruction swear off the intoxicated blurring of self and other. If e-mail tends toward the nonheroic,
does it also tend toward the renunciation of renunciation? The renunciation of sacrifice?

The renunciations of the postmaster and the postrider are occasioned by threats to the letter, threats to its arrival figured as threats to
the nation. Yet asceticism and determination were not sufficient: the
post was, from the beginning, bound up with sacrificial death, particularly
executions and burnings. Robberies of mail stagecoaches and postriders
were news in the early American republic and served to emblematize
the vicissitudes and ultimate triumph of westward expansion. Pony
Express riders *possessed strong wills and a determination that nothing in*

*the ordinary course could balk. . . . The trail was infested with "road agents"
and hostile savages who roamed in formidable bands, ready to murder and
scalp with as little compunction as they would kill a buffalo* (Visscher 28).
By the mid-nineteenth century, rates for sending personal letters became
less prohibitive and the rhetoric of the post shifted from the nation-
binding, civilizing effects of communication between far-flung individuals and their government to the commune between individuals. But
early debates in Congress focused nearly exclusively on the post as it
related to the durability and furtherance of democracy and the republic. For these reasons, mail theft, the interruption of the mail, was deemed
by many representatives to be *depraved* and *a crime of so pernicious a
nature* that it ought to be punishable by death (U.S. Congress 1855, 287).

Capital punishment was much at issue both in the United States and
in Britain as sentiment against the British "bloody code" intensified.
Through the early nineteenth century, British law contained more than
two hundred capital crimes and treated the public to nearly daily executions (Isenberg 26–29). In contrast, the statutes of the original Bay Col-
onies listed only thirteen death penalty crimes including assault, sodomy,
buggery, adultery, and statutory rape. The numbers and kinds of death
penalty crimes varied from state to state, but in 1790 when the first
Congress enacted the General Crimes Act, it named seventeen federal
crimes, only six of which carried a penalty of death: treason, willful
murder, piracy, piracy at the behest of foreign governments, and aiding
or abetting piracy (U.S. Congress 1845, 112–19). By the time the first postal
code was enacted in 1792, a reform movement was well underway led by
Pennsylvania. The death penalty was interdicted for all crimes other
than first-degree murder in 1794. Nonetheless, and attesting to the centrality of the post to the new nation, when the 1792 Postal Act passed, it
prescribed the death penalty for postal employees convicted of stealing
any fiscal instrument (bank notes, letters of credit, stocks, and so on)
from *any letter packet, bag or mail of letters* and for any person who *shall
rob any carrier of the mail* (U.S. Congress 1845, 236–37).

The fact that the post must post, that it must spend time in unknown
hands and in fact may never arrive, that it may be misread or misused
makes it tremble, makes it perverse and occasions the extraordinary
oaths, performances, bureaucracies, and penalties brought to bear upon
it. These oaths, performances, and penalties attest to the sacrificial
structure of the post, one that survives today in the stock image of the

mail deliverer being chased by a dog. As with any sacrifice, postal sacrifices involve the request of a boon. The figures of the post—the ascetic-priestly figure of the postmaster, the ascetic-warrior figure of the postrider, and the outcaste figure of the postal thief—are figures of renunciative sacrifice and literal, bodily sacrifice. The boon for which they sacrifice is that of arrival, of one good arrival over all others, a tipping of the scales in favor of the one correct address and the one true nation. But even this formulation, "one arrival over others," points to the fact that despite seals, oaths, signatures, renunciation, and execution, despite the attempt to link the post to a certain destiny, the post is always open to chance. For any purposes that might be called "posthuman," the postal principle *is* the operation of chance as it exceeds the envelopment of determination, or more precisely, as it accompanies and issues from determinations: the seal, the address, the act of mailing, and the systematicity of the delivery system. If the heroics and sacrifices that accrue to the postal system work toward attenuating the operations of chance, then I want to inquire of e-mail whether it might lend itself both to the renunciation of renunciation and to a greater *openness* to chance.

But before approaching these difficult questions, I want to address a second set of concerns that comes into play most intensely with respect to personal correspondence. These are centered not around the execution or sacrifice of human beings, but around the sacrifice of letters, their burning. Roger Chartier has written that *secrecy versus the family network, spontaneity versus guidelines: these were the main tensions structuring the practice of letter-writing in ancient societies—those prior to the invention of the telephone* (20). The relationship of the letter to illicit love or to prohibited or socially incoherent relations or to an activity that uses public conveyances to escape public stricture or sanction is one of a quasi-public, quasi-private secret that both threatens and longs for eruption, both threatens and longs for destruction, both threatens and longs for preservation. Burning, and more often, a dramatic request for burning, tracks through all of these suspensions. *I* **quiver** *at the thought of their [the letters] existence, and entreat you, in mere kindness to me, to burn them* (Henry Adams to Elizabeth Cameron; quoted in Decker 53; emphasis mine). The figure of the burning letter is, of course, in metonymic relation to the epistolary relation itself, one that only exists on the flickering edge of a leaky hermeticism. The letter, and the relations it carries, are burning secrets that must pass through other hands and that may be preserved for a future beyond the control of either addresser or addressee. If the letter is not burned, what will it burn on exposure to air? At the same time, the body of the letter, its substrate, so long associated with the bodies of those who write them, is made visible in the flames. The near-canonical request for burning, parodied in seriocomic fashion in Derrida's epistolary opus *The Post Card*, performs the letter, and metonymically the senders and receivers, as *quivering* inside the edge of responsibility/irresponsibility—to the family, to the future, to the archives of memory and history, and to the normative relations of power that maintain these.

▼▼ Fire ▼▼

But what of the sacrificial or renunciative structure of e-mail? Is there one? Here I limit myself to the most problematic letter for posthumanism: the letter that has been, until recently, associated with the self, the regulation of the self, the performance of self, with humanistic pursuits, and the letter whose disposition as the constructor of the one-on-one relationship renders it more susceptible to the retention of "older" forms of address and urges toward authentic communication. I am speaking of the friendship letter, the love letter, the letter that has, in its various ways, been subject to burning, the threat of burning, and the promise of burning.

Contemplating present challenges to the humanities, Edward Said charges electronic writing with contributing *to the gradual loss... of a critical model for humanism with a heroic ideal at its core* (286). Said locates this heroic ideal in the *enabling image of an individual human being pressing on with his or her work* (289), and *symbolized in the idea of labor, the sheer unremitting scriptural effort and its physical realization, the total absence of any sort of electronic (or even electric) assistance* (287). Referring this ideal to *dignity* and painstaking *rational processes of judgment and criticism,* Said lauds the abstinence of his *humanista laborans,* stating of the work of this figure, *nor certainly does it have anything to do with self-esteem or feeling good* (290). E-mail, as compared to other forms of electronic communication, affiliates more closely with the history of the letter and therefore with letters and the man of letters as these figures connote both the regulation and dissemination of knowledge and a certain exclusive and virtuously literate relation between men. However, and particularly with respect to the taking up of diaristic e-mail writing as a nonexclusive devotional practice, e-mail breaks with the *scriptural effort* of humanist scholarship. It flauntingly commingles *feeling good* with scholarly inquiry; enables a certain as yet undetermined *lack* of painstakingness to enter into scholarly discourse; is not generally virtuous or dignified; lends itself to less discriminate modes of correspondence, that is, intimate correspondence with strangers; and breaks decisively with *the* book, *the* letter, while refusing to steer clear of either, by inserting itself, folding itself into and around both.

The letter is vulnerable to sacrificial burnings, both literal and rhetorical, because its substrate, paper, passes through various hands and enables a series of literal associations between living bodies and the body of the letter. *The* letter filiates with the book via a powerful tropic regime having to do with the book's filiation with the body. *The book of life, the body of the book, a body of knowledge, the body of the letter, body text.* The holism of the book, its biblical master referent, and its status as both progeny and "self," renders the book a more complete, although still wayward, body than the letter. Fetishes of paper, handwriting, signature, and seal are all supports for the always already failed project of warranting the letter by the authoritative body, a failure that inhabits all writing, but intensifies with e-mail. This failure, however, is also a suspension, a suspension of closeness and separation, of communion and death, and in light of uncertain deliveries, of accident and fatedness. These suspensions allow the letter to be both a fragmented, imperiled body, threatening separation and death, and a nexus for fantasies of mind-to-mind communication, for soul mergings, and transcendental authenticity. As a traveling fragment of both a desiring body and an authentic soul addressed to one person in particular, the letter poses an intensified threat of exposure, of miscontextualization, recontextualization, misreading. Trembling inside a number of edges—the public, the private, the clichéd, the outrageous, the productive, the destructive, the secret, the banal, the perverse, the authentic, the manipulative, the legal, the illegal, the prohibited and the prescribed, the governed and the spontaneous—burning, and sometimes burial, becomes a necessity. As a ritual of bodily immolation, burning signals the death or renunciation of certain relational possibilities, their purification, and the determination that they should continue in some other, more sub-rosa form. The performance of the threat or the entreaty to burn brings to awareness, and causes to burn brighter, all of the fragilities that the letter makes manifest so that they may threaten more, so that the threat may be performatively resisted and thus enjoyed more virtuously.

E-mail cannot burn. Of course, one can print out e-mail and burn it, but one would not be burning *the* letter. A threat or a request to burn e-mail would be nonsensical. Most importantly, the insusceptibility of e-mail to the *rhetoric* of burning significantly impairs my ability to reproduce the heroism of *the* letter. Without burning, I cannot dramatize renunciation and sacrifice; I cannot make visible the relationship of heroism to renunciation, of vigilance to desire. I cannot dramatize my virtue, my dignity, my humanist diligence, that which eschews pleasure in favor of labor even while taking my pleasure otherwise. In effect, *I cannot distinguish what may be preserved and made public from what must abide under the sign of burning.* An entire regime of purification by burning, the purification of human relations, and of scholarship, breaks down.

))) Water

The insusceptibility of e-mail to the tropic regime of burning signals an incipient moral contamination, an anti-asceticism, and a range of disciplinary dissolves operating under the sign of *water*. The substrate of e-mail, while literally telephone wires, routers, and computers, is affectively and rhetorically a liquid contiguous with the space of the mind. Indeed, metaphorics of the oceanic, of unbounded liquid space construct the space of e-mail creation and transmission *as* mind and thus imbue the space of e-mail with Platonic metaphysics. The association of the field of electronic communication with water is well established. Marcos Novak has famously deemed the imaginal space behind the computer a *liquid architecture. Cyberspace is liquid, liquid cyberspace, liquid architecture, liquid cities. Liquid architecture is more than kinetic architecture, robotic architecture, an architecture of fixed parts and variable links. Liquid architecture is an architecture that breathes, pulses, leaps as one form and lands as another* (250). The goal of virtual reality programming is to achieve a sense of *immersion.* Characters in virtual reality novels regularly *sink* into cyberspace. Derrida: *having written something or other on the screen, the letters remaining as if suspended and yet floating yet at the surface of a liquid element* (1996, 26). What does it mean that affectively and rhetorically, e-mail appears as "letters," floating and rapidly propelled through a fluid, global space? What is the significance of encountering letters suspended in this way? To ask this is to ask about how the rhetoric of cyberspace, of virtuality generally affects the letter. This is the rhetoric of seamless connectivity and of the ability to manifest one's will anywhere, instantaneously. In other words, the affective and rhetorical regime of cyberspace imbues e-mail with a certain Platonism, a certain notion that the body of the letter has been transcended and that we are now confronted with a living word, or at least a word freed from physical constraints, a word that is *closer* to the voice of the mind. The Platonism of discourses of virtuality has been widely discussed and might be condensed in the increasingly popular term *telepresence* (see Markley; Heim). These rhetorics relate to those of the letter that invoke the true self, soul affinity, and immortality. However, within discourses of virtuality, the contravening peril and uncertainty of the medium has been underplayed in favor of a scientism that imagines a literal conflatability between digital code and mind, thus enabling fantasies of immortality that are less troubled than related fantasies about the letter and the tenuous connections established via its transits (see Weinstone 1997b). The most it is possible to hypothesize here is that the peril to which *the* letter is subjected may be moderated in favor of some less mediated and mortal aura permeating the scene of e-mail.

■ Flesh ■

At the same time, the absence of paper and its hand-to-hand transit undermines two sources of authority: the authority of the "original" and, more pressingly, the authority of the warranting body that survives in the letter, in its having been touched, and perhaps kissed, by its author and signed by hand. This latter situation only underscores the disposition of all writing, which must, to function, travel and thus slip from the authoritative grasp of its author who is also its first reader. What interests me is how the literal absence of a warranting touch, an absence that intensifies the disposition of the letter as paradigmatic writing, and the frequent situation of an absence of any other prior contact with one's interlocutor, initiates and intensifies uncertainties as to the meaning and origin and truthfulness of a text precisely in a rhetorical milieu that encourages us to think of computer mediated communication as *more present, more intimate, more direct.* Furthermore, as Baron and others have noted, correspondence with an interlocutor one cannot see *enables* personal disclosure and, for better or worse, renders one less cautious (1998a, 147–48). What I propose is that these dispositions, taken together, produce a "living word," but in a sense other than that connoted by the paradigmatic living word of god or *logos,* that is, other than a word that enjoys its effects precisely as it is warranted by a super-authority.

Relatively cut off from their authorities and operating within a context of heightened openness and the expectation of fluid, de-disciplined contact, the suspended words of e-mail constitute a kind of permission to be affected by and to effect language. In other words, the heightened undecidable relation of e-mail texts to warrants of ownership and authority and intent, especially with respect to the diaristic exchange of e-mail between those who have never met, in conjunction with the heightened propensity toward disclosure and hybrid intimacies (intellectual, emotional, sexual, and so on), tends toward heightening awareness and sensitivity to the impacts of language, to the *effectivities* of language over the significatory.

In "A Little Something," the late Michael Current wrote: *A stranger writes to me of the body. Answering my e-mail, he tells me he is skeptical of e-mail, concerned about the detachment of thought and affect from the fleshbonesandblood. An ethical matter, a concern that we will abandon our environment, that our being-in-the-world will be replaced by being-in/being-with/being-one-with/becoming-with the machine* (158). The stranger's fear assumes an ontological disjunct between words and flesh. *As if we could detach thought, detach language from fleshbonesandblood.* This is the presumption that posthumanism has mostly abandoned. The primary questions for ethics, as they have been formulated by posthumanism, deconstruction, and poststructuralism generally, both as capacitation and responsibility, are not about meaning per se but about how meanings, the said, and the saying get, literally, under our skin. How do words make us, shape us, and participate in our becomings, becomings that are always embodied? These questions, this disposition emerged from multiple histories of violence to the body, from traumas of representation. The heightened sensitivity to language that e-mail enables must also enable, in ways we do not yet understand, a heightening of the body's sensitivities. The modal expressivities of words and flesh exist in a state of *involvement*. And while there is never not the possibility of trauma, e-mail opens a space of amorous 2 + n experimentation that does not exclude, indeed that emphatically includes, pleasure, and within a technical structure where the play of distance and merger, language and bodies, may be observed and intensified. Encountering words in "fluidic" space, e-mail correspondence, as a practice, returns me, in your quasi-absence, your quasi-presence, and the relative absence of authority, to the watery encounter between word and flesh. This is a Tantric relational technology for posthumanism.

▼ Who?

But whose words are these? And who sent them? To practice writing with strangers makes these questions quiver even more violently and challenges even more thoroughly regimes of the proper name and address. The suspension of self and other, the heightening of the question "Who?" is facilitated by the confluence of the preconditioned and the recontextualized that structures e-mail correspondences. The rhetoric of transformative power, instantaneity, and mind-to-mind that informs discourses of virtuality encourages urges of the sovereign self, urges such as projection and assimilation *at the same time that* the absence of face-to-face cues and the frequent situation of having never met one's interlocutor, confront me with the processes, images, emotions, sensations, and interpretations emanating from me that are, sometimes drastically, at odds with my correspondent. Inaugurated by the intensification of the absence of both nonverbal cues and richer lived contexts, my own emanations become more visible to myself and others. *I would see myself on the screen and say, "There I go again." I could see my neuroses in black and white. It was a wake-up call* (quoted in Turkle 206). Having *determined* to open myself to this practice, these conflicts become occasions for observing and negotiating under an altered technical and social regime, and an altered temporal-spatial regime.

With regard to the latter, while e-mail is faster than paper post, the time of e-mail, of writing, responding, and reading, is much different than that of live chat or Usenet groups or even listservs. The speed of e-mail allows for a diaristic kind of writing, synchronous with one's lived time, while the storage of e-mail and the ability to write and read offline allows for reflection and rereading, for the maintenance of a malleable archive that, through multiple iterations, calls into question or suspends the question of the authenticity of my words and the whole notion of a "proper" context. Yet, *at the same time*, processes of projection, introjection, and assimilation are built into e-mail both socially and technically. The more conserving rhetoric of *the* letter, of authenticity, and of soul merging that transcends particularities of embodiment exists alongside rhetorics of becoming other, of playful transfiguration. At the level of the text, I am more alert to verbal resonance, coincidence, accidents of confluence *at the same time that* these textual instances become occasions for the ironic interweaving of your words with mine, for deformations of text, and the slow accretion of hybrid vocabularies that create and emerge from a context, from a *shared history, from a shared work.* Projection and assimilation, then, may be reconceived as capacities that open me to the encounter with avatar emanations that are undecidably mine or yours, that open me to self-alteration within a practice of devotion.

One of the few letters that Foucault quotes during his extensive discussion of technologies of self is a love letter from Marcus Aurelius to his tutor Fronto: *Hail, my sweetest of masters.* This is followed by a rather banal list of the day's activities: *slept somewhat late... relieved my throat... luncheon... long chat... bathed... I love you and you are away* (1988, 28–29). Unlike Platonic erotics which had as their *telos* the recognition of one's *true relation to being,* Foucault wants to perpetuate *a multiplicity of relationships* (1989, 308). Ethical modes of being, of relating the self to itself, happen in relation in part because *in relationships, one's own actions become more problematic* (1986, 84). Recounting the acts of the day, I open myself up for scrutiny, comment, renegotiation. For those of us who would indulge in it, e-mail returns us to an every day practice of writing in relation. The taking up of an every day practice of writing in relation is the ritual gesture that the technical structure and social disposition of e-mail encourages through the absence of paper, seal, handwriting, and handwritten signature, through the attenuation of warranting by the authoritative body, the relative ease and speed of access to others, and the various ways in which text may be manipulated.

▼ E-Mail *Mudrā* Ψ

I am proposing, then, as a gesture that would invite a posthuman ethics to come, a commitment to an every day practice of writing in relationship via e-mail, and particularly, a commitment to fostering e-mail relations with those we have never met. This is, of course, a practice of hospitality to strangers within a stylized and ritualized regime of both shared work and pleasure. This, I would argue, is the paradigmatic form of devotion: I "gaze up" without knowing in advance at whom I am gazing. Through a daily practice, a ritual regime, I establish an estranged, yet still porous space of examination and encounter. However, rather than a "warning off," through this constructed distance, this gazing up, I signal my openness to surprise, to *being affected*. I signal my willingness, in advance, to suffer certain forms of death, of abandonment, and transformation that are endemic to postality and to any gesture that might look forward to an ethics of both enhanced capacity and responsibility.

Chris... Two days after I wrote, and you didn't answer, haven't answered, I am imagining you hospitalized. *Immortality, mortality, and the tenuous character of earthly contacts constitute a principal theme of letter writing, a theme that is metonymically reinforced in the text's reference to the letter's artifacticity and to its imperiled passage through time and space* (Decker 42). But when time and space "collapse," into an instant, a micron, isn't it true that the affective distances between us intensify as a result? What am I left with other than my desire for response, my fear of disconnection and death, my struggle to devote myself to you even if you are (always) threatening intractability?

I am reminded of the regularity of such anxieties and of the speed with which they race through my life now that, paradoxically, I participate in these proliferating correspondences. (I am also feeling anxious about a letter and a piece of text I sent to K.) The time of e-mail is supposed to be the instant, the rhetorical field of e-mail is connectivity, and yet I have become sensitized to how this expectation and this mode, casts a brilliant and anxious halo around my fears of loss and death. Barthes disparages the love letter, deeming it mere *correspondence* rather than *relation* (1978, 158). But as we both wrote, at different times before we met: *every letter is a love letter.* I told you how intimately connected I feel to this phrase. Is it because every letter is a gift that renders us vulnerable to misreading, to nonresponse, to the nonreciprocal? Am I willing to risk this? Am I willing to risk your projections, your assimilations, the ones that inevitably change me? The way your words and my flesh, your desires and my sense of self interleaf so that I am always in a suspended state of belonging/belonging to? And who, these days, would consider that projective assimilation might also be a stroke of luck? A welcome downcoming?

Then, I constantly wrangle with myself: what will be my response to nonresponse? Will my letter be devotional or a demand?

I sent you three letters in one day, because I was inspired, but I will leave this fourth one here and wait, hoping for you . . .

June 11, 2000

Dear Ann,

. . . but I wasn't sick at all, I was in the middle of this endless and relentless construction that I seem to be the general contractor of, that is happening simultaneously at my house and two other rehab income properties I bought across the park. The guys who work here don't have cars, so the day begins at 7 and ends 12 hours later with me giving people rides back to their neighborhoods from Hollywood to Highland Park. Then I come home and just collapse. I don't even check the voicemail— what would be the point? It is totally absorbing and I'm getting to speak Spanish—several of these guys are refugees from Salvador and Guatemala, someone else swam across the Tijuana Channel just last week—but apart from hearing all these stories and trying to keep everybody focused and productive, I don't have any other life. I am saving beaucoup $$$ by doing it this way, the left-wing hippie college teacher posing as con-struction boss. Or perhaps vice versa, and your letter, which was so purely intellectual, made me focus on the "vice."

We were talking about how people can assimilate each other. Hospi-tality. And how nice you made me feel when I was visiting at your house, even as I vaguely understood that it was conscious, part of a spiritual practice.

It was so fascinating to find out that we had such parallel experiences when we were living in New York. You were working as a tenant organ-izer. I was in the art world, but kept dipping round the edges of this "community" political stuff. Partly because I believed in it, but also partly because it was an angle on supporting yourself as an artist at the tail end of the Carter years.

Certain artists like myself who didn't have viable (i.e., huge) careers were able to eke out a subsistence living from a byzantine network of government, state, and local grants. An arts administrator named Rochelle Slavin had the brilliant idea that she could use the CETA pro-gram (envisaged as a mechanism to employ the semiskilled employable who'd lost jobs during the recession) to create 200 artist jobs. Not that most of us would be employable in *any* economic climate . . . It was "Art in the Community."

Through the program, we artists were connected with other, more professional scammers in ghetto neighborhoods who were creaming CETA funds themselves to operate nonexistent community centers, educational collectives, etc. Two of the places I was sent to in East New York (a neighborhood distinguished mostly by the highest homicide rate in the five boroughs) did not exist at all. Finally, I dug up a "tenant organizing committee" at the East New York Housing Projects. So great, I'd make a video about the heroic struggle of the self-empowered Wel-fare Mothers . . . but when I got there, there was no tenant committee working there at all. There was only Florence Bell, a woman in her late fifties who'd made a nice garden out beside the parking lot. Florence shared a one-bedroom apartment with her twenty-five-year-old son who was mentally disabled with an I.Q. of 70.

Florence was no more a "tenant organizer" than I was "a professional video artist." But if she was a little bit bewildered by my presence, she was incredibly hospitable. Florence was a nice woman from North Caro-lina who thought the Projects should be better, and I was an anorexic white girl with a CETA job and a borrowed Porta-Pak. On that basis, we got along.

I remember Florence's kitchen, drinking Diet Cokes and visiting with her son. She used to try and make me eat. I went there once a week, and this went on all summer. I remember I was very lost—could barely speak beyond a stammer, guilty that the purpose of these visits was so vague and undefined. But mostly I remember Florence's hospitality, her unquestioning willingness to host these aimless visits: what went on beneath the lines.

How can anyone be sure the Other really is "another" when by simply being there to listen, it's possible to absorb not just their stories (the stories never are the point) but these other *people* too? This kind of journalism can be really spooky. A form of schizophrenia. When other people's lives seem more real than your own and you're too shy to speak, you have no position to observe from, and so you just absorb. To walk a little bit behind . . . Devotion? Disappearance? Terror? All that year I was drinking everyone in massive gulps, listening to other people's stories until I realized: I'm not what I appear to be, I'm what I heard. For years it seemed like an epiphany. It was accompanied by endless weeping (the body's means of letting energy, when it becomes too full) and I made up theories to describe it: Lonely Girl Phenomenology. But I didn't write you back this week because I'm not a lonely girl right now, I'm a construction boss.

Devotedly,
Chris
(Sent via fax and paper post per arrangement by phone.)

Chance ▼

Either you have stumbled indeed, without the aid of LSD or other indole alkaloids, onto a secret richness and concealed density of dream; onto a network by which X number of Americans are truly communicating whilst reserving their lies, recitations of routine, and betrayals of spiritual poverty, for the official government delivery system; maybe even into a real alternative to the exitlessness, to the absence of surprise to life, that harrows the head of everybody American you know, and you too, sweetie. Or you are hallucinating it.

—Thomas Pynchon, *Crying of Lot 49*

In *Archive Fever,* Derrida argues that the archive must destroy in order to produce itself. The archive cannot contain everything: it must select and the principles of selection constitute *patriarchic* functions of hierarchy, titling, consignation, burning, and suppression. Derrida also notes the archaeological urge of the archive, the urge to find the most original, singular, and irreplaceable. He goes on to describe a ***mal d'archive . . . a sickness. . . . It is to burn with a passion. It is never to rest, interminably, from searching for the archive right where it slips away. It is to run after the archive, even if there's too much of it, right where something in it anarchives itself. It is to have a compulsive, repetitive, and nostalgic desire for the archive, an irrepressible desire to return to the origin, a homesickness, a nostalgia for the return to the most archaic place of commencement*** (91). The figure of the archive, and of the anarchive, is fire, the burning book, the burning letter, the burning library, the feverish, desiring brow. How could the nonfascist West distance itself from its own fascist longings if not by drawing a line between the good destruction and the bad destruction of books, between the making and the unmaking of history?

The functions and impulses of the archive are intimately bound up with the functions and impulses of humanism and humanistic scholarship, each of which rely upon and propagate through the creation of archives. Needless to say, the threat that electronic communication and storage pose to archivization is of pressing concern. Electronic data is subject to any number of accidents that, as is well known, render it less durable than paper. The lifetime of various magnetic media, several decades to only several years, is horrifically short compared to paper. Then, magnetic media become obsolete as we are seeing now with floppy disks. The future readability of electronic data is imperiled. Derrida asks: *what is the moment **proper** to the archive?* (1996, 25). It is possible to say with respect to *the* letter, that mainstay of the archive, that there is no longer any *moment* proper to the archive, that the archival gesture has proliferated through repeated savings, sendings, and copyings and furthermore across highly unstable substrates. As Derrida realizes, the advent of e-mail challenges the writing of *a certain* history, the saving of *a certain* history, and potentials for the future as the future are conditioned by the selections and destructions that construct the past. The archaeological impulse of the archivist is controverted by the forms of malleability and dissemination to which e-mail texts are subject. *The massive publication of personal correspondence merits recognition as one of the major events—indeed, one of the great capital investments—of twentieth-century humanities scholarship* (Decker 7).

Executing a poignant and nostalgic reference to *the* letter, the popular e-mail software program Eudora admonishes *Sorry, this text cannot be changed* if one attempts to edit a received letter. But of course, one has only to reply to the letter, a reply which automatically generates a "copy" and inserts it into the reply window, in order for the text to become fully malleable, subject to cutting, pasting, re-signing, and more intimate deformations. The "original" may be deleted, time stamps may be changed. Even the markers commonly used to indicate quoted text may be turned on and off and applied or misapplied to any text. At the other end, I might alter my own letter, resave it with a different date, a different subject, or as a text file; delete it or paste all of it or parts of it into other texts. More perversely, I might anticipate the intrusion of accidents of delivery into my letter by scrambling "packets" of text as if the entire letter had been misassembled at the receiving end. I might even insert the words "NO CARRIER" at the end of a truncated letter, thus initiating a game of Exquisite Corpse by inviting my interlocutor to continue my text where it breaks off. Enabled by the technical capacities and social disposition of e-mail systems and relations, I have done all of these things.

As if the archive were now subject to the actions of water, there is a strange indurable durability to e-mail, a strange duration of what has not survived in a unique, recognizable form. E-mail texts do not burn: they evaporate, erode, break apart, evolve, shift, and are subject to baroque growths, hybridities, the accumulation of waste, debris, redundancy, and critical gaps. And although this applies in some degree to other forms of electronic communication, the archival principles are at work much differently, say, on listservs, where all versions of posts sent to lists are either preserved in threaded archives or are not archived at all. However, with e-mail letters sent between colleagues, friends, and lovers, I mean the quasi-private correspondence that has, up until now, been a mainstay of the humanist archive, all of the possibilities of multiple savings, copyings, disseminations, repetitions with difference, and playful or painful deformations are at work while there are fewer archiving impulses, either technically or in terms of social writing practices, that would urge the retention of anything that might be called an "original" text or a coherent narrative. This dissemination and deformation makes hypervisible the operation of *différance* as texts ratchet from context to context. The technical structure of the mail now conspicuously gives the lie to any notion of a stable whole or of the possibility of correct and comprehensive principles of selection and suppression under the control of any single archivist or archival principle. As e-mail proliferates, it enfolds and surpasses its earlier incarnations, during times when intracity letters, delivered by servants, friends, and later by local postal systems, served as the substrate for daily communication among people of certain classes. As the sheer volume of potential archivable material expands along with the baroqueness of its potential forms, the archive is opened to events of relation, to historical *events*, to chance determinations and determinations of chance that render its consignations and boundary conditions impossibly porous.

Determining to engage in diaristic writing with others impacts the production of scholarly writing, as it has here, in these pages. I am writing to you as I am writing. I write about my writing. I send you unformed ideas, odd images, unwieldy insights, outbursts, fragments. You interrupt me, entangle your words with mine. Often, my writing begins as writing to you. I am pasting text that began as letters into this text. Over time, I can no longer tell why I am using certain words or where they come from. I find what I thought were my ideas in your writing, and vice versa. I can't articulate the status of my most intimate obsessions, and my phrasing begins to sound like an echo from somewhere else. My words take on an uncanny, ghostly quality, doubled or astigmatically blurred. These are effects that, of course, are familiar to many writers working in communities and addressing writers in their fields. Submitting to a daily practice of e-mail writing, particularly with those one hasn't met, intensifies these effects of iteration, of emanation, sensitizing us to these constant and productive openings to chance, to the surprise familiarity of others, and to the suspensions that intensify the question "Who?" It is an opening to encounter through the intensification of postality, one that renounces the true address, the exclusive discipline, the exclusive history, the exclusive family, the exclusive friend, and therefore opens to nonexemption: a renunciation of renunciation, a sacrifice of proper sacrifice.

The join of capacitation and responsibility begins with this hospitality to influx, with the adoption of practices that sensitize me to the coming-from-everywhere of my always uncertain belongings, even of my capacity to make such devotional gestures. My body, my modes of subjectivation are a shared history, a shared work that retains no *zero-point* of possession or accountability, no prophylactic against unauthorized touch. This "coming-from-everywhere" is not a radically elsewhere, a radically other that must be, in the absence of all inducements and proofs, supposed or believed. To renounce the renunciations, the exclusions of sovereignty, we must give up our demands of others and the Other. My forms, potentials, and capacities, from the quantum to the biological to the subjective to the choices and determinations "I" might make, are no more or less "me" than they are the manifestations, the emanations, the downcomings of others. Posthumanist ethics, postdeconstructive responsibility, cannot sidestep these intimacies in favor of absolute difference, in favor of legible individuality. My hope is that we would work together to create the conditions for a posthumanist, postdeconstructive ethics to come by continually exposing ourselves to our entanglements. Not knowing my *self,* not knowing what I mean when I say "I," and you say "I," places us in the most intimate relation of capacitation, of effect, *and thus, of responsibility for everything.* You are my body, too.

Please write back...

weinstone@earthlink.net

Ψ▼ Postscript

Lockup: Inside Colorado State Pen is an investigative report about conditions at one of the United States' super maximum security prisons. The camera opens onto a series of uniformly white interiors beginning with an antiseptic 7 x 9 foot cell and moving outward to a cell block where glossy white walls, ceilings, fixtures, moldings, and floor tiles give the impression of a blindingly lit operating theater for alien abductees. Inmates of the prison are locked down, alone in their cells, twenty-three hours a day, seven days a week. For one hour a day, they leave their cells in shackles in the company only of prison employees. All visits are "no contact," conducted from behind thick glass partitions. New prisoners are tested with a seven-day period of total isolation in an "austere cell." If they survive without incident, they receive personal belongings and a television tuned to a preselected news channel. During his interview, the prison psychologist employs a revealing series of references to denote the relationship of the inmates to larger world as seen through their TV windows. *Most of these inmates have television sets connected to outside news services. They know who Saddam Hussein is, who's the new Chancellor of Germany, and what's happening on the NASDAQ. The only thing they don't have is physical contact with other prisoners.*

Billy Hankins notes the frequency with which the isolation breaks down his fellow inmates. *You have guys crying, pounding on the doors. Most of these guys are on medication. They just can't handle the reality of being in a cell twenty-four hours a day. It gets to them.* Another prisoner says, *I've seen a lot of guys snap. On any given day they could break down, get ulcers, loose their hair. I've seen it tear people down.* Here's one of the facility's few women prisoners in an article about supermax prisons: *This place not only takes your freedom it also takes your very being. Your entire personality is forced to change to the conditions such as loneliness, frustration, and depression* (quoted in Lynd, n.p.).

Prisoners living in near-isolation for years or decades experience severe trauma upon their release into the general prison population. They find it difficult to tolerate large numbers of people and exhibit symptoms of post-traumatic stress syndrome. Larry Reid, Program Manager: *We were hearing from people that these inmates are freaked out. They're in this huge environment with all these other people and they're having a hard time adjusting.* In response, the prison institutes a series of graduated levels designed to break down and then reacclimatize inmates prior to their release. Level 1: total isolation. Level 2: isolation with limited privileges. Level 3: isolation with work detail. Level 4: meeting with other prisoners in small groups. Level 5: classroom-based resocialization training. Prisoners descend to the depths and are then slowly lifted to the surface: a precaution against the bends. Some prisoners subsist in lockdown for decades or a lifetime. Twenty thousand inmates, the overwhelming majority of them people of color, live in super maximum security prisons nationwide. Colorado State Penitentiary is one of the most lenient. The word that tears through me is *Gulag.*

A federal court in California wrote about the relationship between mental illness and confinement under supermax conditions at the Pelican Bay prison. The court concluded that if prisons *inflict a serious mental illness, greatly exacerbate mental illness, or deprive inmates of their sanity, then defendants have deprived inmates of a basic necessity of human existence—indeed, they have crossed into the realm of psychological torture* (quoted in Lynd, n.p). The supermax prison doesn't punish the person; it punishes what makes a person possible. It punishes the organism.

I watch the flat, impassive face of Billy Hankins as he describes the distress of his fellows. The terror is in the details. The suggestion of a tremor in his voice. A tremulous breath. The sheen of sweat. The way his eyelids flutter closed, looking inside at what he doesn't want to see. My body begins to change in response. A torsion, a twisting, a burn in my chest and throat. A sickening vertigo in the center of my head. The image of dark fists pounding white metal, mouths stretched with cries. Billy's words, his pictures are indistinguishable from an emotion, a sensation. The categories begin to blur. The terror is in the details. Pulse in the fingertips, iron taste on the tongue. I can't think anymore. I'm breaking down. It's me, pounding on the inside of a locked door. It's my panic of isolation, the deathly loneliness, this dread of total withdrawal that is also cellular, corpuscular: a rhythm, a rushing, a scattering beyond, the nightmare free fall. I'm falling. As *nothing* rushes up, it's the closest I will ever get to feeling myself as *one*, here at the edge, where the thread of human connection threatens to break, where *nothing* threatens.

This nothing, this total withdrawal—an absolute absence, an absolutely impervious exterior—punctures the interior while threatening to render me radically alone. *Spacing* designates **nothing**, *nothing that is, no presence at a distance; it is the index of an irreducible exterior, and at the same time of a* **movement**, *a displacement that indicates an irreducible alterity* (Derrida 1981, 81). Puncturing, the interruption by the abyss, threatens to reduce me to one. This *oneness* occasions death, insanity, suicide. To avoid it, my body/psyche, for lack of a better term, exercises a capacity, enacts a *necessity* for a state of indistinction between myself and another. I am not empathizing *with* him; I *am* him in some undecidable way. Even though Billy shot a grocery clerk at point-blank range, something moves abruptly toward him, to keep us both safe from this raw harm of condemnation to *one*. Responding to his terror, *the terror,* my body rushes to announce itself as an iteration of his body. The breakdown of the "I," the shrinking of flesh, relates this starvation to other starvations; it conserves "me" in the face of death, conserves me in the form of a nonsubjectivable connection, in the form of a terrified assimilation *to* this other man. As "I" break down, something else, something prior, hastens to be *taken in.* A whole history of a vexed separation/nonseparation rises up to overwhelm me in this moment of threatened break. My body/psyche acts preemptively to fit itself undecidably into the place of the other, to reestablish the conditions permitting the continuation of anything that could be called "me." *That condition is entanglement.* I am returned, through my body/psyche's incapacity for sustaining radical aloneness, to a company, even to a company in terror.

In the crack of trauma, the space of horror, when I am, as Levinas says, thrown out of subjectivity, away from consciousness, into confrontation with an impersonal *there is,* something stretches to become the other, not brutishly, but announcing a dependency, an enmeshment, a thread, a liaison, a vibration that stretches between us as a matter of life and death. At the limit of the survivable self, something here tends toward you, becomes you, and it is at the extremes of an aloneness that is beyond loneliness, that this necessary nonseparation becomes most palpable. In anticipation of the horror of absolute rupture, I am not passively exposed to the *wholly other*, or what Derrida lately calls "God," but to a resolute *capacity*, belonging to whom I don't know, that insists on my survival as a category breakdown between my *self* and the world.

At the edge of the break, of the rupture, "I" cannot tolerate the condition of oneness, the encounter with an absolutely other, an other with whom I have no contact, an other *who is* this prohibition on contact as many of us have thought the other. Rather than inaugurating experience, inaugurating subjectivity, this brush with absolute difference, with the space of *nothing*, causes my body/psyche to shut down. "I" cannot face such an unmitigated withdrawal. To survive at all, "I" must be stretched, thrown, dizzied, blurred *into* you. Reaching the true rupture, "I" would become insane or die. There would be no experience: "I" would have no means left to move toward you, to answer your call.

Derrida makes a double gesture of renunciation: *It is ethics itself: to learn to live—alone, from oneself, by oneself* (1994b, xviii). I want to suggest that this "oneself," even in its deconstructing form, is a luxury that comes after. My "oneself" is a *capacity*, a formulation of self as a relation of nonrelation made possible by a prior entanglement, a prior undecidability that literally keeps me alive. What comes from elsewhere, this intensity of expression, of emanation, this avatar body, loses its capacities for various forms of survival when it is ripped from the company of the others, when it is confronted with radical separation from those with whom it exists in an undecidable and necessary relation that can never be *nothing*. How could the *absolutely nothing to do with each other*, or the space of *nothing*, or the *no contact*, or the *absolute difference* answer to this cry? I asked, earlier in this text, *but will I feel less lonely when we speak the language of the membrane? When we are "together"?* Instead I find I want to follow loneliness toward the breakdowns of both terror and pleasure. I want to devote myself to this capacity, to our profound intimacy and the thread of my undecidable belonging to you.

Works Cited

Acker, Kathy. 1984. *Algeria: A Series of Innovations Because Nothing Else Works.* London: Aloes Books.

——. 1988. *Empire of the Senseless.* New York: Grove Press.

Agamben, Giorgio. 1993. *The Coming Community.* Translated by Michael Hardt. Minneapolis, MN: University of Minnesota Press.

Alper, Harvey P. 1979. "Siva and the Ubiquity of Consciousness: The Spaciousness of an Artful Yogi." *Journal of Indian Philosophy.* 7:345–407.

Altieri, Charles. 1985. "Plato's Performative Sublime and the Ends of Reading." *New Literary History* 16, no. 2: 251–73.

Amato, Joe. 1997. *Bookend: Anatomies of a Virtual Self.* Albany, NY: State University of New York Press.

Badiou, Alain. 2000. "What Is Love?" In *Sexuation,* edited by Renata Salecl, 263–81. Durham, NC: Duke University Press.

——. 1999a. *Deleuze: The Clamor of Being.* Translated by Louise Burchill. Minneapolis: University of Minnesota Press.

——. 1999b. *Manifesto for Philosophy.* Translated by Norman Madarasz. Albany: State University of New York Press. Original edition, 1989.

Bacon, Leonard. 1843. "The Post-Office System as an Element of Modern Civilization." *New Englander* 1:9–27.

Bagchi, P. C., ed. 1986. *Kaulajñāna-nirṇaya of the School of Matsyendranātha.* Varanasi, India: Prachya Prakashan.

Barkan, Leonard. 1991. *Transuming Passion: Ganymede and the Erotics of Humanism.* Stanford, CA: Stanford University Press.

Baron, Naomi S. 1998a. "Letters by Phone or Speech by Other Means: The Linguistics of Email." *Language & Communication* 18:133–70.

——. 1998b. "Writing in the Age of Email: The Impact of Ideology versus Technology." *Visible Language* 32, no. 1: 35–53.

Barthes, Roland. 1975. *The Pleasure of the Text.* Translated by Richard Miller. New York: Hill and Wang. Original edition, 1973.

——. 1978. *A Lover's Discourse: Fragments.* Translated by Richard Howard. New York: Farrar, Straus and Giroux.

Baty, S. Paige. 1999. *E-Mail Trouble: Love and Addiction @ the Matrix.* Austin: University of Texas Press.

Baudrillard, Jean. 1993. *The Transparency of Evil: Essays on Extreme Phenomena.* Translated by James Benedict. London: Verso.

Bhandarkar, Sir Ramkrishna Gopal. 1936. *Collected Works of Sir R. G. Bhandarkar.* Poona, India: Bhandarkar Oriental Research Institute.

Biardeau, Madeleine. 1989. *Hinduism: The Anthropology of a Civilization.* Translated by Richard Nice. French Studies in South Asian Culture and Society 3. Oxford: Oxford University Press.

Biggs, Donald C. 1956. *The Pony Express: Creation of the Legend.* San Francisco, CA: private printing.

Bolter, Jay David, and Richard Grusin. 1999. *Remediation: Understanding New Media.* Cambridge, MA: MIT Press.

Boundas, Constantin V. 1994. "Deleuze: Serialization and Subject-Formation." In *Deleuze and the Theater of Philosophy,* edited by Constantin V. Boundas and Dorothea Olkowski, 99–116. New York: Routledge.

Bowker, Geof. 1993. "How to Be Universal: Some Cybernetic Strategies, 1943–70." *Social Studies of Science* 23:107–27.

Braidotti, Rosi. 1994. "Toward a New Nomadism: Feminist Deleuzian Tracks; or, Metaphysics and Metabolism." In *Gilles Deleuze and the Theater of Philosophy,* edited by Constantine V. Boundas and Dorothea Olkowski, 159–86. New York: Routledge.

———. 1997. "Meta(l)morphoses." *Theory, Culture & Society* 14, no. 2: 67–80.

Braude, Stephen E. 1991. *First Person Plural: Multiple Personality and the Philosophy of Mind.* London: Routledge.

Brockman, John. 1995. *The Third Culture: Beyond the Scientific Revolution.* New York: Simon and Schuster.

Burckhardt, Jacob. 1929. *The Civilization of the Renaissance in Italy.* Translated by S. G. C. Middlemore. London: George G. Harrap.

Burgin, Victor. 1995. "The City in Pieces." In *Prosthetic Territories: Pressolitics and Hypertechnologies,* edited by Gabriel Brahm Jr. and Mark Driscoll, 5–20. Boulder, CO: Westview Press.

Burroughs, William S. 1981. *Cities of the Red Night.* New York: Henry Holt.

———. 1987. *The Western Lands.* New York: Penguin.

———. 1993. *The Letters of William S. Burroughs.* New York: Penguin.

Burroughs, Williams S., and Brion Gysin. 1978. *The Third Mind.* New York: Viking Press.

Caillois, Roger. 1960. *Méduse et Cie.* Paris: Gallimard.

Chartier, Roger, Alain Boureau, and Cécile Dauphin. 1997. *Correspondence: Models of Letter-Writing from the Middle Ages to the Nineteenth Century.* Translated by Christopher Woodall. Princeton, NJ: Princeton University Press.

Chasin, Alexandra. 1995. "Class and Its Close Relations: Identities among Women, Servants, and Machines." In *Posthuman Bodies,* edited by Judith Halberstam and Ira Livingston, 73–96. Bloomington: Indiana University Press.

Chatterji, J. C. 1986. *Kashmir Shaivism.* Albany: State University of New York Press.

Cheah, Pheng, and Bruce Robbins, eds. 1998. *Cosmopolitics: Thinking and Feeling beyond the Nation.* Minneapolis: University of Minnesota Press.

Cixous, Hélène. 1991. *Readings: The Poetics of Blanchot, Joyce, Kafka, Kleist, Lispector, and Tsvetayeva.* Translated by Verena Andermatt Conley. Minneapolis: University of Minnesota Press.

Clifford, James. 1992. "Traveling Cultures." In *Cultural Studies,* edited by Lawrence Grossberg, Cary Nelson, and Paula Trichler, 96–116. New York: Routledge.

Critchley, Simon. 1996. "Prolegomena to Any Post-Deconstructive Subjectivity." In *Deconstructive Subjectivities,* edited by Simon Critchley and Peter Dews, 13–45. Albany: State University of New York Press.

Current, Michael. 1996. "A Little Something." In *Being On Line: Net Subjectivity,* edited by Alan Sondheim, 158–60. New York: Lusitania Press.

Davies, Tony. 1997. *Humanism, the New Critical Idiom.* London: Routledge.

Decker, William Merrill. 1998. *Epistolary Practices: Letter Writing in America before Telecommunications.* Chapel Hill: University of North Carolina Press.

Deleuze, Gilles. 1988a. *Foucault.* Translated by Seán Hand. Minneapolis: University of Minnesota Press.

———. 1988b. *Spinoza: Practical Philosophy.* Translated by Robert Hurley. San Francisco: City Lights Books.

———. 1990. *The Logic of Sense.* New York: Columbia University Press.

———. 1992. *Expressionism in Philosophy: Spinoza.* Translated by Martin Joughin. New York: Zone Books.

———. 1993. *The Fold: Leibniz and the Baroque.* Translated by Tom Conley. Minneapolis: University of Minnesota Press.

———. 1994. *Difference and Repetition.* Translated by Paul Patton. New York: Columbia University Press.

———. 1997a. "Desire and Pleasure." In *Foucault and His Interlocutors,* edited by Arnold I. Davidson, 183–92. Chicago: University of Chicago Press. Original edition, 1994.

———. 1997b. "Immanence: A Life . . ." *Theory, Culture & Society* 14, no. 2: 3–7.

Deleuze, Gilles, and Félix Guattari. 1983. *Anti-Oedipus: Capitalism and Schizophrenia.* Translated by Robert Hurley, Mark Seem, and Helen R. Lane. Minneapolis: University of Minnesota Press.

———. 1987. *A Thousand Plateaus: Capitalism and Schizophrenia.* Translated by Brian Massumi. Minneapolis: University of Minnesota Press.

———. 1994. *What Is Philosophy?* Translated by Hugh Tomlinson and Graham Burchell. New York: Columbia University Press.

Deleuze, Gilles, and Claire Parnet. 1987. *Dialogues.* Translated by Hugh Tomlinson and Barbara Habberjam. New York: Columbia University Press.

Derrida, Jacques. 1978. *Writing and Difference.* Translated by Alan Bass. Chicago: University of Chicago Press.

———. 1981. *Positions.* Translated by Alan Bass. Chicago: University of Chicago Press. Original edition, 1972.

———. 1982. *Margins of Philosophy.* Translated by Alan Bass. Chicago: University of Chicago Press.

———. 1987. *The Post Card: From Socrates to Freud and Beyond.* Translated by Alan Bass. Chicago: University of Chicago Press.

———. 1988. *Limited, Inc.* Translated by Samuel Weber and Jeffrey Mehlman. Evanston, IL: Northwestern University Press. Original edition, 1977.

―――. 1992. "Force of Law: The 'Mystical Foundation of Authority.'" In *Deconstruction and the Possibility of Justice*, edited by Drucilla Cornell, Michel Rosenfeld, and David Gray Carlson, 3–67. New York: Routledge.

―――. 1994a. "The Deconstruction of Actuality: An Interview with Jacques Derrida." *Radical Philosophy* 68 (Autumn): 28–41.

―――. 1994b. *Specters of Marx: The State of the Debt, the Work of Mourning, and the New International.* Translated by Peggy Kamuf. New York: Routledge. Original edition, 1993.

―――. 1996. *Archive Fever: A Freudian Impression.* Translated by Eric Prenowitz. Chicago: University of Chicago Press.

―――. 1997a. "On Responsibility: An Interview with Jonathan Dronsfield, Nick Midgley, Adrian Wilding." *PLI: Warwick Journal of Philosophy* 6 (Summer): 19–36.

―――. 1997b. *Politics of Friendship.* Translated by George Collins. London: Verso. Original edition, 1994.

―――. 1999a. *Adieu to Emmanuel Levinas.* Translated by Pascale-Anne Brault and Michael Naas. Stanford, CA: Stanford University Press. Original edition, 1997.

―――. 1999b. "Hospitality, Justice and Responsibility: A Dialogue with Jacques Derrida." In *Questioning Ethics: Contemporary Debates in Philosophy,* edited by Richard Kearny and Mark Dooley, 65–83. London: Routledge.

―――. 2002. "The Animal That Therefore I Am (More to Follow)." *Critical Inquiry* 28:369–418.

Derrida, Jacques, with Alexander Garcia Düttmann. 1997. "Perhaps or Maybe." *Responsibilities of Deconstruction. PLI: Warwick Journal of Philosophy* 6 (Summer): 1–18.

Derrida, Jacques, and Jean-Luc Nancy. 1991. "'Eating Well,' or the Calculation of The Subject: An Interview with Jacques Derrida." In *Who Comes after the Subject?* edited by Eduardo Cadava, Peter Connor, and Jean-Luc Nancy, 98–119. New York: Routledge.

Doniger, Wendy. 1973. *Śiva: The Erotic Ascetic.* New York: Oxford University Press.

Dyczkowski, Mark S. G. 1987. *The Doctrine of Vibration: An Analysis of the Doctrines and Practices of Kashmir Shaivism.* Albany: State University of New York Press.

―――. 1992. *The Stanzas on Vibration.* Translated by Mark S. G. Dyczkowski. Albany: State University of New York Press.

Encyclopaedia Britannica Online. 1999. S.V. "Socrates." http://www.eb.com:180/bol/topic?artcl=109554&seq_nbr=1&page=n&isctn=2 (accessed May 14, 1999).

Feuerstein, Georg. 1998. *Tantra: The Path of Ecstasy.* Boston: Shambhala.

Flood, Gavin D. 1993. *Body and Cosmology in Kashmir Śaivism.* San Francisco: Mellen Research University Press.

Foucault, Michel. 1985. *The Use of Pleasure: History of Sexuality, Volume 2.* Translated by Robert Hurley. New York: Random House.

―――. 1986. *The Care of the Self: History of Sexuality, Volume 3.* Translated by Robert Hurley. New York: Random House.

―――. 1988. "Technologies of the Self." In *Technologies of the Self: A Seminar with Michel Foucault,* edited by Luther H. Martin, Huck Gutman, and Patrick H. Hutton, 16–49. Amherst: University of Massachusetts Press.

―――. 1989. *Foucault Live: Collected Interviews, 1961–1984.* New York: Semiotext(e).

Gashé, Rodolfe. 1994. *Inventions of Difference: On Jacques Derrida.* Cambridge: Harvard University Press.

Gibson, William. 1984. *Neuromancer.* New York: Ace Books.

Golding, Sue, ed. 1997. *The Eight Technologies of Otherness*. London: Routledge.

Gray, Chris Hables, and Steven Mentor. 1995. "The Cyborg Body Politic and the New World Order." In *Prosthetic Territories: Politics and Hypertechnologies*, edited by Gabriel Brahm Jr. and Mark Driscoll, 219–47. Boulder, CO: Westview Press.

Griggers, Camilla. 1997. *Becoming-Woman*. Minneapolis: University of Minnesota Press.

Grimes, John. 1996. *A Concise Dictionary of Indian Philosophy*. Albany: State University of New York Press.

Grosz, Elizabeth. 1994. "A Thousand Tiny Sexes: Feminism and Rhizomatics." In *Gilles Deleuze and the Theater of Philosophy*, edited by Constantin V. Boundas and Dorothea Olkowski, 187–210. New York: Routledge.

Gulik, Robert Hans van. 1961. *Sexual Life in Ancient China: A Preliminary Survey of Chinese Sex and Society from ca. 1500 B.C. till 1644 A.D.* Leiden, The Netherlands: E. J. Brill.

Gupta, Sanjukta, Dirk Jan Hoens, and Teun Goudriaan. 1979. *Hindu Tantrism*. Leiden, The Netherlands: E. J. Brill.

Halberstam, Judith, and Ira Livingston, eds. 1995. *Posthuman Bodies*. Bloomington: Indiana University Press.

Hallward, Peter. 1998. "Generic Sovereignty: The Philosophy of Alain Badiou." *Angelaki: Journal of the Theoretical Humanities* 3, no. 1: 87–111.

Haraway, Donna J. 1985. "A Manifesto for Cyborgs." *Socialist Review* 2:65–108.

———. 1991. "The Biopolitics of Postmodern Bodies: Constitutions of Self in Immune System Discourse." In *Simians, Cyborgs, and Women: The Reinvention of Nature*, 203–30. New York: Routledge. 1997.

———. 1997. *Modest Witness@Second Millennium. Female Man© Meets OncoMouse™.* New York: Routledge.

Hardt, Michael. 1993. *Gilles Deleuze: An Apprenticeship in Philosophy*. Minneapolis: University of Minnesota Press.

Hassan, Ihab. 1977. "Prometheus as Performer: Toward a Posthumanist Culture?" *Georgia Review* 31, no. 4: 830–50.

Hayles, N. Katherine. 1993. "The Seductions of Cyberspace." In *Rethinking Technologies*, edited by Verena Andermatt Conley, 173–90. Minneapolis: University of Minnesota Press.

———. 1999. *How We Became Posthuman: Virtual Bodies in Cybernetics, Literature, and Informatics*. Chicago: University of Chicago Press.

Heim, Michael. 1993. *The Metaphysics of Virtual Reality*. New York: Oxford University Press.

Isenberg, Irwin, ed. 1977. *The Death Penalty*. The Reference Shelf 49, no. 2. New York: H. W. Wilson Company.

Jameson, Fredric. 1991. *Postmodernism, or, The Cultural Logic of Late Capitalism*. Durham, NC: Duke University Press.

John, Richard R. 1995. *Spreading the News: The American Postal System from Franklin to Morse*. Cambridge: Harvard University Press.

Kafka, Franz. 1996. *The Metamorphosis*. Translated by Stanley Corngold. New York: W. W. Norton.

Kant, Immanuel. 1963. *On History*. Indianapolis, IN: Bobbs-Merrill.

Khanna, Madhu. 1979. *Yantra: The Tantric Symbol of Cosmic Unity*. London: Thames and Hudson.

Kinsley, David. 1997. *Tantric Visions of the Divine Feminine: The Ten Mahāvidyās.* Berkeley and Los Angeles: University of California Press.

Kirby, Vicki. 1997. *Telling Flesh: The Substance of the Corporeal.* New York: Routledge.

Konish, Nancy. 1999. "So You Can't Keep Up with Your E-Mail? Check This Out." *Electronic Design,* July 26, 1999, 32.

Kraus, Chris. 1997. *I Love Dick.* New York: Semiotext(e).

————. 2000. *Aliens and Anorexia.* New York: Semiotext(e).

Lacoue-Labarthe, Philippe. 1990. *Heidegger, Art, and Politics: The Fiction of the Personal.* Translated by Chris Turner. London: Basil Blackwell.

Lakshmanjoo, Swami. 2001. *Shiva Sutras: The Supreme Awakening Audio Study Set.* Universal Shaiva Fellowship: Culver City, CA. 17 compact discs.

Latour, Bruno. 1999. *Pandora's Hope: Essays on the Reality of Science Studies.* Cambridge: Harvard University Press.

Lem, Stanislaw. 1987. *Solaris.* Translated by Joanna Kilmartin and Steve Cox. San Diego: Harcourt Brace Jovanovich.

Levinas, Emmanuel. 1969. *Totality and Infinity.* Translated by Alphonso Lingis. Pittsburgh, PA: Duquesne University Press. Original edition, 1961.

————. 1998. *Otherwise Than Being or Beyond Essence.* Translated by Alphonso Lingis. Pittsburgh, PA: Duquesne University Press. Original edition, 1974.

Lispector, Clarice. 1988. *The Passion According to G. H.* Translated by Ronald W. Sousa. Minneapolis: University of Minnesota Press. Original edition, 1964.

Litvak, Joseph. 1997. "Strange Gourmet: Taste, Waste, Proust." In *Novel Gazing: Queer Readings in Fiction,* edited by Eve Kosofsky Sedgwick, 74–93. Durham, NC: Duke University Press.

"Lockup: Inside Colorado State Pen." 2000. *MSNBC Investigates.* Original airdate July 13.

Luhmann, Niklas. 1990. *Essays on Self-Reference.* New York: Columbia University Press.

————. 1995. *Social Systems.* Translated by John Bednarz Jr. with Dirk Baecker. Stanford, CA: Stanford University Press.

Lynd, Alice. *What Is a Supermax Prison?* 1996. http://www.spunk.org/texts/prison/sp001611.txt (accessed July 20, 2000).

Markley, Robert. 1996. "Boundaries: Mathematics, Alienation, and the Metaphysics of Cyberspace." In *Virtual Realities and Their Discontents,* edited by Robert Markley, 55–78. Baltimore: Johns Hopkins University Press.

Massumi, Brian. 1995. "The Autonomy of Affect." *Cultural Critique* 31:83–109.

————. 1996. *A User's Guide to Capitalism and Schizophrenia: Deviations from Deleuze and Guattari.* Cambridge, MA: MIT Press.

Maturana, Humberto R., and Francisco J. Varela. 1980. *Autopoiesis and Cognition: The Realization of the Living.* Boston Studies in the Philosophy of Science 42. Dordrecht: D. Reidel.

————. 1987. *The Tree of Knowledge: The Biological Roots of Human Understanding.* Translated by Robert Paolucci. Boston, MA: Shambhala.

May, Todd. 1994. "Difference and Unity in Gilles Deleuze." In *Gilles Deleuze and the Theater of Philosophy,* edited by Constantin V. Boundas and Dorthea Olkowski, 33–50. New York: Routledge.

Merleau-Ponty, Maurice. 1962. *Phenomenology of Perception.* Translated by Colin Smith. London: Routledge.

———. 1968. *The Visible and the Invisible.* Translated by Alphonso Lingis. Evanston, IL: Northwestern University Press. Original edition, 1964.

Miller, Richard C., ed. n.d. *Mudra: Gateways to Self-Understanding.* Sebastopol, CA: Anahata Press.

Mookerjee, Ajit, and Madhu Khanna. 1977. *The Tantric Way: Art, Science, Ritual.* New York: Thames and Hudson.

Muktananda, Swami. 1992. *I AM THAT: The Science of Hamsa from the Vijnana Bhairava.* South Fallsburg, NY: SYDA Foundation.

Muller-Ortega, Paul. 1989. *The Triadic Heart of Siva.* Albany: State University of New York Press.

Murphy, Timothy S. 1997. *Wising Up the Marks: The Amodern William Burroughs.* Berkeley and Los Angeles: University of California Press.

Nehamas, Alexander. 1999. *Virtues of Authenticity: Essays on Plato and Socrates.* Princeton, NJ: Princeton University Press.

Nietzsche, Friedrich. 1978. *Thus Spoke Zarathustra.* Translated by Walter Kaufmann. New York: Penguin.

———. 1994. *On the Genealogy of Morality.* Cambridge: Cambridge University Press.

Novak, Marcos. 1991. "Liquid Architectures in Cyberspace." In *Cyberspace: First Steps,* edited by Michael Benedikt, 225–54. Cambridge, MA: MIT Press.

Padoux, André. 1990. *Vac: The Concept of the Word in Selected Hindu Tantras.* Translated by Jacques Gontier. Albany: State University of New York Press.

Parker, Jo Alyson. 1992. "Gendering the Robot: Stanislaw Lem's 'The Mask.'" *Science Fiction Studies* 19:177–91.

Parrinder, Geoffrey. 1970. *Avatar and Incarnation: The Wilde Lectures in Natural and Comparative Religion in the University of Oxford.* New York: Barnes and Noble.

Pearson, Keith Ansell. 1999. *Germinal Life: The Difference and Repetition of Deleuze.* London: Routledge.

Poster, Mark. 1990. *The Mode of Information: Poststructuralism and Social Context.* Chicago: University of Chicago Press.

Pynchon, Thomas. 1966. *The Crying of Lot 49.* New York: Harper and Row.

Rai, Ram Kumar. 1983. *Kulārnava Tantra.* Varanasi, India: Prachya Prakashan.

Rasch, William, and Cary Wolfe, eds. 1995. "The Politics of Systems and Environments, Part I." Special issue, *Cultural Critique* 30.

———. 1995. "The Politics of Systems and Environments, Part II." Special issue, *Cultural Critique* 31.

Richter, Gerhard. 2000. *Walter Benjamin and the Corpus of Autobiography.* Detroit, MI: Wayne State University Press.

Rotman, Brian. 1997. "Circa 2000: Material Consciousness in the Transmodern Age." Presentation at Interactive Media Group, Stanford, CA, May.

———. 1999. *Becoming Beside Oneself.* http://www.cgrg.ohio-state.edu/~brotman/becoming.html (accessed September 3, 1999).

Rush, Benjamin. 1787. "Address to the People of the United States." *American Museum* 1:8–11.

Ryman, Geoff. 1996. *253.* New York: Saint Martin's Griffin.

Sagan, Dorion, and Lynn Margulis. 1991. "The Uncut Self." In *Organism and the Origins of Self,* edited by A. I. Tauber, 361–74. The Netherlands: Kluwer Academic Publishers.

Said, Edward. 2000. "Presidential Address 1999: Humanism and Heroism." *PMLA* 115, no. 3: 285–91.

Sanderson, Alexis. 1985. "Purity and Power among the Brahmans of Kashmir." In *The Category of the Person: Anthropology, Philosophy, History,* edited by Michael Carrithers, Steven Collins, and Steven Lukes, 190–216. New York: Cambridge University Press.

Saraswati, Satyananda Swami. 1982. *Sannyasa Tantra.* Bihar, India: Bihar School of Yoga.

Sarduy, Severo. 1989. *Written on a Body.* Translated by Carol Maier. New York: Lumen Books.

———. 1995. *Christ on the Rue Jacob.* Translated by Suzanne Jill Levine and Carol Maier. San Francisco: Mercury House.

Sartre, Jean-Paul. 1956. *Being and Nothingness.* Translated by Hazel E. Barnes. New York: Washington Square Press.

———. 1964. *Nausea.* Translated by Lloyd Alexander. New York: New Directions.

Sedgwick, Eve Kosofsky, ed. 1997. *Novel Gazing: Queer Readings in Fiction.* Series Q. Durham, NC: Duke University Press.

Shaviro, Steven. 1995. ".Two Lessons from Burroughs." In *Posthuman Bodies,* edited by Judith Halberstam and Ira Livingston, 38–54. Bloomington: Indiana University Press.

Shaw, Miranda. 1994. *Passionate Enlightenment: Women in Tantric Buddhism.* Princeton, NJ: Princeton University Press.

Simmel, Georg. 1950. *The Sociology of Georg Simmel.* London: Free Press of Glencoe.

Sinha, Indra. 1993. *The Great Book of Tantra: Translations and Images from the Classic Indian Texts with Commentary.* Rochester, VT: Destiny Books.

Sivananda, Swami. 1957. *The Practice of Bhakti Yoga.* Shivanandanagar, Himalayas, India: Divine Life Society.

———. 1986. *Spiritual Experiences.* Shivanandanagar, Himalayas, India: Divine Life Society.

Smith, Brian K. 1990. "Eaters, Food, and Social Hierarchy in Ancient India: A Dietary Guide to a Revolution of Values." *Journal of the American Academy of Religion* 58, no. 2: 177–205.

Spanos, William V. 1993. *The End of Education: Toward Posthumanism.* Minneapolis: University of Minnesota Press.

Spinoza, Benedict de. 1994. *A Spinoza Reader: The Ethics and Other Works.* Princeton, NJ: Princeton University Press.

Stockton, Kathryn Bond. 2000. "Narrative Luxuries and Punctured Politics: Tucked in the Cut in *Pulp Fiction* and *Hoop Dreams.*" Paper presented at the annual meeting of the Modern Language Association, San Francisco, CA.

Stone, Allucquère Rosanne. 1995. *The War of Desire and Technology at the Close of the Mechanical Age.* Cambridge, MA: MIT Press.

Strawson, Galen. 1997. "The Self." *Journal of Consciousness Studies* 4, no. 5–6: 405–28.

Trinh T. Minh-ha. 1989. *Woman, Native, Other: Writing Postcoloniality and Feminism.* Bloomington: Indiana University Press.

Turkle, Sherry. 1995. *Life on the Screen: Identity in the Age of the Internet.* New York: Simon and Schuster.

Ulmer, Gregory L. 1985. *Applied Grammatology: Post(e)-Pedagogy from Jacques Derrida to Joseph Beuys.* Baltimore: Johns Hopkins University Press.

Urban, Hugh B. 1988. "The Torment of Secrecy: Ethical and Epistemological Problems in the Study of Esoteric Traditions." *History of Religions* 37:209–48.

——. 1997. "Elitism and Esotericism: Strategies of Secrecy and Power in South Indian Tantra and French Freemasonry." *Numen* 44:1–38.

——. 1999. "The Extreme Orient: The Construction of 'Tantrism' as a Category in the Orientalist Imagination." *Religion* 29:123–46.

——. 2001. *Songs of Ecstasy: Tantric and Devotional Songs from Colonial Bengal.* New York: Oxford University Press.

U.S. Congress. 1845. *Public Statutes at Large of the United States of America.* Vol. 1. Boston: Charles C. Little and James Brown.

——. 1855. *Annals of the Congress of the United States, Oct. 24, 1791–March 2, 1793.* Washington: Gales and Seaton.

Varela, Francisco J. 1991. "Organism: A Meshwork of Selfless Selves." In *Organism and the Origins of Self,* edited by Alfred I. Tauber, 79–107. The Netherlands: Kluwer Academic Publishers.

——. 1999. *Ethical Know-How: Action, Wisdom, and Cognition.* Writing Science. Stanford, CA: Stanford University Press.

Varela, Francisco J., Evan Thompson, and Eleanor Rosch. 1991. *The Embodied Mind: Cognitive Science and Human Experience.* Cambridge, MA: MIT Press.

Visscher, William Lightfoot. 1946. *A Thrilling and Truthful History of the Pony Express, or Blazing the Westward Way.* Chicago: Charles T. Powner Co. Original edition, 1908.

Ward, William. 1815. *A View of the History, Literature, and Mythology of the Hindoos: Including a Minute Description of Their Manners and Customs, and Translations from Their Principal Works.* Serampore, India: The Mission Press.

Weinstone, Ann. 1997a. "Death and E-Mail@Modest Manifesto." Paper presented at the annual meeting of the Society for Literature and Science, Pittsburgh, PA.

——. 1997b. "Welcome to the Pharmacy: Addiction, Transcendence, and Virtual Reality." *Diacritics* 27:77–89.

White, David Gordon. 1992. "You Are What You Eat: The Anomalous Status of Dog-Cookers in Hindu Mythology." In *The Eternal Food: Gastronomic Ideas and Experiences of Hindus and Buddhists,* edited by R. S. Khare, 53–93. Albany: State University of New York Press.

——. 1996. *The Alchemical Body: Siddha Traditions in Medieval India.* Chicago: University of Chicago Press.

Wiener, Norbert. 1948. *Cybernetics: or Control and Communication in the Animal and the Machine.* Cambridge, MA: MIT Press.

——. 1956. *I Am a Mathematician: The Later Life of a Prodigy.* Garden City, NY: Doubleday.

Wolfe, Cary. 1995. "In Search of Post-Humanist Theory: The Second-Order Cybernetics of Maturana and Varela." *Cultural Critique* 30 (Spring): 33–70.

——. 1998. *Critical Environments: Postmodern Theory and the Pragmatics of the "Outside."* Minneapolis: University of Minnesota Press.

Wood, David. 1999. "The Experience of the Ethical." In *Questioning Ethics: Contemporary Debates in Philosophy,* edited by Richard Kearny and Mark Dooley, 105–19. New York: Routledge.

Woodroffe, Sir John. 1969. *Śakti and Śakta.* 7th ed. Madras, India: Ganesh and Co.

Ann Weinstone (Lalita Sarasvati) is assistant professor of literature and new media at Northwestern University. She received the Chelsea Award for Fiction and is the author of numerous scholarly articles.